A Practical Guide to Managing Tourist Experiences

This book provides students with a concise and practical guide that presents key understandings of the tourist experience and provides strategic guidance on how to develop an impactful and memorable experience.

Chapters follow the path of the tourist journey, firstly exploring consumer behaviour, the decision-making process and the tourist's need for escape, and providing insights into the strategic implications of consumer behaviour and the concept of immersion in tourism. Subsequent chapters look at the impact of experiences; consider trends in tourism experience such as wellness, sustainability, authenticity and fantasy; and provide experience design models. The final chapter offers a unique ten-step approach to designing impactful and memorable tourist experiences. Highly practical and engaging, this book is packed full of case studies and examples, from forest bathing in Finland to truffle hunting in Italy, as well as tools and exercises to guide the design process.

This book offers students a full understanding of how the experience is lived from the tourist perspective, how tourism providers can manage that process and how to develop successful experimental marketing interventions. This is essential reading for all tourism students and future tourism managers.

Isabelle Frochot has been a course leader since 2000 of a Master in Tourism Destination Management at the University Savoie Mont Blanc and is now the director of studies for its six Masters. She is currently supervising four PhD students. Isabelle has recently been welcomed back onto the TTRA Europe Board, and will certainly be actively involved in this association for years to come. Isabelle specializes in the study of tourist behaviour and started her research career by investigating psychographic segmentation in heritage management, rural tourism and service quality scales with the creation of HISTOQUAL. Isabelle completed her PhD at Manchester Metropolitan University and then worked as a lecturer at the Scottish Agricultural College and the Scottish Hotel School (Strathclyde University, Scotland) for five years. Since returning to France in 2000, Isabelle has moved her research focus to mountain tourism, concentrating on the analysis of the consumer experience (experience sequencing, nesting dynamics in a holiday context, immersion, and disconnection/reconnection processes in tourism consumption). She has recently been involved in projects investigating the conceptual framework of escapism, the role and evolution of memory in tourism experiences and the place of videos as a new tool in qualitative research.

A Practical Guide to Managing Tourist Experiences

Isabelle Frochot

Routledge
Taylor & Francis Group

LONDON AND NEW YORK

First published 2022
by Routledge
2 Park Square, Milton Park, Abingdon, Oxon OX14 4RN

and by Routledge
605 Third Avenue, New York, NY 10158

Routledge is an imprint of the Taylor & Francis Group, an informa business

British Library Cataloguing-in-Publication Data
A catalogue record for this book is available from the British Library

Library of Congress Cataloging-in-Publication Data
A catalog record has been requested for this book

ISBN: 9780367894467 (hbk)
ISBN: 9780367819828 (pbk)
ISBN: 9781003019237 (ebk)

DOI: 10.4324/9781003019237

Typeset in Iowan Old Style
by Deanta Global Publishing Services, Chennai, India

To Julie and Benjamin

Contents

Figures

Tables

Acknowledgements

I would like to warmly thank all the people and all the actors who participated in the production of this book. I was sensitive to the confidence and interest shown by tourism professionals and academics who agreed to contribute to the book and share their work. I would particularly like to thank Julie Masset and Alain Decrop (Namur University), Francesco DeParis (Couchsurfing), Françoise Forsans (Paris Greeters), Katarina Rainer and Mark Stickdorn (Smaply), Daniel Charbonnier (Null Stern) and Philippe Bourdeau (Labex ITTEM). I also thank all the researchers with whom I have spent days and days observing, interviewing, videoing and interacting with tourists. This has been the best way to keep on unravelling our understanding of the tourism experience and engaging in valuable research investigations. Thank you Dominique Kreziak, Mélanie Marcuzzi and Pauline Muller for the time we spent together investigating tourists in all kind of situations and weather conditions. Thanks to all the tourists who keep on taking the time to answer our questions and devoting time to us, you are magic! Thanks to my students: motivated, interested, smart and amazingly creative.

Last but not least, I thank my family and close friends for their patience and unwavering support.

Introduction

The term *experiential marketing* has become a common feature in academics' and consultants' spheres of expertise. It seems that experiences have become the key feature of any service delivery and the new consumption vocabulary. Experiences do not represent another marketing trick or a new fashion trend; the notion of experiential marketing encapsulates a different vision of consumption processes and develops specific models to understand those processes more efficiently. Originally, the experiential approach was developed to analyse different consumption behaviours observed in specific forms of consumption, such as art and leisure, and it fits perfectly within the context of tourism consumption. Experiential marketing is interested in the spheres of consumption where consumers seek to escape from their normal lives by experiencing services that engage their emotions and have strong symbolical and esthetical values. Experiences differentiate companies and allow them to charge premium prices, thereby providing unique business opportunities.

Nowadays, experiences are developed as a consumption offer in their own right, but they are also associated with products and services. For instance, a computer might be sold within premises that offers a range of experiences associated with the product. In society, a trend for experiences has been slowly emerging, and they have become a common feature of contemporary consumer demand. In the United Kingdom, consumers have been identified as purchasing fewer physical goods (furniture, vehicles and household appliances) and more experiences. For instance, consumption in pubs has increased by 20%, in restaurants by 16% and in theatres and cinemas by 13% (Usborne, 2017). There is therefore a shift among consumers who consider that life is made richer by experiencing and living intense encounters rather than by owning goods. This shift will necessarily be deepened by the pandemic, which has refocused consumers on what really matters to them in life, and experiences are necessarily part of this equation.

DOI: 10.4324/9781003019237-1

Because experiential marketing investigates the nonrational and emotionally laden consumption occurrences, it corresponds perfectly with the understanding of tourism consumption dynamics. The field of tourism research has been investigating the idea of experiences for decades. Tourism consumption carries some specificities that make it a perfect field for experimenting and with understanding the scope of experiential marketing. The tourism industry provides experiences that are different from everyday life, have strong emotional resonance, create deep involvement and strong connections and have the potential to transform consumers. This book aims to understand how the combined knowledge gained on experiences can assist experience designers, in tourism companies or in destinations, to develop powerful experiences.

Considering that several books exist on experiential marketing and that the knowledge that has been accumulated over the years is rather rich, this book does not aim to synthetize this large field of expertise. The book will present the key information necessary to understand the consumer experience and will introduce a range of examples and some exercises to engage the reader in the experience design process. The book also aims to provide readers with a practical understanding of experience design. To this end, the book offers models and practical tools and exercises that will serve as guidance for this design process.

The book is divided into six chapters. The first chapter sets the scene by providing a general framework for consumer behaviour. The chapter details why the investigation of consumer behaviour is strategic, and which specificities have been identified in the tourism context. It then investigates consumers' decision processes and the different influences that impact behaviour (socio-economic influences, evolution through the life cycle, cultural influences and how consumers behave at the individual level). The chapter then addresses the strategic implications of consumer behaviour in terms of targeting and positioning, communicating efficiency and anticipating the evolution of consumer demand.

The second chapter investigates in detail the specificities of the tourism consumption process. It addresses the dialectics of tourism consumption, a process motivated primarily by the need to escape various realities. Because this need for escape is fundamental to understanding the tourist experience, the chapter investigates its various dimensions, from the escape from everyday lives and duties to the escape from more general work and societal spheres. The notion of liminality brings an insight into the opportunity that holidays provide to escape usual norms and obligations, to develop a new identity and to build new connections. Finally, the concept of immersion provides an understanding of the mechanisms that allow tourists to immerse themselves in a holiday context and thereby forget their everyday lives.

The third chapter provides a deeper insight into tourists' experiences by investigating the core experiences that impact most consumers. The notion of optimal and peak experiences, understood as deep experiences, will be addressed in order to understand what characteristics of an experience create the most impactful and memorable outcomes. The contribution of positive psychology in better understanding experience triggers will also be addressed. The chapter will investigate how episodes of flow and of awe can energise the experience, and under which conditions. This third chapter will investigate the extent to which tourism experiences can transform visitors. Finally, it will address how memories are constructed and how they evolve over time.

The fourth chapter aims to situate tourism experiences within the context of consumer trends. The chapter addresses ten trends which will be examined and illustrated with various examples. These trends are playfulness, well-being, once-in-a-lifetime experiences, nature, sustainability, authenticity, localhood, simplicity, fantasy and all-inclusive holidays.

The fifth chapter then presents the main experiential models created by different academics and consultants. The chapter presents its own model with six experiential cues that should be taken into consideration when designing experiences. These cues are the five senses, creating a surprise, involving consumers, creating souvenirs, contextualizing and relatedness. The chapter then details each of these components and provides a "generator" exercise that will assist designers in developing each of the six cues.

The last chapter aims to combine all the information, tools and techniques addressed in the book into a ten-step approach that can serve as guide to designing experiences. The model invites experience designers to first identify resources and key markets and then to design experiences by taking current trends into consideration. Once the experience has been created, the design of the experience needs to be investigated with the actors in mind, and tourism networks that contribute to the experience. Finally, the marketing mix encourages experience designers to contemplate the promotion, distribution and pricing of the experience. The last part of the chapter presents one example and details how an experience was created following the ten steps.

This book aims to combine academic and consultancy expertise in order to provide readers with models that can assist them in delivering impactful and memorable experiences. The different examples, exercises and tools provided will help experience designers in that process. The last chapter combines all this knowledge into a practical ten-step model to design experiences, but the previous chapters are also essential to understand this process.

1

Investigating vacation behaviour

Introduction

This book is set within the broader framework of consumer behaviour. Before addressing the notion of experience, it is essential to go back to the roots of behaviour: what it means, how it is conceptualized, its implications in terms of marketing and management strategies and how it is specifically investigated in the field of tourism. This chapter will address in the first place how behaviour is defined and its characteristic models, and it will then explain why behaviour is a strategic marketing weapon. The chapter will then address the specificities of tourism behaviour and why it necessitates a specific focus. Finally, the chapter will address the special characteristics of tourism segmentation and how it helps managers to strategically better understand their markets. Last but not least, we will address the notion of experience and experiential marketing.

1.1 What is behaviour?

The field of consumer behaviour investigates how consumers make their decisions at an individual or group level and why they decide to purchase, use and/ or reuse products and services. Necessarily, looking at decision-making means that companies and destinations also need to understand when consumers are

DOI: 10.4324/9781003019237-2

likely to purchase products and services, how they are going to purchase them, where they will purchase them, with what regularity, etc.

The field of consumer behaviour is a rich field that has developed over several decades and has accumulated a vast field of knowledge. The complexity of human behaviour has called for a scientific knowledge coming from various fields. For instance, psychology has been a key contributor, bringing valuable knowledge in understanding the human mind and behaviour, helping to understand feelings, ideas and behaviours and how decisions and actions are fuelled. Sociology has also brought a rich comprehension of social behaviour, society dynamics and social interactions, and helps us understand how behaviour relates to broader cultural and social influences. Other fields bring an interesting insight into consumer behaviour, such as Consumer Culture Theory (CCT), which conveys a very pertinent outlook on consumption from social and cultural perspectives. CCT looks at consumption not just as a commercial transaction, but also as a source of social integration and identity formation. Other disciplines also provide valuable insights; for instance, the fields of human geography, neuroscience, and economics all bring their own contribution to the general understanding of consumer behaviour.

1.2 The tourism specificities

If the various disciplines contributing to the understanding of consumer behaviour bring a rich understanding of its dynamics, why study specifically tourism behaviour? The field of tourism is a multidisciplinary field which concentrates extensive knowledge on the various dimensions of the tourism phenomenon. Within the broad spectrum of consumption, tourism stands apart due to the characteristics it has that not many other consumption contexts share.

1.2.1 Tourist behaviour is unique

Tourism consumption takes place far away from consumers' homes. The different contexts and opportunities that can be encountered at the destination create the source of tourism demand and the competitive advantage of receiving destinations. New landscapes, new cultures, new communities all bring novelty and tourists' desire to discover other ways of living. Nonetheless, some forms of tourism have been recognized as providing limited contacts with destinations whilst still producing consumer satisfaction (some all-inclusive resorts, cruising, etc.). The distance between tourists' location and the destinations they visit implies that consumers cannot see a service in advance of its consumption (brochures, videos and 3D representations might assist their understanding, but the destination will be fully discovered only once the actual holiday starts).

By definition, holidays often take place in environments that can be drastically different from consumers' habitual environments. Physically, culturally, socially, the holiday experience usually projects consumers into different environments that necessitate adaptation, skills and understanding that not many other consumption situations entail.

Holidays are a temporary period away from the usual constraints and pressures where consumers can behave differently, find a new self and experience new activities that can lead to profound transformations.

1.2.2 The tourism context is specific and unique

From a strategic perspective, other characteristics of the tourism industry necessitate approaches that are different to those of traditional marketing. For instance, tourism is a highly seasonal industry. This seasonality is in many instances a weakness: the more seasonal a tourism sector is, the more difficult it will be to sustain strong economic activity. Highly seasonal sectors call for more seasonal workers, workers who might not live locally all year round, and the resorts/destinations' physical capacities (accommodation and catering facilities, for example) will only be used for a fraction of the year. Expanding tourism over the four seasons is a solution that many destinations would like to achieve because it means developing more economical and social stability for their economy. Seasonality also means that strategies need to be developed to target different consumers across different seasons. It also implies that tourism products will be sold at variable costs and marketed differently to these different markets. The tourism industry has high infrastructure costs and because it is a service; perishability is an inevitable feature of the industry (an unsold hotel room for a day is a revenue that is lost forever). Whilst revenue management techniques bring a powerful strategic approach to increase facilities' (and destinations) occupancy rates, they cannot resolve the broader question of seasonality on their own. Reducing seasonality is an objective that needs to be managed at destination level, and that involves different competencies, including planning, facilities development and governance.

The tourism industry encapsulates different questions because it involves both private and public actors. The dynamics of tourism relies on the efficiency of the interrelationships between these economic spheres. Public actors, from local tourism information centres to destination marketing organizations and tourism ministries, drive the tourism industry at destination level. Public actors manage the destination, taking into account the destination facilities but also taking on board broader competitive and geopolitical issues. They also have at their core the aim of developing tourism in harmony with the inherent needs of the local population and actors' networks at the destination. Public organizations might decide to boost specific tourism sectors and activities rather than others. They might consider improving the destination's image by monitoring some developments more closely and restricting them within their own destinations (for instance, Amsterdam is a key example of a destination that is aiming to improve its image by reducing its coffee-shop reputation and minimizing the visibility of the prostitution sector). Public organizations also increasingly manage their tourism industries with local populations' living conditions at heart. Whilst this aspect had been less considered in the past, it has become a real concern, especially with questions of overtourism, which have clearly shown that tourism developments can have negative impacts on local populations that need to be managed.

The public sector, however, cannot manage a tourism industry on its own. It can give direction and promote and federate tourism actors, and it works intimately with networks of private actors at their destinations. Actors' networks have been the object of increased attention over recent decades; they are at the heart of service provision, contributing to the destination's image and to the production of the holiday experience, providing services from accommodation and catering facilities to activities of various types and travel management operators (with travel agencies and tour operators as distribution agents). The tourism industry features a large proportion of fairly small enterprises (SMEs), and tourism actors are spread across vast territories. The role of destination management systems is therefore not just to act on strategic and marketing decisions for their destinations; Destination Marketing Organisations (DMOs) also have a central role to play in federating the range of actors that are involved in their tourism provision.

The tourism industry cannot be conceived in isolation from the rest of the world. Tourism markets are interdependent, and occurrences of crises have demonstrated how events taking place in one part of the world have strong implications for other destinations. For example, the Arab spring reduced the demand for northern African tourism destinations and witnessed a shift of tourism demand for other seaside destinations in the Southern European Mediterranean destinations of Croatia and Turkey. The pandemic that shattered the tourism industry in 2020 has had dramatic impacts on international tourism demand. However, it has also boosted domestic demand, and many tourism destinations managed to keep their tourism sector afloat by catering to the needs of domestic visitors.

The tourism industry is therefore a particularly vast sector, one that combines a multiplicity of tourism actors, but it is also an industry that always evolves and needs to integrate local needs and economic balance in the development of tourism. This chapter will focus primarily on tourist demand, which is the preliminary knowledge necessary in order to better understand experiential marketing.

1.3 Consumers as decision makers

The process of consumer decision-making has been investigated in the marketing field and has produced a dense field of knowledge that this book cannot fully report. Decisions are influenced by various personal, societal and individual elements and we shall address in this chapter how decisions are taken and the different influences that impact them.

1.3.1 The decision process

The recognition of a need is at the origin of the process of consumer choice. Once this need is recognized, the consumer will be motivated to embark on a process of purchasing a tourist product. This process then integrates a search for information, which will lead to the identification of a set of products able to meet the needs of the consumer (Figure 1.1).

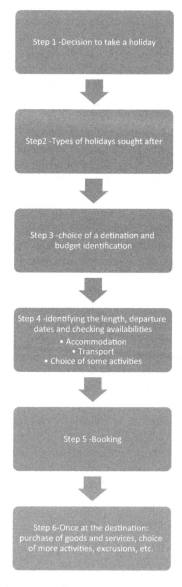

Figure 1.1 The tourist decision-making process. Source: Adapted from Woodside and King (2001).

Individuals only know a fraction of the total set of options available in the market and only retain those that they know and that are feasible within their time and budget limits. Then the selected destinations are evaluated on the basis of a series of attributes in limited number (generally three to four). Certain tourism decisions, such as the organization of an independent trip, are made up of a multitude of subdecisions (choice of transport, accommodation, dates, duration, activities, budget, etc.), the whole of which is particularly complex. On the other hand, package tours, resorts or cruises are products sold in their entity. In these situations, the decision will have fewer elements and will be limited to a choice by product type, destination or brand.

It is believed that a profusion of products and destinations can meet the first two stages of tourism choice. The finalization of the choice of a destination takes place mainly during the third and fourth stages. The choice is made on a set called a "consideration set". This set brings together destinations capable of satisfying consumer needs. It is estimated that this set does not include more than seven destinations (Moutinho, 1987).

UNDERSTANDING TOURISTS' TRAVEL DECISIONS

The Travel Industry Association of America conducted a survey that aimed to identify factors that play a major role in the leisure travel planning process. The survey divided the study population into four subsets based on the purpose of travel: pleasure; business travel coupled with pleasure travel; visiting relatives and friends; and vacations with outdoor activities. The survey was conducted among 5,000 American tourists who had taken an overnight trip in the past year.

The results show that when planning their vacations, American tourists first make decisions about where to go and then about how long to stay, before deciding how much to budget. Decisions on activities and transportation come last.

The factors that influence the decision-making process vary depending on the purpose of travel. In the context of a pleasure trip, the factors having the most influence are the partners who will be part of the trip (53%), the available budget (48%), the time and the period of the year available (44% each) and rates (42%). The purpose of the trip only influences the decision by 33%.

For an outdoor vacation, the importance of each of these factors is relatively similar, except for the time of the year, which has a stronger weight (52%). The importance outdoor vacationers attach to the season is easily explained by the search for certain climatic conditions for practising activities. On the other hand, in the context of vacations controlled by an element (visiting friends and relatives and business trips), the purpose of the trip is the most

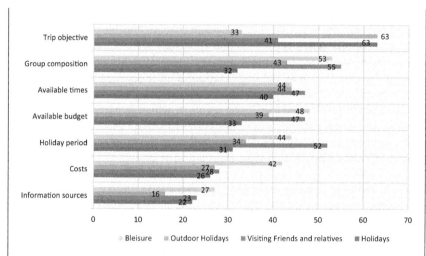

Figure 1.2 Planning characteristics for American tourists (in percentage of sources influencing most the decision. Source: Author.

influential factor (63%), followed by the time and budget available and then the group composition (Figure 1.2).

The study indicates that holiday planning periods vary a lot from one individual to another: 22% of the tourists surveyed start planning their vacations 1–2 months in advance, 15% from 3 to 6 months and 15% from 6 to 9 months. However, 18% prepare for their stay 1–13 days in advance and 14% from 2 weeks to 1 month. Depending on the mode of transport, car vacations require little preparation (48% are decided less than a month before departure) whilst 45% of tourists travelling by plane plan their trip 3–6 months in advance. Finally, the higher the income, the longer the preparation period. This aspect is partly linked to the fact that tourists with higher incomes take more self-catering holidays, travel by plane more often and carry out more extensive preparations for their trip.

Source: Translated from: Peloquin C. (2005) Comprendre les décisions de voyage, Réseau de veille en tourisme, Chaire de tourisme Transat https://veilletourisme.ca/ 2005/08/17/comp rendre-les-decisions-de-voyage/

1.3.2 Various decision-making processes

The stages of the decision-making process as we have described them so far are not necessarily always present in all tourists' purchases. The nature of decisions varies along a continuum, with decisions characterized as routine on one hand and decisions that involve extensive decision-making processes on the other. It is commonly believed that tourism decision-making, due to its financial and personal implications, inevitably responds to extensive decision processes, but reality shows that it can also be the result of shorter processes (Figure 1.3).

The understanding of the decision continuum is important to be able to assess the various components that will be used to various extents by potential consumers. According to individual personal situations, previous holiday experiences and personal motivations, the decision will vary from being an extensive one down to a routinized one. In tourism, the range of decisions is a broad one, as we shall explain (Figure 1.4).

Routinised decision	⟵——————⟶	Extensive decision
Low	Problem resolution	High
Low	Information needs	High
Short	Length of the decisional process	Long
Low	Product comparison	High
Low	Number of choice criteria	High
Low	Number of products evaluated	high

Figure 1.3 The decision-making continuum. Source: Adapted from Mayo and Jarvis (1981) and Peter and Olson (1987).

Figure 1.4 A happy family holiday on the beach. Source: Photo by Natalya Zaritskaya on Unsplash.

1.3.2.1 Decisions characteristic of an extensive process

This type of decision corresponds to products that consumers believe carry a certain "risk". They often represent a significant financial and personal investment; in other words, they are products that have far-reaching implications. They induce a relatively comprehensive search for information (particularly from external sources) and an extensive comparison of the alternatives offered on the market. Seeking information can be a first step in a trip, and some tourists find it a real source of pleasure; some might even say that this is when the travel experience begins. This mode of decision takes place in the case of destinations for which tourists have a limited knowledge and previous experience, and those which may involve elements of risk. The physical and cultural distance as well as the perception of the exotic character of a destination will add elements of uncertainty, which will lead to an extensive choice process. The same goes for independent trips, which require a fairly complex organization, an understanding of what the destination has to offer and logistics that require a lot of information.

The extensive process is the only one where people undertake additional information research shortly before departure, using specific sources such as brochures, contacting tourism office centres at the destination and tourist guides. This desire for information will continue during the trip with a greater collection of information taking place on the spot. Decision planning is the longest of all forms of decision making. A study of the holiday decision-making process used by Dutch tourists showed that the extensive process took between 4 months and 2 years before the purchase was made (Bargeman & van der Poel, 2006).

1.3.2.2 Limited decision-making process

This characterizes situations where the tourist considers that the product represents little risk and the decision does not require an extensive search for information. Limited decision-making is also at stake when tourists purchase the same product again (for example, if the tourist has already stayed at a hotel or a destination). It is also characteristic of decisions concerning some vacation packages (for example, going to a resort in a destination A or B will have few differences in the eyes of the consumer if his/her primary choice is directed by a resort brand or a tour operator). The same form of decision-making applies to short-term products such as short stays and local stays. A limited decision can also apply when the consumer is already familiar with the product but a part remains unknown – for example, a tourist who is going to travel to a different region of the same country.

In a limited decision-making process, the tourist uses fewer external sources of information and evaluates a more limited number of products than in the extensive process. It is believed that this process responds to a decision-making mode with a limited number of criteria and a search for information which is also limited but nevertheless present.

1.3.2.3 Routine decision-making process

Routine decisions are undertaken quickly and with limited mental effort. They generally relate to a repeated purchase, either of an already known product or of a relatively simple product. The purchase is made on the basis of satisfactory past experience and good knowledge of the product/destination/brand. Routine purchasing is characterized by little or no search for information, and a limited comparison between products (the product concerned carries little or no incertitude in the eyes of the consumer). Planning for the decision can take from a year to a week before going on vacation, but if people travel to the same destination every year, the reservation can be made at the end of the vacation of the previous year.

It is considered that visits to relatives and friends, a weekend in a completely familiar destination, a vacation taken each year in the same place or a vacation in a second home fall into this category.

1.3.2.4 Impulsive decision-making

Impulse buying is characterized by its sudden and unplanned character, and this does not necessarily apply to holiday purchasing. It can be argued that last-minute holidays fall under this type of decision to an extent. The consumer surfs a website or comes across an advertisement selling an attractive holiday destination package at a very low price. The consumer knows that the offer won't last and that their decision has to be made quickly. When a tourist consults a supersaver travel site or even shows up at an airport ready to go on a discounted trip immediately, part of the decision to travel will have already been made. Certain destinations or certain characteristics of destinations (seaside resorts, for example) will have already been preselected by individuals, whether consciously or unconsciously.

The decision-making processes that we have presented in this section vary according to holiday characteristics, but also from one consumer to another; tourists' socioeconomic and cultural characteristics influence the way they choose and consume tourism products. In the next section, we will discuss the influence of some variables (socio-professional category (CSP), income, family cycle and culture) on tourism consumption.

1.4 Different influences on behaviour

Consumer decision-making is impacted by different variables at several levels. For instance, individual consumers are characterized by different demographic and socioeconomic characteristics which impact their behaviour. Consumers are also individuals in their own right, which means that they are characterized by specific personalities, attitudes, values and motivations.

When we consider the ways in which consumers undertake their decisions, we also need to take into account the fact that those consumers might be taking a decision at an individual level, but they may also need to take into account a family context (for instance, integrating the needs of a spouse and children when making a holiday-taking decision). Consumers are also influenced by the society they live in, which inherently reflects a specific culture. At a more individual level, consumers also belong to reference groups. Consciously or unconsciously, consumers will behave and take decisions in a way that will be seen as more favourable by some groups and cultures than others. This section will present those various influences and how they impact holiday taking.

1.4.1 Socioeconomic influences

First and foremost, tourism consumption takes place within the broader framework of various social and economic influences that shape tourism demand.

Tourism demand is the result of industrialized societies. Industry has created the means and the reasons for tourism consumption as we know it nowadays. With industrialization, populations suddenly moved to large urban centres *en masse*. This shift meant that populations had to live in cramped conditions and faced a heavy work load, often heavier than in rural societies. The decrease in general health and hygiene and the increasing problems of violence and alcoholism motivated the industry and governments to develop social policies to take better care of their citizens' living conditions. Among those initiatives, a time devoted to holidays emerged, and then the idea of paid holidays materialized. Nowadays, most countries have a minimum amount of paid holidays per employee. The time available to go on holiday is therefore an important variable to consider when looking at tourism demand. Across the world, inhabitants have access to different holiday entitlement schemes. If, in Europe, the average entitlement covers 5 weeks a year, it can be less than this in other countries. Nowadays, the combination of minimum holiday entitlements and public holidays means that consumers can have 36 days a year in the United Kingdom, 32 days in Italy and 20 days in the Netherlands. At the same time, free time and flexible working practices (which are dramatically being revised in the light of the Covid 19 crisis) are redistributing access to the periods of time devoted to holidays. A mix of business and leisure ("bleisure") has also been observed in the work sphere, and the emergence of digital nomads has become a new and steady trend.

Industrialization has also meant that the concentration of populations in urban centres has created the necessity to escape increasingly stressful living conditions. We will address in Chapter 2 what this notion of escape entails, while we will focus here on the profile of typical holiday consumers. Through the advent of industrialization and tertiarization, it has become clear that some key socioeconomic dimensions are crucial influencers on departure rates. For instance, consumers' level of education is a central pivotal variable that helps explain different holiday behaviour. With higher levels of education, consumers are keener to travel abroad; they master at least one foreign language and might undertake business travel, and their level of education gives them an opening to the world, a level of curiosity and the confidence to travel independently. Those consumers are also known to be more attracted to cultural products and encounters with local communities.

1.4.2 The influence of income and social classes on departure rate

Available income is necessarily a key element shaping tourism demand. The inequalities in terms of holiday consumption reflect broadly the inequalities observed in society. The level of income primarily influences the rate of departure on vacation, a rate which is also influenced by socioprofessional category (CSP).

For the purposes of surveys, travellers are differentiated according to their frequency of travel. By definition, nonparticipants do not take any trips per year, small travellers one to two trips per year, medium travellers three to ten trips and frequent travellers more than ten trips per year. We will use here statistics produced by the French government (Direction du Tourisme, 2002) since they are very pertinent to understanding how tourism demand is structured in terms of the number of trips taken by consumers.

- Frequent travellers account for 6% of the French population and 35% of all trips taken. They are executives, retirees or people exercising a higher intellectual profession. Not only are these categories of the population more likely to travel through their work, but their income and their social environment also favours travelling. Coming from small households (two people) whose net monthly income fluctuates between €1,900 and €5,300, half of these travellers take trips between 11 and 14 times a year for an average length of stay of 4.5 nights. They are overrepresented among those aged 25–34 and 55–64 and come from large urban areas. Half make trips abroad and, in 73% of cases, their accommodation is non-commercial (58% stay with family and friends and 14% in second homes).

- Medium travellers are represented by retirees, employees or those in intermediate professions who are between 25 and 44 years old or over 64 years old. They consist of one- to two-person households with net monthly incomes of €1,500 to €3,500. Of these, 37% have gone at least one trip abroad or in the Dom Tom (Départements d'outre-mer, Territoires d'outre-mer [French overseas departments and territories]), 57% choose noncommercial accommodation and 17% live in hotels.

- Small travellers (55% made only one trip) leave for 9–10 nights on average. They are retirees and employees or workers aged 15–24 and 35–54. Travelers from rural communities are overrepresented in this segment. Of small travellers, 19% travel abroad and 59% opt for noncommercial accommodation.

- Nontravellers are mainly unemployed people under 25 or over 65 years old. They come from a household of one or two people with a monthly net income of less than €2,300. They come from smaller agglomerations (less than 100,000 inhabitants) and rural municipalities.

- Income also plays a role in the type of vacation chosen. Higher income levels will correspond to longer vacation times as well as high participation rates in specific activities, usually those associated with the travellers' social status. For example, the higher the occupation, the more consumption of cultural products and outdoor activities will be observed. There is also, for those tourists, a predilection for independent trips and tours.

These statistics relate only to an analysis of the French holiday-making market. However, they are to some extent representative of the shape of demand according to socioeconomic factors in a lot of European countries. When looking at tourism demand, it is evident that deep differences exist between different countries across the world. This is evident when investigating holiday departure rates and, more simply, when identifying the reasons mentioned for not taking holidays. On average across Europe, 42.6% of inhabitants state "lack of money" as the main reason for not taking holidays (Mergoupis & Steuer, 2003). Those differences are also very much present within countries, even when they are considered to be fairly developed countries. If we take again the example of France, the inequalities of access to holidays need no demonstration. In France, more than 80% of upper social classes take at least one holiday a year, while less than 36% of the poorer classes go on holidays.

The divide in terms of holiday access is therefore very steep and, considering that holiday taking contributes to the general quality of life, it is a question that governments have aimed to address. In this regard, social tourism aims to develop facilities, activities and events and/or increased access to holidays for the more deprived strata of the population.

1.4.3 The evolution of tourism demand over the life-cycle

The concept of the life-cycle takes into account the impact on consumption of the evolution of an individual through life by taking into account his/her personal situation (single, in a couple, with or without children, etc.) and his/her professional life. Typologies in this area abound and have even passed into everyday language. Beginning with Table 1.1, the tables here present some of

Table 1.1 The family life cycle from birth to early adult life

Stage	Characteristics	Tourist behaviour
Childhood	Totally dependent on parents. Keen to indulge in activities with children of same age range.	Parents search for destinations and resorts (either seaside, backcountry, rural, mountain) with facilities for young children.
Adolescents	Stronger influence on parents' decisions but still dependent on them. This is a difficult age for the family unit. Adolescents are keen to spend time with friends of a similar age range.	Enjoy holidays in resorts with entertainment and activities, and most importantly with other adolescents. Semi-independent, they enjoy active holidays (sports), in groups and "adventurous" travel.
Young adult	Young, single and no longer living with parents (Single Income No Kids or SINKS). When at university, they will travel on a tight budget with friends of similar age. When they have their first employment, they will experience an increase in earnings, but they might not have purchased residential property yet, hence they have available income for holidays. They enjoy spending their earnings on leisure and travel.	Holidays depend on the time and resources available and are therefore varied. Young adults have a thirst for discovering the world, but if they still have a student status, they might be on a limited budget. They might undertake a world tour and backpacking experiences across various countries at the end of their studies. With their first employment, available time for holidays reduces but their salary allows them to plan some travel. They are active consumers of adventure, backpack holidays and experiences. They are also active consumers of party destinations such as Ibiza or the Tomorrowland Festival, and they like attending big festivals. This is a growing market, and the tourism industry has grown to consider backpacking as an important market deserving of more attention. Various products and services can serve this market: youth hostels, round-the-world plane tickets, low-cost airlines, interrailing, etc.

Source: Adapted from Lumsdon (1997)

the key stages individuals go through in their lives and the implications that those changes have in terms of tourism consumption.

The stages described so far identify the early years of a traveller, from being totally dependent on their parents to gradually gaining autonomy and starting travelling by oneself, especially in the student years (Table 1.2).

Inevitably, children will leave the household and parents will carry on travelling but with different patterns (Table 1.3).

We have provided a general overview of the different stages in the life-cycle of an individual. These are necessarily broad indications which do not account for the variation among individual demands that might not correspond to this broad average. But it does give an indication of the dynamics of the life-cycle and of all the personal, family and work elements that impact holiday choice.

In order to illustrate the life-cycle, we have chosen to shed light on the backpackers' market. Whilst backpackers often call to mind an image of penniless students travelling the world, they represent a very large market. The next case study describes the specifics of this market in the state of New South Wales in Australia (Figure 1.5).

THE BACKPACKING MARKET FOR THE STATE OF NEW SOUTH WALES (AUSTRALIA)

Despite their reputation as travellers on a budget, backpackers actually spend more, travel further and stay longer than other categories of tourists. Backpackers are typically young (18–35 years old), have a good level of education and are adventurous and thrifty. Their travel style is characterized as follows:

- They prefer **low-cost accommodation**: They use youth hostels but they are looking for good value for money, which does not necessarily lead them to always choose the cheapest option.

- Backpackers want to mix with **other travellers**: Social contacts (including making friends and partying) are an essential component of the backpacking lifestyle. Meeting other backpackers is also a way to exchange information on future trips. In regard to their activities, 94% cite "eat out, dine at a restaurant or café" as their prime activity; this is closely followed by "going to the beach" (88%) and sightseeing/looking around (88%).

- **Thrifty**: Even though they pay attention to prices and try to make their budgets last as long as possible, their average spend is $2,511 per visitor and $79 per night in NSW. Overall, backpackers contribute to 13% of the total tourism spend in Australia (https://www.thebyte.com.au/latest-backpacker-stats-from-tra/). NSW attracts 75% of backpacker visitors coming to Australia.

- **Flexible itinerary and long stays**: Backpackers visiting Australia stay longer than international travellers – 65 nights compared to an average of 26. They arrive in Australia with loosely planned routes and very few advance bookings.

- **Active adventurers**: The products of particular interest to them are adventure circuits and any service that requires active physical participation. Typical Australian activities that do not fall under the purview of mass tourism are particularly popular. Backpackers also seek information on and interactions with Aboriginal culture.

- **Working holiday**: A large proportion of backpackers aim to work during their stay to replenish their budget (working visas allow this easily).

- **Accommodation preferences**: The increase in backpacker demand for Australia has fuelled a supply of good-value, clean and secure youth hostels. Some of these may belong to international networks (YHA), but private hostels have also developed rapidly. Backpackers look for accommodation in the heart of cities close to the sights. In New South Wales, a trend has been noticed whereby backpackers move away from hostels and prefer rented apartments, which also correlates with the significant proportion of backpackers on a working visa. They can look for isolated accommodation, but only if they are close to established tourist attractions and if there is access by public transport.

- **Transport**: Given the size of Australia, a good public transport network is essential. Carriers have set up preferential rates and multi-day pass cards. The bus is the most popular mode of transport for backpackers because it is cheap and flexible. Incoming tour operators have set up offers for a few days or "jump-on, jump-off" bus options which have been met with great success. The train, because of its price, is less in demand while air travel is on the increase due to the lower prices charged.

- **Nationalities**: Backpackers are primarily British (18%), followed by Germans (13%) and Americans (9%). Of backpackers, 36% are between 20 and 24 years old and 30% are between 25 and 29 years old.

Source: Destination NSW (2015) International Backpackers to New South Wales, Tourism Research Australia.

Table 1.2 The family life cycle from early adult life to family life

Stage	Characteristics	Tourist behaviour
Couples with no children	Couples living together; they don't have children yet, they cumulate two salaries and they have not purchased a house yet. They have busy lives (they need to plan holidays in advance). They are at the start of their careers so they invest a lot of time and energy at work. Holidays are important periods to relax and be rewarded from their hard-working schedule. They are also called Double Income No Kids or DINKS.	This market exists in continuation from the previous one. Varied holiday behaviours exist but there is still a strong appetite for discovering other destinations. Compared to the previous segment, they will take short trips (city breaks) but they might also have a strong demand for "exotic" and memorable trips. DINKS have high tourist purchasing power and still have few financial burdens (no children, no high home loans and time available). They can afford favourite purchases of high-end products. They are curious and want to discover various countries before they settle down. DINKS are a lucrative market for the tourism industry.
Young family	The young couple is now settling down and is starting a family. Young family refers to the stage where the children are still young. The arrival of children might put pressure on the family's resources: they might buy a house, and childcare and other factors will contribute to a reduction in total income. Some parents might take time off to raise the children, which diminishes resources further. School rhythms also create another constraint, especially when it comes to booking holidays. Young families search for holidays with good value for money.	If both parents are working, they might feel frustration at not being able to spend enough quality time with their spouse and children. Days go by fast, and between work schedules, commuting, picking up children from school and various other duties, families might struggle to free up time for each other. For those reasons, holidays have increasingly become one of the last refuges of family life. Young families nourish expectations for those holidays where burdens and duties will be removed so that the family can make time to be truly with each other.

	When families separate, the financial strains upon single parents are stronger and will impact holidaying capacity and choices.	Families might book their holiday independently, and are avid consumers of products that offer a wide range of possibilities such as campsites and/or resorts. Between the full board option, the range of facilities and activities, and the capacity for their children to mix with children of the same age, resorts have created an offer that suits families.

The main holidays are particularly important for the family to be with each other. The family unit might also expand to include three generations (with the grandparents). |
| Mature family | Children's schooling is still a major constraint upon holiday taking. The children are growing and are reaching adolescent age. Connections with parents might not be as strong as before, and the teenagers are keen to spend time with friends of the same age. | With the children growing up, the family's holiday needs might also evolve. Resorts and cruises are still efficient at providing an interesting offer for mature families, they might even offer activities or spaces dedicated to teenagers.

With children growing older, however, a taste for the unknown and a sense of adventure will motivate families to engage with more adventurous travel. This means that independent travel is also an interesting option for mature families. |

Source: Adapted from Lumsdon (1997)

Table 1.3 The family life cycle in later life

Stage	Characteristics	Tourist behaviour
Empty nesters	Children leave home and parents have more freedom and greater purchasing power. Indeed, by the time the children have left the family home and finished their studies, the parents will have experienced a change in life. They will be better off financially (they might have finished paying their mortgage, they might still have two incomes, and their children are now financially independent).	The types of holidays chosen are very varied but there is a higher propensity to buy more expensive, cultural and discovery products as well as an increase in holidays during the year. "Empty nesters" are one of the most lucrative markets for the tourism industry. They have a high purchasing power and still have the desire to travel and discover. If they are in good health, they are ready to travel and carry on discovering the world. They also want to reward themselves for their strenuous work life but, with the departure of their children, they also enjoy getting back time to themselves. They demand products of a certain standard and they like their comfort.
Retirees	Both parents gradually retire. Their income is now set at a certain level but the time available to them increases significantly. They might become grandparents, in which case they will integrate the desire to spend time with their children and grandchildren into their holiday schedule.	Advancing in age, retirees will still have the desire to travel, but facilities, amenities, levels of security and comfort are elements that will weigh more strongly in their holiday choice. They might also favour group travel, seek quality and, with age, look for less active holidays. An advanced age is no longer automatically a hindrance to travel as it might have been for previous generations. It is noted, however, that over the age of 75, the propensity to travel drops tremendously. Overall, health incidents play a crucial role in holiday decision making. If a retiree experiences a health scare, he/she will become less confident about travelling, especially to far-away destinations.

Source: Adapted from Lumsdon (1997)

Figure 1.5 Resting on the beach and embracing the landscape. Source: Photo by Engin Akyurt on Unsplash.

1.4.4 Cultural influences

Beyond socioeconomic influences, consumers never exist in isolation. The country in which they were born, their region and their local area will have shaped how they behave to some extent. Family and social class will also influence consumers' profiles, behaviour and expectations.

Culture, taken in its broadest sense, is a wide, rich, multisource element that can provide an extremely rich insight into consumer behaviour. The influence of culture is considered as an external influence, an overarching element that is acquired when growing up. It is acquired through everyday life encounters and in family life, but also in the professional sphere and through education systems. Culture is comprehensive; it encapsulates a range of beliefs and practices that, together, constitute a cohesive culture. Culture is a very subtle universe, as investigated by Bourdieu. In his book on social class distinctions (2018), Bourdieu investigated how even in detailed aspects of everyday life, social class differences could be ascertained.

DISNEYLAND RESORT THROUGH A DIFFERENT CULTURE

In 1992, Disneyland developed a new resort at the heart of Europe, near Paris. Originally the project aimed to develop an ambitious park, along the same lines as those parks already in existence in the United States; the plan was to gradually open several parks and various resorts, along with shopping malls, golf courses, etc. The objective was also to position the resort as a destination in itself, one where consumers would holiday for several days or at least a week.

Nearly 30 years later, the average length of time spent by visitors is slowly reaching 2 nights and 3 days. The difficulties encountered by Disney in the implementation of this new park have been mostly linked to a misunderstanding of cultural perceptions of theme parks throughout Europe.

Indeed, first and foremost, different nationalities across Europe have very different perceptions of what a theme park should be. In France itself, theme parks were considered as an activity for children, to be consumed on a day out. It took a very long time to expand the customer base to include larger strata of the population: teenagers, young adults and families of all kinds. Across Europe, whilst Nordic consumers are the bigger consumers of theme parks, the same could not be achieved across some southern European destinations.

At another level, Disney discovered that each nationality had different expectations in terms of merchandising.

For instance, the company discovered that each country favoured different Disney characters, preferred a different visibility of Disney characters and logos on items bought, purchased different types of items and was keen to participate in events echoing their national cultures. As a result, Disney redesigned its merchandising and event strategies to develop an offer closer to different nationalities' expectations.

Culture is by definition a very strong component of tourism experiences because individuals from different cultures will encounter each other on different occasions.

On one hand, this necessitates integrating the fact that visiting tourists will "carry" with them their own culture, which is most likely to be different from the destination's culture. Whilst this is what creates destinations' richness and attractiveness, it is also what might create difficulties on both sides of the equation. On one side, tourists might fail to understand how their behaviour might not be seen favourably by local populations. Whether this refers to their style of dress, their eating habits, their behaviour in public or many other differences, visiting tourists are likely to display different behaviours. This might cause difficulties of various intensity for local inhabitants and can produce unnecessary friction. In order to encourage visiting tourists to adapt further to local cultures, destinations and operators alike have drawn up codes of conduct that assist their consumers in integrating some behavioural codes that can be beneficial to both parties (see example given thereafter on codes of conduct). These codes of conduct also have the objective to attempt to reduce culture shock. Culture shock happens when tourists experience a new culture that is radically different from theirs, and this confrontation might translate into an unpleasant experience. Culture shock might be felt physically and emotionally. Oberg (1960) identified five symptoms of culture shock: strain as a result of having to adapt to the new culture, a sense of loss and deprivation of usual social spheres (friends, work and social spheres), feeling rejected by the new culture, confusion in role expectations and, finally, feeling unable to cope with the new context.

DESIGNING A CODE OF CONDUCT FOR TOURISTS

Apus Peru is a travel agency based in Cusco, Peru. Every year, this agency welcomes tourists of various nationalities and is well aware of the difficulty that visitors and hosts might have in understanding what is expected behaviour, especially when they are in contact with the local population. The agency's website is rich in advice for travellers.

One interesting element of the communities' culture is their gift-giving philosophy, called *ayni*. Ayni is both a philosophical and legal principle of reciprocal exchange: "today for me, tomorrow for you". Gift-giving with no reciprocal exchange can break this fundamental principle in Queshua society. If giving gifts, travellers are advised to avoid giving sweets, loose change or anything packaged (which will become litter).

Recommended gifts are fresh and dried fruits, hats, tee-shirts, shampoo, toothbrushes and toothpaste, Spanish language reading and picture books, etc. Travellers are advised to give the books to the local schools and not to individuals.

The company also encourages its clients to be watchful about the pictures they show of their lifestyles back home. A steep difference between the tourists' and locals' lifestyles can only create frustration and incomprehension.

The agency also advises its customers not to try to eat with or spend time with porters and muleteers. Queshua people are extremely shy and would much prefer to spend time with each other and speak in their own language. This need has to be respected by tourists.

Source: https://www.apus-peru.com/why-choose-apus-peru/
being-a-responsible-tourist

On the other hand, local inhabitants might have difficulty in accepting the different behaviour and habits that tourists display while on holidays and which might conflict with their own culture. The codes of conduct mentioned above might also be beneficial in reducing this incomprehension but they might not be sufficient. If tourism is massified and the ratio between the number of visitors to a destination and the local destination capacity in absorbing this tourism influence is too high, difficulties might arise. Pearce (1982) also identified that this impact might be particularly strong if host communities are small, unsophisticated and in fairly isolated locations. This might lead to a phenomenon of the rejection of tourism and local communities expressing resistance by firmly closing off one's culture. This phenomenon has been exemplified vividly in the overtourism debates that have taken place across the globe. When tourism becomes overwhelming for a destination, local inhabitants might feel that they have lost their quality of life and no longer recognize their own city/destination. This might lead them to reject tourism (the infamous "tourists go home" tags seen in Barcelona, for instance) and/or to develop parallel lives in enclaves that are free from tourist intrusions. Recently, destinations have increasingly been willing to reduce the negative impacts of tourism on local populations and consider that local inhabitants' quality of life is also an element that they need to integrate in their policies.

Overall, the notion of culture shock is an important one to consider when designing tourism experiences. It calls for service designers to integrate this potential shock into the design of their service delivery and to prepare consumers for those potential differences by disseminating codes of conduct. When frictions come to dominate the situation, destinations might also decide to rethink their tourism development with the quality of life of their inhabitants in mind (see example here on Amsterdam).

EXAMPLE: AMSTERDAM AND OVERTOURISM

Whilst, in the minds of many, overtourism has often been associated with tourist destinations in Mediterranean countries such as Barcelona or Venice, it has also been a key issue in other destinations such as Copenhagen

(Denmark) or in natural areas such as the Banff National Park (Canada) or on the Isle of Skye (Scotland). Overtourism does not only refer to situations where the levels of tourism flow can no longer be absorbed by a destination. It also highlights the fact that tourism can disrupt local life and the social balance of local destinations. In other words, in overtourism occurrences, life becomes unbearable and residents find it increasingly difficult to live a normal life, the life they had been accustomed to. In many ways, overtourism impacts local quality of life and in its worst forms it might lead local residents to move away from the destination.

In Amsterdam, local authorities are well aware of the impacts that tourism has had and have aimed to develop several measures in order to overcome those shortcomings. Amsterdam welcomed 20 million visitors in 2018 for a local population of 820,000 inhabitants. As often, tourists concentrate on a limited range of areas, and this has put tremendous pressure on some neighbourhoods. Identifying a real problem for the quality of life of its inhabitants, Amsterdam has taken radical decisions in relation to various issues.

First of all, tourism pressure encourages local businesses to move away from traditional shops and cater for the more prolific tourist needs. Restaurants (of local feature or not) and souvenirs shops gradually replace traditional services. Businesses such as local corner shops, chemists and laundry services will gradually be pushed out of those neighbourhoods. This not only diminishes the traditional ambience of those areas but more importantly, for local inhabitants, creates a sense of frustration of not recognizing their own neighbourhood, the one they once enjoyed living in. Amsterdam has therefore aimed to strictly regulate the new opening of shops catering only to tourists in order to guarantee that local communities maintain a local quality of life by having access to their usual local shops. Hotel relocation is another strategy to redirect tourist flows to less touristic areas, and the famous "I Amsterdam" destination brand sign has been moved to a site near Schiphol airport.

The rise of short-term tourist accommodation rental (typically Airbnb flats) has led to a steep increase in rents and house prices, pushing out traditional inhabitants from some areas. In consequence, the city has decided to ban Airbnb rentals from the historic centre.

Other issues are associated with young people's stag and hen parties and their antisocial behaviour (drunkenness, urinating, noise, littering). As a result, Amsterdam has decided to reduce the provision of alcohol on its streets. Beer bikes serving alcohol have been banned. Antisocial behaviour is also the object of heavy fines.

Amsterdam is also aiming to change its image. The city wants to be known for the right reasons, and the attraction of drugs and prostitution is an image that the city needs to get rid of. Amsterdam wants to shift its coffee-shop image and aims to restrict coffee-shop use only to locals (as is the case for the rest of the Netherlands). Amsterdam also wants to shift the red-light district to the outskirts of the city; in the meantime, it has already banned organized tours of the red-light district.

The strategy adopted by Amsterdam results from a deep analysis of what tourism has brought to the city but also its negative externalities. The decisions that have been taken in terms of tourism management aim both at restoring quality of life for local inhabitants and redressing the image of Amsterdam itself. The various decisions taken are also the result of a city that is willing to take radical decisions and implement them. Whilst tourism naturally brings income and employment, this cannot be at any cost, especially for the populations that live at the heart of popular destinations.

Within the overarching notion of culture, smaller groups can be identified that are referred to as *subcultures*. The idea of a subculture is that communities of consumers can share common interests and are more likely to be attracted to similar categories of products. Subculture groups transcend traditional segmentation criteria to identify consumer communities according to common passions and interests. They share a common sense of identity and they share similar behaviour. Subcultures can be identified by their generation (an age range such as generation Y, for instance), their sexual orientation or their regional belonging. They might also be defined by a passion they share. Backpackers can be defined as a subculture, but so can volcano lovers, who design their travelling career around visits to volcanoes across the world; or kite surfers, who equally live and breathe their passion for their sport and make travel choices accordingly.

Consumers might belong to several subcultures. For example, a consumer might be a generation Y kite surfer from a middle social class.

The interesting aspect about subcultures is the ability to identify tourists according to the cultures they cherish or their common lifestyles, independently from some other variables.

Subcultures will share specific codes (dressing styles, language, values, etc.). Some subcultures can be quite subtle in their set of references and values; therefore, precise consumer research data is needed in order to fully understand their subcultural sphere. Even if they might be a smaller subset group within a culture, they can be a correct target for marketers as they will be active consumers if the products match their subculture expectations.

EXERCISE: UNDERSTANDING THE SENIOR MARKET

Age is a simple criterion to segment consumers but it can be a pertinent one, especially when it points to the emergence of new markets such as generation Z (born from the late 1990s to the early 2010s) and millennials (born from the early 1980s to the mid-1990s). Those generations, born with the Internet, are more likely to travel independently and more often than previous generations (millennials take four or more trips per year) and assign more value to experiences than possessions. These new generations have achieved a certain independence in terms of their travel (a result of experience and access to information).

When analysing the senior market, it might be tempting to consider it as a global market with similar expectations. However, the senior market carries many subtleties and subgroups that need to be fully understood in order to appreciate more finely which products are best targeted to which categories of senior people. In order to understand those subtleties, you are encouraged to investigate consumer intelligence that you can identify over the Internet. With a good search engine and pertinent keywords, you will quickly find some very relevant reports that can assist you in strategically reading the senior market. To drive your analysis, you might want to consider the following questions and challenges:

Can you identify different age ranges within the senior market? Do these categories have different types of expectations? Which tourism products are they most likely to consume?
What characterizes them in terms of activities, lifestyle and expectations?
Is age and perception of age an important component to understand this market?
The outcome of this first step is to identify the key segments of senior consumers.

Once you have established this, you might want to undertake the following challenge:

In relation to your destination, can you identify one existing product for each of the senior segments identified in the previous step?

Secondly, can you create what you feel would be the ideal package offer for one of those segments? You can create a 3-day package and it should include a choice of accommodation, a catering experience and two activities. This package needs to be coherent, and the products you identify need to answer, together and cohesively, the needs of that market.

1.5 The consumer at the individual level

At the individual level, consumer behaviour investigates consumers from various angles such as their values, perception, personality, attitude and learning.

1.5.1 Values, motivations and lifestyles

Consumers can be defined by their values, motivations and lifestyles. The study of motivation has been the object of ample research in tourism marketing and will be detailed in the following chapter. Motivation helps in understanding the key leverage elements to appreciate what consumers are seeking when choosing some products and services, and this can serve as a powerful basis to segment consumers (see Chapter 6, Section 6.9). Motivations have also been recognized as a strong dynamic that allows practitioners to understand consumers' goals and thereby understand more clearly to which extent products and services fulfil those goals and fuel satisfaction.

Consumers' lifestyles also mean that they can be inclined to choose holidays that reflect their general style as consumers and individuals. Belk (1988) has long identified that brands could be considered as an extension of the self. Holidays are equally a consumable that project an image of consumers and supports this image to the outside world. The advent of social networking has reinforced this process, and sharing holiday snapshots has become for some a key outcome of holidays to strengthen their image on those networks. This evolution has also meant that consumers are increasingly looking to reinforce this identity by consuming specific holiday sites and destinations. For instance, the trend of the "bucket list" has seen consumers touring the world in search of key sites that will reinforce their public image, up to the point that seeking those snapshots (in the Grand Canyon, up Mont Blanc or at Uluru) constitute the main holiday objective.

1.5.2 Perceptions

Consumer behaviour also looks at individual processes within consumption. For instance, perceptions have been the object of research to understand how sensory information is stored and interpreted by consumers. Whilst sensory inputs fuel perceptions, those perceptions are also translated by consumers' previous experiences, knowledge and cultural influences. In other words, individuals will perceive sensory stimulus differently according to their own schema, patterns and culture.

1.5.3 Attitude

The notion of attitude refers to the fact that human beings have predispositions to evaluate positively or negatively a product, service or experience. There has been much study of attitudes since they play a key role in predicting purchases. Attitudes are made up of three main components: affective (the feeling one has towards a certain consumption), cognitive (thoughts and beliefs about a consumption) and behavioural (the actions actually undertaken by consumers). For instance, in relation to holidays, a consumer might have a positive attitude towards travelling independently because travelling and meeting with local communities is important to them (affective); when they travel, they always aim to interact with local inhabitants (behavioural), because it is important to engage with local communities to improve their understanding of the world (cognitive).

1.5.4 Personality

Consumers' personalities also strongly influence their holiday choices and expectations. This dimension has been the object of various studies over the years. The most recognized study in this regard was produced by Plog in an investigation of American Express card owners in the late 1970s. Plog identified that travellers could be differentiated according to different personalities and that this categorization could help providers predict their holiday destination choices. According to Plog (1974), travellers could be organized along a continuum ranging from allocentrics to psychocentrics. Psychocentrics were identified as rather conservative, broadly risk-averse consumers who were keen to stay in their comfort zone and, as a result, tended to use the car rather than flying, to travel less frequently and to be mostly domestic consumers. At the other end of the continuum, allocentrics were identified as being more self-confident and preferring adventurous experiences and novelty. They were more frequent travellers, took longer holidays and were more likely to fly. While Plog's model is now rather dated, and the information gained on flying and distance travelled might be different nowadays, it still has relevance in order to understand consumer markets. For instance, it might help us to understand why some consumers prefer some forms of travel rather than others. As an example, the consumption of cruises and all-inclusive resorts answers the needs of stressed individuals who seek an all-inclusive offer that will give them access to holidays located within an enclaved setting that answers their psychocentric needs for reassurance. On the other end, the demand for independent travel, road trips or backpacking answer the needs of allocentrics.

1.5.5 Learning and memory

Learning is a key understanding of the consumer experience, relating to the analysis of how consumers develop understanding, knowledge, behaviour and skills. Those components are essential to be able to feel at ease with a new holiday environment and/or activities, to understand how consumers can or cannot immerse themselves (do they need specific competences, skills, previous knowledge, etc.?). Those elements will be addressed in Chapter 2.

The aspects associated with memory will be addressed in Chapter 3.

1.6 Why study behaviour?

The analysis, measure and understanding of behaviour is a strategic weapon for enterprises and destinations alike. Indeed, behaviour informs strategic decisions at different levels of marketing functions. Whether it aims to identify the right customer targets or tailor communication according to strategic aims, develop a new product, reposition a product or predict future behaviour, the understanding of consumer behaviour is at the heart of and the driving force behind efficient strategies.

1.6.1 Identify the right consumer

The analysis of different behaviours across the range of consumers is the object of market segmentation. Segmentation concentrates a range of techniques that allow decision-makers to understand how to identify clusters of behaviour among their consumer markets. The basic principle of segmentation is to identify, within a consumer market, segments of consumers displaying similar behaviour. A wide range of criteria can be used in segmentation techniques. Whereas traditionally, segmentation techniques looked at socioeconomic demographic criteria to segment customers, over the years techniques have greatly evolved and are now integrating lifestyle and psychological elements that allow decision-makers to have a much more precise choice of criteria to segment efficiently consumers. See Chapter 6 for more detailed information on segmentation approaches.

Once the segments have been identified, decision-makers will then choose one or several markets where they will aim to concentrate their strategic efforts. This choice of market targeting is a crucial decision because it has to be achievable by the company or destination. One has to evaluate to which extent a segment is attractive on a commercial basis and make sure that it will not cannibalize other segments. The commercial viability of a segment depends on the size of the segment but also necessarily on its purchasing power.

Nowadays, it would be difficult to imagine a company with no targeting strategy. Even though mass tourism is the easiest broad and holistic marketing strategy, most tourism strategies involve the identification of key consumer segments and a marketing strategy devoted to one or several segments.

The strategic choice for a tourism enterprise or destination lies also in questioning its capacity to be able to target several segments. Indeed, since each segment will require a specific marketing mix, it can be a heavy financial and managerial load to target several segments.

In order not to blur the image of a product, companies often choose to develop several brands that will position their products in different markets. Choosing those different brands allows the companies to be able to portray a different image and value proposition in different markets.

In the 2000s, New Zealand recognized the growing demand from the Chinese market for its destination. This is the fastest growing market and its second most important international visitors' market. This market, like any other, has specific needs that the tourism authorities have recognized. As a result, they have developed recommendations and tool kits to assist tourism providers in targeting and serving this market efficiently.

The China Visitor Insight program has been commissioned by the New Zealand Ministry of Business, Innovation and Employment (MBIE), estimating that Chinese visitors' expenditure will rise to $16 billion by 2022 (predictions pre-Covid 19 pandemic). This program stemmed from the recognition that the Chinese market is evolving, witnessing the rise of independent travellers (rather than tour-group visitors). Independent travellers are likely to stay longer, and their economic impact on destinations is greater and more localized than that of group tours. The program also hopes to encourage visitors to travel during off-peak seasons.

The China Visitor Insight program was set up in 2015 and provides various online services and a series of webinars to assist tourism providers in understanding the expectations of these visitors and to develop products specific to their needs. It details the types of destinations and tourism products and services attractive to those consumers. The webinars present general data about the growth of this market and the specificities of its demand.

The advantage of webinars is also their capacity to provide travel updates especially in times of crisis. Webinars are a very pertinent mode of communication to reach providers who are often burdened by their daily activities and might not find the time to read lengthy reports.

1.6.2 Communicate efficiently

Communication strategies have become an extremely complex field whereby companies and destinations have to identify the types of messages to convey and the media that are best suited to their message. Indeed, various tourism players are using increasingly varied communication strategies to promote themselves and assert their positions with their customers. As the means at their disposal have evolved, they now have a particularly wide range of tools to achieve their goals.

The objective of communication is to move the consumer from a stage of non-recognition or knowledge of a product to the ultimate stage of action, that is to say of purchase or even re-purchase. The formulation of the objectives must be clear and realistic because they will guide the entire communication process (the creative aspect, media planning, etc.), and they will often serve as a basis for subsequently evaluating the effectiveness of the advertising campaign. The objectives must already contain a formulation of the communication intention, the intended target and the expected time frame. Some objectives can be identified very precisely; for example, a company might aim to increase awareness of its products and services by x%.

The objectives are determined in conjunction with the identification of a communication target. This target corresponds to all the individuals a company or destination wants to reach through the communication campaign. It is not limited to customers; it can also target opinion leaders who will, in turn, influence consumers (journalists, travel agents, influencers, etc.).

Private actors (tour operators [TOs], travel agencies, hotel groups, etc.) and destinations have very different means and communication strategies. Destinations promote their territory, but they are often at a certain distance from source markets (apart from their offices abroad). They must promote their destination to multiple markets, and in each of those markets, they compete with other destinations. Their mission is not limited to promotional actions since they must also take into account the social, economic and environmental imperatives that these developments induce in their own territories. Conversely, TOs offer a wide choice of products and destinations for a well-defined clientele. Depending on their size, they might have larger promotional budgets than destinations.

Most importantly, communication has become a complex strategy because the means of communication have multiplied over the years, and each might provide a platform to achieve different objectives (Figure 1.6).

Media planning constitutes an important item of the communication budget (often the most important) and, as such, deserves special attention. The proliferation of media has made the choice of media mix more complex. Cable and satellite channels have been added to the terrestrial channels, the magazine market has exploded into a multitude of specialized magazines and outdoor and indoor advertising media have diversified (back of parking tickets, laser projections, counters, etc.). The possibilities on the Internet have multiplied. However, this explosion in the media mix has also made it possible to have tools that can reach much more targeted markets than before.

Media planning is the tool that makes it possible to implement the strategic communication directions for a company or a destination. It optimizes the quality and quantity of the media tools used. The media plan looks at the options chosen within each media, seeking to maximize the match between the image of the medium and that of the product. Other decisions will concern the format of the advertisement: length and frequency of exposure per week/month/day and

Figure 1.6 Communication strategy. Source: Author.

hourly for each medium, optimization of the length of the advertisement within the limits of the budget, geographical coverage, amount of investments, etc.

1.6.3 Develop new products

Another outcome of consumer behaviour is to be able to identify needs in the market, gaps that will serve as a basis for strategic development. The development of new products requires extensive market intelligence to be able to identify those needs and how tourism providers can respond to them. The creative process detailed in Chapter 6 gives a further indication of the different steps involved in the creation of new experiences.

1.6.4 Reposition a product

Repositioning a product and changing an image are probably the most difficult strategies to develop. Products and services cultivate set images among their key consumers, and those images might have been acquired and established over several decades. Changing an image requires careful thinking, a clever marketing strategy and very convincing argument to achieve this objective. The Club Med example underneath serves as an illustration of a brand repositioning strategy.

THE EVOLUTION OF THE IMAGE AND CONCEPT OF CLUB MED

The Club was founded by Gérard Blitz, who was then joined by Gilbert Trigano, in the early 1950s. When it was created, its objective was to meet a need for total relaxation coupled with active and sporting vacations for an audience of single people in their early 20s and 30s. At first, the comfort was rudimentary and the emphasis was more on the offer of sporting activities, and socialising, in an attractive natural setting. The aim was also to encourage interactions between tourists during their stay, and to break down social barriers between them as much as possible. Originally the accommodation was provided in tents, which were replaced in 1955 by huts, and then bungalows from 1965 onwards. Club Med was the forerunner in terms of all-inclusive packages, long before this offering spread throughout the world. The purchase price included travel, accommodation, activities and entertainment and catering. The only additional charges were individual drinks taken at the bar, and excursions.

As it evolved, the concept of Club Med changed from having the image of a young and unfussy club to that of a more family-oriented and adult resort from the end of the 1960s onwards. The clubs then equipped themselves with children's areas, and then, later on, with adolescent clubs.

After 2002, Club Med moved its offer to an all-inclusive holiday (all on-site consumption and activities are included in the price) to respond to a growing trend in consumer demand across the planet. This offer was generalized to all villages (sea and snow) from 2006 onwards.

The real strategic turning point was taken in 2004, notably under the leadership of its CEO, Henri Giscard-d'Estaing, by moving towards a high-end, friendly and multicultural positioning. The idea was to keep the notion of "living together" which has made the Club so successful, but without enrolment (less familiarity and no more collective tables) and in a much more luxurious setting than before. Most of the offer is centred on the values of refinement, generosity, and service personalization (à la carte service). The change was backed up by using renowned experts to design and conceive the new resorts. The renovation of the village clubs was undertaken by renowned architects and designers, the chefs were trained at the Lenôtre school and the rooms were redesigned with different levels of comfort (Club, Deluxe or Suite). The objective for the club has been to meet expectations of refinement, prestigious activities and majestic landscapes.

This repositioning was promoted through a large-scale communication campaign. The television advertising campaign focused on playing the card of the dreams, emotions and well-being that can be experienced on Club-Med vacation. Few images of resorts, rooms or services were presented; the essence of the message was based on the feeling of satisfaction and total relaxation that often only vacations can achieve.

If the objective was the same in the professional press, the tone used was more direct. The aim was to convince the professionals who would be selling Club Med's upscale products. The press campaign was carried out with six-page supplements that bolstered the new brand signature "There are still so many to discover". The message to professionals was clear and straight-forward: "Club Med has changed and metamorphosed. Some doubted this change. And then very quickly, they discovered exceptional sites, a refined à la carte vacation experience, etc. don't wait to change your outlook on Club Med".

In 2010, we can consider that the repositioning of Club Med was a success and that it was able to change its image, which was nevertheless very ste-reotypical and firmly anchored in French culture. Now, the Club's offering is considered to be a perfect match for that of global luxury resorts. However, the price increase was not without its challenges. Thus, in March 2010, Club Med announced a reduction in its prices of between 5% and 19% in 36 of its 80 villages. If the very upscale villages have gained customers, the two- and three-trident villages have lost some. With the move upmarket, Club Med has alienated part of its core target group, namely families (which represent 30% of the group's turnover), which it must now win back.

Internationally, Club Med is opening up to the BRIC countries (Brazil, Russia, India and China), particularly in the case of China, where the group opened a resort in Yabuli (North-East China) dedicated to skiing in 2010. A second hotel was been opened in Guilin in 2013. In 2014, a new complex opened on Dong'ao Island with other openings in the pipeline. Club Méditerranée wishes to capitalize on the Chinese people's openness to vacations and their need to escape particularly stressful and polluted urban environments.

Source: Adapted from Wermes R. (2007); Orsoni T. (2007)

1.6.5 Predicting future behaviour

Chapter 4 is devoted to current trends observed in tourism markets, so this will not be addressed here.

Nonetheless, the interest in mastering and understanding behaviour lies also in the capacity to foresee forthcoming demand. For instance, in a "math-ematical" vision, if one understands what fuels tourism demand, then one can foresee where the demand is most likely to emerge in the future. Therefore, when analysing the world, looking at economies entering different levels of industrialization and tertiarization will give pointers to the next emerging markets. For instance, the BRICS have long been identified as key growth markets. National policies regarding holiday entitlement and holiday visas have also contributed to energizing national tourism demand. Political influences can also be major influences in shaping both tourism offer and tourism demand. Political strategies can have strong impacts on the development of tourism within destinations. Planning and economic strategies and marketing strategies will impact the shape and development of a tourism industry nationwide. For instance, some countries will engage in vast programs to develop tourism infrastructures in specific areas, but they might also choose to restrict tourism in other areas.

HOW THE OECD INVESTIGATES MEGATRENDS SHAPING FUTURE TOURISM BEHAVIOUR

The Organization for Economic Co-operation and Development (OECD) plays a central role in assisting tourism professionals to foresee future trends. Their analysis relies on four key dimensions:

- **People**: this dimension investigates key changes in demographics and also integrates evolutions in health, labour and social cohesion. The evolution of those data reflects broadly the evolution of tourism demand, looking at the age shape of populations and the evolution of social classes.

- **Planet**: this dimension investigates the state of the planet and its major evolutions (the environment and climate change, for instance). This information helps managers to understand how resources are evolving across the globe and how it impacts sustainable tourism.

- **Productivity**: this element looks at economies' dynamics, such as evolutions in technology and innovation, and how they impact tourism demand. For instance, new technologies are necessarily important (sharing economy platforms, automization, new distribution developments) and so are evolutions in business models that allow a wider access to transport (low-cost models, for instance).

- **Policy**: this variable investigates evolutions in political orientations, especially those impacting access to tourism such as travel mobility, access to visas, to which extent states facilitate travel and support international transport, etc.

Source: OECD Tourism trends and Policies (2018); for a full report, see: www.oecd-library.org

Conclusion

This introductory chapter aimed to establish the foundation needed for the following chapters. It has examined the basis of consumer behaviour and its various facets and has aimed to point at the various elements that help marketers understand better why and how their consumers make their consumption choices. The marketing value of this comprehension was demonstrated through the implications that a better understanding of consumers can bring in terms of marketing strategy. We will devote the next two chapters to a more detailed analysis of behaviour specifically in the case of tourism. Before we develop a detailed analysis of experiential marketing (Chapter 5), we will investigate further the consumer behaviour specificities associated with the holiday universe. The next chapter will aim to analyse the processes that take place during holidays. Holidays are a very specific part of individuals' lives, and it is essential that readers understand this specificity, because it conditions the understanding and strategic development of successful experiences.

Chapter 2

Unlocking the dynamics of the holiday experience

Why consumers travel and how they engage with the experience

Introduction

Holiday consumption is unique in individuals' lives. It is a set period in their life, one that is outside their ordinary living conditions, one that is motivated by the need to leave behind everyday life and its various frustrations. Whilst this is an evident component of tourist demand, this need to escape the everyday should not be overlooked because it has strong implications for the design of experiences. This chapter will first go back to the roots of tourist demand, not only the need to escape daily life in its most fundamental frustrations, but also how holidays liberate consumers from their cultural constraints. This escape process is one of the key ways that consumers can rediscover their true selves, another important outcome of the holiday experience. The process of embarking on the holiday experience and its immersive essence will then be addressed, and finally the chapter will present some research technics that allow experience designers to gain a valuable insight into experiences as they unfold.

DOI: 10.4324/9781003019237-3

2.1 Push and pull factors

Motivation is the engine of human behaviour. Motivations are at the root of behaviour; they create, maintain and direct consumers' actions. Motivations are often considered as a unifying variable which concentrate the influence of various factors internal and external to the consumer. In the context of tourism consumption, this concept has been widely studied and its different facets are well understood. Tourists' motivations are divided into two main components: on one hand, the push factors that motivate the desire to leave; and on the other hand, the pull factors that explain the choice of a destination or a type of tourism product.

In 1977, Dann established that tourism consumption achieves the fulfilment of both anomie and ego-enhancement needs. Anomie corresponds to a break from a feeling of isolation, a feeling which is characteristic of contemporary societies and motivates consumers to get away from it all. Ego-enhancement needs refer rather to the need to boost one's ego through recognition and social interactions, for instance, and those might be achieved through the consumption of holidays. Therefore, according to Dann, holidays offer both an escape from cold and solitary contemporary life and the opportunity to enhance one's ego through the holiday.

Crompton (1979), in a well-known study on tourists' behaviour, identified that motivations could be separated into two broad types: socio-psychological and cultural. Socio-psychological motives incorporate the needs for escape from a perceived mundane environment, exploration and evaluation of self, relaxation, prestige, regression, enhancement of kingship relationships and facilitation of social interactions. In Crompton's approach, cultural motives referred to novelty and education. Various studies have investigated motivations over the years, and overall, motivations seem to revolve around five central themes: relaxing, companionship (quality time with family and friends), cultural discovery, novelty and physical activities. There are more subtle approaches to the study of motivations but we shall not develop them further in this chapter. The main focus of this chapter is to concentrate on the push factors – in other words, the deep reasons why people want to get away from it all.

Krippendorf (1987) has often argued that vacations should be advised by medical prescription as they represent a safety valve in our stressful living conditions. According to Krippendorf (1987), vacations equal "escape aids, problem solvers, suppliers of strength, energy, new lifeblood and happiness" (page 17). Studies perfectly corroborate this vision of tourism: a break from everyday life and the need for renewal remain the primary motivations for tourist consumption. The push factors are essential to understand because they not only constitute the root of tourism demand, but also drive tourists' behaviour and expectations throughout the holiday.

The notion of being able to get away from everyday life is investigated in studies addressing the dynamics of the concept of escape. Escape can be defined as a state experienced during a tourist experience; it results from a commitment to the experience, characterizes the escape felt by consumers from their everyday life and induces specific assessments and behaviours (Lenglet & Frochot, 2021). The concept reflects a state of escape from everyday routines in general (Uriely 2005), and engaging in activities allowing tourists to distance themselves from civilization, routines or responsibilities, as well as from the self (Cova et al., 2018; Wang, 1999).

Overall, these studies identify common aspects of the idea of escape, such as playing a different character, escaping daily routines and pressures and being in a different place or time.

2.1.1 Escaping everyday life

The need for relaxation is often defined in opposition to everyday life and reflects both mental and physical relaxation: the ability to stop stressing, to rest body and mind, to forget everything, to let matters take their course, etc. Thus, tourists seek to leave the many frustrations experienced on a daily basis behind them: "In consumer research, escape is akin to breaking away from mundane reality because that reality cannot be transformed" (Cova, Carù & Caila, 2018, page 3).

Frustration with and tiredness of daily life are lived at different levels. On a very basic level, consumers want to escape a broad range of daily chores. For instance, running a home involves various duties such as cleaning the home, cooking meals, looking after the garden, paying bills, engaging in various DIY and house maintenance duties, etc. On a second level, being a family involves various duties such as taking children to school and other activities, finding time to look after children's education, taking care of oneself with various leisure activities and medical appointments, etc. Considering that 70% of the world's population will be leaving in urban areas by 2030, one might also want to consider that urban living conditions bring another range of tensions: congestion on the roads, queues, dependence on the car, stress in the city, a lack of free time and regular and unavoidable daily rhythms (metro-work-sleep). The work sphere equally brings many satisfactions but also stresses and pressures: uncertainties about employment, short-term (even zero-hours) contracts, pressures from responsibilities, etc.

Consumers' everyday lives also have to be viewed from the perspective of the society they live in. Societies bring many positive elements but they can also create pressure on individuals. Political changes in a country, social instability, crime, etc. can all create an oppressive atmosphere. On a more general level, global issues can create a lot of stress: wars, terrorism and civil unrest, global warming issues and pandemics all contribute to a tension that one might want to escape from during a holiday.

The need to escape from those various levels of tension is even more essential nowadays because of the living conditions individuals are experiencing. As an example, a study carried out in 2003 by CSA/Télérama indicates that, if tourists had the choice, 64% would like to take more holidays during the year (even if their duration was limited) and only 11% would prefer an increase in salary to a reduction in time off. The survey also indicates that 96% believe that the priority on vacation is to decompress, 76% that holidays allow them to forget about work completely and 68% that they allow them to forget about problems at work. It should be noted that this demand is just as strong among retirees, 93% of whom rely on vacations to decompress and 80% of whom take advantage of their vacations to simply rest (CSA / Télérama, 2003).

Figure 2.1 can fuel creative thinking for tourist experience designers, allowing them to understand the extent to which the experience can take consumers away from those various stresses. As such, the tourist experience opens a period of time where consumers will act and behave differently and adopt not only a new identity but also different rules and practices. However, "There are subtle differences between mundane routines that are fun and part of the holiday, and

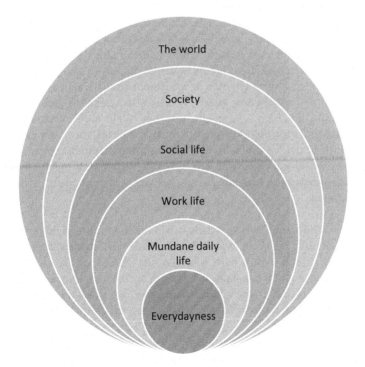

Figure 2.1 Escaping different levels of pressure. Source: Author.

those that are a reminder of daily and temporarily unwanted lives" (Frochot, Kreziak & Elliot, 2018, page 334). Some mundane routines will remain present (and necessary) during the holiday – those pertaining to daily life (preparing meals, minor cleaning, etc.) – but other chores will disappear. For instance, elements such as DIY activities, ironing clothes or in-depth cleaning of the house are absent from holiday routines.

If consumers feel that they are often under pressure of time in their daily lives, they will appreciate, on holidays, being cut free from those imposed rhythms. For instance, on vacation, tourists often refer to the pleasure of no longer having imposed rhythms. The resorts have understood this demand and offer catering possibilities at any time of the day, late breakfasts, all-day snacking, etc. The ideal is to provide schedule-free days where tourists can behave as they please: lie in late, eat at times that suit, undertake activities when they wish, etc. Daily cleaning of rented appartements and hotel rooms also eases the pressure on tourists. Resorts can also organize day excursions and a range of activities (never imposed) from which tourists can choose at their leisure.

In terms of easing services, resorts – and particularly all-inclusive resorts – have developed a key strategic understanding of the tourist experience and how they can develop services to ease and fluidify its process. Necessarily, the same reasoning is harder to achieve for destinations that would like to offer some form of inclusive and fluid offer, but face the challenge of composing the tourist offer from a broad range of public and private providers that the destinations do not own. In the last decade, conciergerie services have emerged that aim to combine service provision from different providers either directly to tourists or to accommodation providers (such as villas or apartment providers). For accommodation owners, they can welcome guests, maintain and clean the accommodation, provide bedding and baby equipment, and they might even manage bookings. They can also provide services directly to tourists. For instance, they can provide bikes or skis and deliver them directly to the tourist accommodation. They can also partner with local chefs who can either deliver cooked meals to tourists' accommodation or even provide a local chef who can cook meals within their accommodation.

For a tourist who wants to escape daily urban life, no longer having to use a car during a resort stay can be an essential criterion of satisfaction in some destinations. Making sure that some parts of a resort or destination are car-free, that a network of bicycle rental companies is on offer and that cycling lanes have been designed can, together, create a holiday universe that gives consumers a more appealing experience, far from the usual car-bound dynamics of their daily lives.

In many ways, the experience designed for tourists is an inversed mirror to the daily frustrations they have come to escape. Figure 2.1 is a good starting base to engage a whole range of thinking about service provision that can be attractive to tourists. Strictly speaking, there is no specific destination capable of meeting these expectations, as any context that is different from that of usual life or work is sufficient; the important dynamic is to offer a universe that sets consumers free from everyday life. This type of reasoning is at the heart of the task of the experience designer, who needs to identify the range of frustrations that consumers are escaping in order to develop an efficient experience (see the next exercise).

DEVELOPING INVERSED-MIRROR EXPERIENCES

In this exercise, the objective is to rethink the various frustrations that tourists experience in their daily lives and understand how experiences can be designed in order to counteract those frustrations. For each of the items listed in the table (and which were explained in Figure 2.1), develop at least one answer that your product/destination can develop. Be creative and thoughtful about the ways in which you can provide a different universe, activity or service that will be attractive to holiday-makers because it will exist in opposition to daily frustrations and stresses.

Everydayness	• Think of service provision that will allow your consumers to ease off from everyday chores even if it might seem anedoctical
Mundane life	• A life involves various tasks, obligations and organisation skills that can be tiring, can you think of ways to remove those from the holiday experience?
Work life	• If work life intrudes on the holiday experience, it is an inhibitor to the holiday mood. Can you think of kind ways to encourage your consumers to cut free from the temptations to connect to this world?
Social life	• Holidays provide quality time with friends and loved-ones. Can you develop opportunities and/or activities that will boost those connections?
Society	• Society brings a structure in which individuals do not necessarily mix with each other. Can you think of opportunities, during the experience, where tourists might meet and develop an understanding of other individuals they might never meet otherwise?
The world	• The world and life in general is a beautiful but also a stressful place. Can you think of activities and encounters that might reunite your consumers with the inherent and natural beauty of our world?

Now that we have listed the range of tensions and pressures that consumers want to leave behind, we shall dig further into the experience to understand what "being on holiday" means for contemporary consumers. The next chapter will look at optimal experiences that fuel tourists' memories, but at his stage we will concentrate on the state that consumers experience when they are on holidays, often referred to as *touristhood*.

2.1.2 Liminality: Escaping everyday roles

Another aspect to consider in holiday consumption is liminality. We have already addressed the basic everyday pressures that individuals escape through their holidays, and we shall now expand this reasoning at another level. Liminality is a very interesting concept that offers another reading of what lies behind the need to escape the everyday. Beyond daily life, travel can also evoke an escape from social norms and a temporary disconnectivity which is captured by the notion of liminality (Van Gennep, 1960; Turner, 1969; Turner & Turner, 1978). Within liminality, Urry (1990) argues that consumers cast aside their obligations, move away from rational decisions and behaviours and develop a new and temporal identity that is different from their everyday identity, both socially and work-wise. The liminal space is therefore a space where one can let go of one's everyday roles and identities (Figure 2.2).

According to van Gennep, the liminal process involves three stages: separation from the usual environment, transition to a new stage and reintegration in one's life. The liminality framework helps us understanding the value of a holiday as a specific time during which a tourist can shake off his/her usual identity and temporarily behave differently and free themselves from familiar pressures. During this period, tourists will engage in *communitas*: bonding and sharing with other tourists. Camaraderie that forms among consumers while consuming holidays creates a new sphere where normal social roles are cast aside and

Figure 2.2 Partying till dawn and engaging into a liminal experience. Source: Photo by John Thomas on Unsplash.

participants engage in relationships where the usual statuses no longer exist (Belk, 1988). Holidays generally respond to this need for escape from the usual structures.

Following from the liminality concept, Jafari (1987) has identified that during a holiday period, tourists will enter a different state named touristhood. In this vision, the holiday corresponds to a phase called *animation*, in which tourists will separate from their usual lives (emancipation) and move to a new experience, escaping from the various roles and obligations mentioned previously. Jafari (1987) describes the emancipation phase as representing a growing distance from the ordinary world, which is also called *encapsulation* (Jansson, 2007) or engagement (McKercher & Lui, 2014).

THE BURNING MAN FESTIVAL

The Burning Man Festival was moved from a beach to the Nevada desert in 1990. This event is more than a festival. Over the course of 9 days at the end of August, it establishes a temporary city where a community can meet and live a very different life for the duration of the festival. The burning man refers to a statue or temple that is burned at the end of the festival; the temple is a memorial dedicated to those who have died and are remembered by their loved ones.

Several principles have been established by its creator, Larry Harvey, and include inclusion, gifting, self-reliance and self-expression, communal effort, immediacy, radical participation and civic responsibility. During the Burning Man Festival, the usual structures of life are set aside to lead a different life away from the usual constraints and structures and reunite with the authentic self. The idea is also to engage in sharing and giving in a collective spirit.

There is a willingness to move away from society's traditional commercial spheres by encouraging gift-giving, and for some of the products purchased onsite, the profits go to various associations. Nonetheless, various commercial services and packages are on offer within the festival site.

Due to its location in a harsh desert with very few facilities, the festival asks its participants to be self-reliant and bring their own tents, water, food, etc. The festival aims to leave no trace and has a strong environmental engagement even though it does have impacts of various types (participants traveling to the site, garbage, etc.).

First and foremost, attending the Burning Man Festival is a temporary experience that sets outside traditional societal boundaries. It encourages participants to disengage from their traditional lives and selves to come and live in a different place, with a different community and identity. The festival creates a sense of re-enchantment by encouraging participants to participate in creative activities (art, theatre, music, etc.). Participants also create muting artistic vehicles (cars, vans, bicycles, etc.). The festival has a fairly tribal atmosphere, most of the music responding to the universe of electronic dance music and electronic music, and drums are another basis for dancing.

The Burning Man Festival is an extreme example in the broad sphere of tourism services' offerings, but a very interesting one. Kozinets's ethnographic study of this festival (2002) investigated how consumers live this experience away from the usual structures and identifies how participants are able to distance themselves from market logic and develop alternative practices away from the usual tenets of efficiency and rationality. Kozinets identifies how participants are able to develop an alternative and temporary community that establishes its own social logics and practices. The creative dimension of the festival and its anti-structure allow participants to liberate themselves from various tyrannies, express themselves differently and achieve some form of transformation. Kozinets insists on the temporary nature of the experience, which allows for its participants to let go – for a certain amount of time and within a well-defined context – of their ordinary selves and their daily lives:

> The speed of hyper community, the urgency of performativity, and the inversion of the festival all overlap to enthrone the disorderly, chaotic, anarchic, creative, risk-taking, and innovative forces of human nature, as against its orderly, planned, pre-programmed, boring, and imitative aspects. For practical reasons communities of this sort can only be temporary. Yet the illumination of taken-for-granted market logics, the flashes of inspiration and transformation to individuals and groups may be longer lasting.
>
> (Kozinets, 2002, page 57)

A video produced by Kozinets on the Burning Man Festival can be watched at https://www.youtube.com/watch?v=ZA6LEsJXYzg (Kozinets, 2012).

2.1.3 Authentic self

Holidays have been conceptualised as representing a quest for the authentic self. The context of liminality translates consumers' need to free themselves from various obligations and roles. Beyond getting away from pressures, holidays also open up the possibility of returning to one's true self, to escape all the behaviours and actions that are often associated with one's role and place in society and at work. These pressures blur the vision of what is actually important in an individual's life and distorts the link with who consumers really are and the direction they want their lives to take. Wang (1999) identified the role of authentic tourist experiences in individuals' lives:

> Existential experience involves personal or intersubjective feelings activated by the liminal process of tourist activities. In such a liminal experience, people feel they themselves are much more authentic and more freely self-expressed than in everyday life, not because they find the toured objects are authentic but simply because they are engaging in non-ordinary activities, free from the constraints of the daily.
>
> (pages 351–352)

The tourist experience is therefore a separate time in life, one where the liminal process allows individuals to step away from their normal lives and to rediscover their true selves. For this process to take place, extreme activities or contexts can play a major role (see the example of the Burning Man Festival), but the consumption contexts do not necessarily need to be so extreme to provide similar results. In Chapter 3, we shall address, in the section on simplicity, how simpler and more spontaneous experiences appear to allow consumers to reunite with their true selves. Experiences that take place in nature, adventure tourism and, more generally, tourist experiences that take consumers out of their comfort zone create fantastic opportunities for consumers to reconnect with their true selves (see the example on mountain hut experiences in Chapter 3).

2.1.4 Escaping reality carries different meanings

While the need to get away from everyday life and structures has been clearly identified, it is important to point out that this need does not translate into the same realities for different types of consumer.

In fact, the desire to leave daily environments behind does not necessarily translate into a search for a total change of scenery and an abandonment of the usual comforts. Consumers are diverse in their capacity to embrace change or not. In this regard, segmentation can help to understand those differences (as we will see in Chapter 6), but for now we will concentrate on two elements that can assist experience designers in understanding consumer differences. On one hand, Plog (2001) segmented consumers according to their personalities in order to predict their choice of destinations. Cohen (1972) also presented a theory based on the capacity and willingness that consumers have to embrace the unknown, called the *environmental bubble*.

Plog's work was based on the idea that consumers' personalities were pertinent pointers to the types of travel they might be attracted to. The model positions individuals on a continuum that identifies consumers' main personalities from allocentrics to psychocentrics. On one hand, consumers characterized as allocentrics are highly independent travellers who seek adventure, independence and novelty. Those tourists seek holidays that will move them outside their comfort zone and provide unfamiliar encounters and adventures, travelling in a road-trip style that leaves space for novelty and unplanned experiences. On the other hand, psychocentrics are individuals who fear the unknown, do not want to step out of their comfort zone and prefer familiar environments. Evidently, these tourists will prefer more packaged and resort-based forms of travel and will also prefer familiar and closer destinations. Plog's model is efficient in explaining travel choices and why tourists opt for specific forms of travel and destinations. Whilst Plog's work is quite old, it has kept its popularity over the years, and it is very common nowadays to find tourist destinations and tour operators offering personality quizzes that allow visitors to be offered a choice of itineraries/destinations tailored to their personalities.

Taking another perspective, Cohen investigated how tourists relate to destinations and proposed another form of categorization of tourists. Cohen's typology (1972) classifies tourists according to their relationship to the tourism industry and to the destination during their trip. Even if this typology is old, it allows us to decipher the behaviour of tourists and the products offered on the market.

According to Cohen, some tourists find it very difficult to escape their everyday environment and all the facilities that come with it. As a result, they travel within an "environmental bubble" that represents the consumers' cultural, behavioural and value system baggage, which they carry with them even on vacation. Based on this observation, Cohen identified four typologies that represent different categories of tourists depending on their desire to escape this environmental bubble or, on the contrary, to take refuge in it. These four categories are grouped into two large families: institutionalized and non-institutionalized tourists.

2.1.4.1 Institutionalized tourists

Trips taken by these tourists are usually organized by tourism operators (tour operators, travel agencies), and if tourists are looking for holidays abroad, those holidays should have many similarities with their daily environment. Within the category of institutionalized tourists, Cohen differentiates between the organized and the independent mass tourist.

2.1.4.1.1 The organized mass tourist

This type of tourist buys products on a package basis and makes few decisions about the course of the vacation. Excursions are pre-organized on air-conditioned buses, the hotel closely resembles consumers' usual surroundings and contacts with the local culture are rare. In the case of seaside holidays, the tourist moves between the hotel, the swimming pool and the beach, often not seeking to venture outside this space. He wants to eat the same food and speak the same language as in his country of origin. The tourism experience is planned, controlled and managed by the tourism industry. Each element of the vacation is planned, "packaged" and predictable, and the notion of discovering the country is often reduced to an inauthentic and mass-produced version of the local culture.

Many examples of this type of tourism exist in southern Europe in destinations that have developed under the impetus of northern tour operators. The products found there generally represent low-cost package offers that are consumed with the aim of being in a sunny destination but with all the comforts of home. Taking the example of the British market, English breakfast is served in most hotels, newspapers are imported from the UK, satellite television broadcasts football matches and famous TV shows, restaurants can serve British food, and fish-and-chip shops or pubs are often run by British owners. These aspects testify to this strong desire to find comfort and daily habits at the destination. It is by all means not representative of all British tourists and it is not only specific to this nationality; other nationalities consuming mass tourism display similar expectations and behaviour.

The organized mass-tourist segment largely represents the products offered by general tourism operators (TOs), mass tourism products like those developed in the 1960s and 1970s. Demand for these products remains very strong, but service standards are changing: aging resorts in the Mediterranean area are having to face increased competition from new resorts developing in other European regions and across the planet.

2.1.4.1.2 The individual mass tourist

Those tourists can still be considered mass tourists but there is a certain degree of individuality in relation to their trip. They will aim to use the tourist system at their disposal but will occasionally want to escape from it. Therefore, they wish to combine elements of familiarity (their environmental bubble) with a dimension of novelty, spicing up the trip by integrating personal choices and a certain degree of autonomy and flexibility.

For example, the individual mass tourist might purchase a packaged trip but with the possibility of integrating personal choices such as a short excursion organized by the tourist. One can also classify in this category tourists who organized their own trip but with the help of a tourist organization. For instance, self-drive tour packages are a relevant example whereby individuals maintain contacts with their environmental bubble (the hotel choice, itinerary and rental of a car of recognized standing are all pre-organized by a tour operator), and at the same time have a degree of flexibility (the flexibility of organizing each day, the choice of sites visited, etc.). Numerous TOs offer these products, whether they are small TOs specializing in a type of product or a type of destination or generalist TOs.

2.1.4.2 Non-institutionalized tourists

Those tourists prefer to travel individually, and their contact with the tourism industry is kept to a minimum and only when necessary. They want to meet new cultures and have different experiences than they are accustomed to in their daily life.

2.1.4.2.1 The Explorer

This tourist seeks to escape mass tourism in order to meet the local populations and customs. This contact search translates into an effort to speak the language of the country, finding local restaurants and having limited contacts with the tourism industry. However, this tourist wants to make sure that the facilities and safety provided by the tourist industry are available if needed. Thus, a minimum level of comfort must be present and the concept of security is also preponderant (easy access to care, contact with banking organizations, subscription to insurance, etc.).

This category of tourist tends to be found in destinations less explored by mass tourism. However, mass destinations may also have geographically limited tourist development (coastline, ski resorts), and areas outside these developments may attract the explorer. For example, an explorer could visit regions of the Cypriot hinterland by organizing their own itinerary and choice of accommodation (in lodges, homestays or in independent hotels), while completely omitting the nearby development areas of mass tourism. This category of tourist stays for longer periods of time and has a higher social status. The tourist does not buy package tours but can use receptive travel agencies for the organization of certain excursions on site. Again, for this category of tourist, the Internet is a widely used tool that facilitates planning and puts the traveller in direct contact with a multitude of local tourism providers, regardless of their size. The destinations have also invested heavily in their websites to be able to provide the necessary elements (information, booking facilities, itinerary suggestions, etc.) to cater for this type of holidaymaker.

2.1.4.2.2 The dinghy

This category, the least common, groups together individuals who want to dissociate themselves completely from mass tourism. They consider themselves to be real travellers and totally refute the denomination of tourist. The dinghy is looking for real contact, or even full integration, with local populations. He/she therefore seeks to completely escape his/her environmental bubble and thus to have as little contact as possible with the tourism industry (the trip to get to the destination ideally being the only contact this tourist category will have with the tourism industry).

It should be noted that Cohen's typology does not provide an explanation for the observed changeable behaviours which result in clienteles changing the type of tourist products they consume in the same year. For instance, a consumer can be classified as an explorer during his/her main vacation, but he/she will also be able, in the same year, to consume an organized mass product. Some TOs have adapted their offer to this need by offering combined products that allow, during the same stay, to spend, for example, a week in a resort by the sea and then a week in cultural discovery of a country or on a safari.

Cohen's typology has based its reasoning on the idea that consumers can develop a level of flexibility in the organization of their holidays. The role of consumers and the possibility of their playing a role in the provision of a service is also known under the umbrella of "consumer agency", as we will now discuss.

2.2 Consumer agency and co-construction

The theory of consumer agency describes the consumer as a competent agent capable of autonomy; a consumer can use their own resources to choose, accept or even transform those made available by the various market offers, in order to build their own experience (Kreziak & Frochot, 2011). A consumer pursues a personal consumption project, often by selecting, modifying or diverting the offer provided by a service provider. Tourists explicitly use the resources offered by the resort to accomplish the goals they set for themselves and which make sense to them. They place themselves in the position of co-producer (Prahalad & Ramaswamy, 2004) by putting in place strategies that allow them to optimize the resources offered by a destination and ensure that their objectives are achieved. In other words, the tourist is an experience co-producer and a value co-creator.

In recent years, several currents of research have focussed specifically on the consumer's role as co-creator of the consumption experience. The terms used to refer to these dynamics include seeing consumers as co-creators, actors, pro-sumers (producer/consumers), protagonists or even post-consumers (Cova and Dalli, 2009). A more collaborative marketing logic is emerging, known as service dominant logic or SDL (Vargo & Lusch, 2004). This approach distinguishes and enhances the resources of each party – consumers and producers – and assumes that the customer is always a co-creator of value. Producers provide supports, most often material and tangible, which allow clients to create both the function and the meanings of their experience, based on their own resources (their culture, their skills, etc.).

However, in many experiences, the client is seen as mostly passive and at best as a co-producer in a process that remains focussed on the company and the supply itself. The consumer agency approach goes beyond this vision to focus even more on consumers' cultural resources rather than just serve as suppliers. Service offers are seen as means that allow consumers to shape the experiences or carry out the projects they have chosen in the first place. In this vision, the suppliers need to understand what the cultural projects are that drive consumers in relation to their products, the goals they seek to achieve more generally in their consumption projects and the meaning they give to this consumption. It is then up to the providers to be creative and envisage how their offers' characteristics can fit into these projects and to help consumers achieve them. To some extent, it is not just the company who helps consumers enjoy the service delivery; consumers and producers find themselves in a situation of balanced power (Kreziak, & Frochot, 2011). The consumer is presented as a competent agent, that is to say a consumer capable of reflection and discourse on their own actions, capable of intentions and decisions and capable of autonomy in relation to the offers and proposals of producers.

Consumers don't just react to offers; they pursue goals and, in this process, specific offers' characteristics allow them to achieve those goals. Consumers deploy their own skills and objectives and use the resources of material culture and consumption to implement them, in order to create their own identity, whether individual or collective (Kreziak, & Frochot, 2011). Consumers construct their own discourse and their experience from the raw materials offered by the offer, mixing their own actions with it. Providers can suggest avenues for interpretation through the setting or the performance, but the consumers do the rest (Sherry, Kozinets & Borghini, 2007).

Consumer agency encompasses various modes of behaviour and has been investigated in the context of different consumption universes. Agency has deep implications in terms of socialization, individual and collective identities, the definition or redefinition of roles, the possibility of reconnecting with one's authentic self, etc. The consumer's experience, the stories they tell about it and the goals they pursue go well beyond what the providers expect, but it is also what gives these offerings their real and full value (Kreziak & Frochot, 2011).

We have so far analysed how consumers want to escape their daily lives, and the various elements that can be integrated in this notion of escaping. For an escape to be successful, consumers need to find, during their holiday, an environment that absorbs them fully. The basic tenet is that the more consumers are immersed in that new universe, the more they will distance themselves from everyday life and have a fulfilling experience. The next section presents this dynamic by introducing the concept of immersion.

2.3 Immersion

2.3.1 The role of immersion in escaping daily life

Beyond the notion of escape, the concept of immersion is particularly interesting in understanding how consumers engage in a tourist holiday. It is essential to understand the immersive process since the more tourists are immersed, the more they will be able to distance themselves from everyday life and achieve a feeling of escape. The notion of immersion has been investigated within research streams such as consumer culture theory (CCT). CCT has been a rich field, exploring different dimensions of consumer cultures and behaviour. This field is interesting for tourism researchers and practitioners because it has investigated how consumers can view consumption as an escape from reality, so the parallel with tourism consumption is evident. We have already addressed, earlier in this section, the notions of liminality and communitas. Immersion looks at the ways in which experiential contexts allow consumers to escape from the everyday by being absorbed into a new universe that can allow them to reveal a different identity, bond with others, release their true selves and eventually experience transformation. In other words, immersion is a process, one in which a door is closed on everyday life and a door opens on the experience universe.

Does immersion necessitate a service provision? Carù and Cova (2006) point out that it is not necessarily the role of a company to create and manage experiences, strictly speaking; it is rather a matter of putting everything in place so that immersion can take place spontaneously. For example, a resort might notice that tourists enjoy a viewpoint in a specific location that is rather windy. The resort might decide to construct some shelters so that tourists can enjoy the view and be protected from the wind. Tourists will then be able to sit comfortably, be protected from the wind and indulge in the view. Some tourists might even come across other tourists, and a social exchange might take place, which will bring another touch to the experience. This very simple example indicates how a destination can co-construct an experience with its consumers and create an opportunity so that they can gradually immerse themselves in the destination and their holiday experience. Again, the more immersed consumers are in their holiday environment, the more they can detach themselves from their everyday lives and responsibilities, and the more they will be available to fully enjoy their holiday experience.

Immersion is therefore a process that gives access to experiences. A broad range of contextual elements can contribute to the immersive process. For this immersion to take place, the servicescape is important but it is also a matter of putting in place mechanisms to support the experience. We shall investigate two of those mechanisms: theming the holiday universe and activities.

2.3.2 Immersion steps to assist consumers into the experience

The new holiday universe can provoke immersion through various approaches. Spontaneously, an outstanding landscape or heritage feature might create an unprompted immersion experience. An outstanding performance from a guide or a genuine encounter with a local inhabitant are also experiences that contribute to immersing consumers in the holiday context. We won't debate those elements in the present chapter, and the experiential cues given in Chapter 5 all contribute to create immersion. However, immersion is a process, and this section presents the immersive process and its managerial implications.

According to Carù and Cova (2006), for an experience to be successful, consumers must be able to take ownership of it, and this dynamic requires an appropriation process. Appropriation refers to the process that allows tourists to feel "at home" in a new experience universe. Appropriation has been studied by Carù and Cova (2006) in a study that investigated how new consumers developed a feeling of immersion in a classical music concert. They studied consumers attending a classical music concert for the first time to understand how they managed, or not, to feel immersed in this new experience context. They modified the guidance given by the maestro: in the first part of the concert, the maestro introduced the musical piece that was going to be played; he was dressed informally, and he explained the storyline and pointed to the role that each instrument would play in the music piece (one instrument represented birdsong, another the wind in the leaves, etc.). In other words, the maestro gave the codes that would help this new audience make sense of and feel more at ease with the concert flow. In the second part, the maestro returned to the concert hall dressed formally; he turned his back to the audience and launched his orchestra. The researchers then interviewed the visitors to understand to what extent they managed, or not, to feel at ease with the concert – whether they got "into it" and how they reacted to the two maestro performances. Through this study, Carù and Cova (2006) identified three appropriation steps: (i) nesting (recreating home); (ii) investigating (exploring surrounding space); and (iii) stamping (the personal meaning assigned to the experience).

- **Nesting** refers to the human need to feel "at home" in new situations: "the individual feels at home because part of the experience being faced has been isolated, a part that is already familiar because of one's accumulated experience and existing foothold in it" (Carù and Cova, 2006, page 7). Nesting equals a search for and identification of anchorage points and can be experienced through physical and mental sensations. In Carù and Cova's study (2006), the referents given by the maestro in his introduction to the classical music concert helped consumers identify points of anchorage. Because they were given those codes, they felt more at ease with the experience, stepped into it and made sense of it.

- **Investigating** refers to any action that, from the nest, will see consumers exploring physically the surroundings provided by the experience, and identifying other products/services that will create new points of anchorage and control, called "signposts" (Carù and Cova, 2006). This process involves observing, describing and exploring, and in doing so, consumers feel more comfortable because they have extended their territory. In Carù and Cova's study (2006), the consumers mention that the maestro's directions given before the concert help them to "find their way" through the concert by being able to understand which sounds come from which instruments and what they refer to in the music storyline. It also refers to the fact that they observed other participants and felt more at ease with the context (the decor of the concert hall, the seats, finding their own seat again after the interval, etc.).

- **Stamping** refers to the personal meaning consumers attach to their experience. In Carù and Cova's study (2006), stamping refers to the personal and imaginative meaning that consumers will attribute to the concert, based on the pre-conceived image they have of it and their personal experience with similar products (Figure 2.3).

Figure 2.3 Taking a picture to settle souvenirs. Source: Photo by Silas Baisch on Unsplash.

We mentioned earlier the fact that consumers escape the everyday, but some practices remain during the holiday. Despite the extraordinary dimensions of tourism consumption, mundane routines still take place on a daily basis within the liminal state of the holiday. The concept of appropriation is particularly relevant to the study of tourist practices as it brings an understanding of the processes involved in anchoring oneself and feeling comfortable in a new setting. Among these practices, some are totally mundane, reflective of a tourist's daily life. These daily routines, far from the most exciting side of tourism consumption, are, understandably, less researched. In other words, tourists will have some new routines during the holiday, and some of them will be similar to those in their everyday lives. Chores are kept to a minimum, but are necessary for the smooth unfolding of a holiday. There is therefore a different everydayness to the holiday whereby tourists recreate an alternative home while on holiday (Larsen, 2008). Those mundane routines are not a secondary side of tourism consumption but rather a set of practices that are part of a holiday. Those practices play a crucial role in allowing tourists to anchor themselves in their new holiday universe.

THE THREE APPROPRIATION STEPS IN DESTINATION RESORTS

In a study of mountain resort consumers, Frochot, Kreziak and Elliot (2018) identified how the three immersion steps occur for consumers that have made the choice to stay in rented accommodation. Their study identifies the following components for the three steps.

Nesting

This first phase involves primarily nesting within the new home: moving in to the apartment, allocating the rooms to group members, unpacking suitcases, taking note of the facilities within the rented accommodation, starting to cook the first meal, etc. This step might also involve allocating responsibilities between members of the group to ensure a smooth organization of the group. After 2–3 days, these routines are acquired and become a "new normal" reality for the group members. Tourists might encounter inhibitors to the nesting process such as outside noise altering sleep quality or faulty appliances that create a feeling of uneasiness during the nesting process.

Investigating

A holiday destination, unless it has been experienced previously, is necessarily a new place that necessitates that newcomers identify their location and the general set up of the destination they are staying in. Investigating skills are solicited right away upon arrival at a destination: finding one's way to the resort, locating one's apartment, finding parking facilities, etc. Once the tourists have moved in to their accommodation, they will then explore the resort to first identify convenience shops that will be necessary for their stay (grocery, store, local information centre, bus stop, etc.). Frochot et al.'s study (2018) identifies that consumers encounter various inhibitors to their investigating process. As a matter of fact, they often get lost, discover facilities in a haphazard way and eventually get help from fellow tourists or locals; there is a general lack of efficiency in investigating the resort. This lack of efficiency might take the form of tourists wasting time when trying to find their way around; it also potentially means that they might fail to identify services that could have been very beneficial in terms of the enjoyment of their stay. As a matter of fact, destinations often develop maps or phone applications to help visitors discover their key resources (a region, a forest, a national park, etc.). They often fail to recognize that directions are also essential to make the investigating phase easier.

Both those steps, nesting and investigating, can take up tourists' precious time. Whilst they are inevitable, it is essential to understand that the more time tourists devote to both these steps, the less time there will be for the enjoyment of their experience. Destinations' strategies in providing assistance and directions at every stage of both those steps are welcome since they allow individuals to put aside those two steps and get around more quickly to concentrating on their holiday.

Stamping

Stamping is a broader notion; it refers to the individual meaning that individuals assign to an experience. It might encapsulate the discovery of new cultures, or more simply the desire to strengthen family ties within the privacy of tourist accommodation or through bonding activities.

2.3.4 Nesting and empowerment

Going back to one of the appropriation steps mentioned in the previous section, nesting is a particularly important step, one that can guarantee the success of an experience, especially because it facilitates immersion. Echoing Carù and Cova's work on classical music concerts, nesting refers to the understanding that consumers might need to master in order to better understand and immerse themselves in a consumption universe. Understanding the nesting process implies that tourism providers and destinations alike need to develop an understanding of the skills and competencies that consumers might need to master in order to grasp fully the specificities of a destination. Transmitting those skills guarantees that consumers will engage more deeply with the destination and immerse themselves more fully with the new universe. Beyond the fact that nesting guarantees a more satisfactory experience, it also, and more importantly, develops a deeper satisfaction with the experiences undertaken and an emotional attachment to the destinations visited. In itself, adopting a nesting approach necessitates considering in the first place which skills consumers might or might not possess. Local inhabitants and tourism providers often assume that tourists possess skills and competences that they don't actually have. Understanding those competences is a basic step from which the experience can be more successfully designed.

One of the most noteworthy initiatives in this regard was developed by Iceland Academy, who produced a series of videos to transfer competencies to their visitors. Their videos were produced in response to the increasing international tourist demand for Iceland, which had resulted in difficulties of various types. The videos have three purposes:

- To assist visitors in enjoying their experience:

  - What to put in their suitcases to suit the weather conditions

  - How to take pictures of the northern lights

- To encourage visitors to behave respectfully:

  - How not to trample on nature

  - Where to drive and not to drive

- To encourage visitors to behave safely:

  - How to take safe selfies

  - How to drive on dirt roads

  - How to walk on ice in winter, etc.

By definition, tourists are not familiar with the holiday universe and they don't always have all the skills that are necessary to truly enjoy their holiday. Learning those skills might also be a strategy to develop better integration of newcomers to an area. Migrating populations encounter the same difficulties as tourists: they are confronted with a new universe and practices that they do not have the skills for. In a similar line of thinking, urban inhabitants often lack the basic skills to enjoy elements of nature. In many ways, nesting is a very interesting subject that aims to identify consumers' missing skills and competencies and to develop programs to transmit them to those consumers (see example on Canadian national parks).

LEARN TO CAMP BY PARKS CANADA

Canadian national parks have engaged in a strategy to more fully engage Canadian populations with national parks and outdoor activities. In Canada, 80% of inhabitants live in cities, and 90% of their time is spent indoors. The average area that a 9-year-old has in which to play has been reduced by 90% since the 1970s. Ethnic minorities are not big consumers of national parks, and 77% of campers are non-ethnic inhabitants. Whilst cost and accessibility might be limiting factors, the lack of familiarity and perception of camping are other limiting factors. Practices learnt during childhood seem to have a strong influence on those undertaken in adulthood. Of adult outdoor consumers, 41% learnt the practice during their childhood (against 18% of those who never practiced it during their childhood).

Various Canadian authorities have undertaken initiatives to tackle these various issues. Classes on the environment have been reintroduced in child education. Better transport connections to national parks have also been established. Canadian authorities also identified that engaging local inhabitants with outdoor facilities was a real issue in terms of the inclusion of migrating populations (i.e. non-Canadian inhabitants who had no culture of the country's outdoors). From an analysis of inhabitants' needs, the authorities identified that consumers had limited skills for enjoying the outdoors, especially camping skills. They set up a program called "Learn to Camp" in Ontario. This programme is run by rangers and aims, over the course of a weekend, to share camping skills with the participants. The programme is sponsored by camping equipment brands, and the rangers engaged in outdoor classes teach participants how to set up a tent, organize sleeping equipment, safely light a barbecue, etc. The target consumers are individuals who have never or barely camped in their lives and need this course to gain or regain confidence that they can master a camping experience on their own.

Source: Levasseur M. (2018) L'amour de la nature ça s'apprend, Réseau de veille en tourisme, Chaire de tourisme Transat, https://veilletourisme.ca/2015/03/27/lamour-du-plein-air-ca-sapprend-2/.

As an interesting exercise, can you identify the skills that consumers might need to master in order to enjoy your destination? Do you feel that consumers might miss out on some interesting destination features? Do you feel that they could improve their experience if they could master some of those skills? Identify the range of skills that could be beneficial to your visitors and then also identify the tools that could be used to provide them with those skills. Maybe a phone

Figure 2.4 Alone in the mountains in communion with nature. Source: Photo by Jarhead Core on Unsplash.

app could be sufficient, or a set of introductory videos (see Iceland Academy, for example), or a guided session teaching important skills to visitors, etc. If the tourists master those skills, they are more likely to feel more at ease with the destination, enjoy their experience, immerse themselves in the holiday and ultimately develop an attachment to the destination (Figure 2.4).

2.3.5 The immersion rhythm

How long does it take for tourists to cut free from their daily lives and immerse fully in the holiday context? This is a tricky question that has no definite answer. The few studies that have investigated this process have commonly identified that it takes on average 3–5 days for tourists to cut free from their daily lives and responsibilities. Frochot, Kreziak and Elliot (2018) identified that it takes several days for tourists to unwind. In their study on mountain resort visitors, they revealed that it was only from the third day onwards that tourists showed clear signs of detaching themselves from everyday life and also from the functional activities associated with nesting and investigating.

Similar results have been identified in a study on Canadian visitors to Hong Kong. In this study, McKercher and Lui (2014) identified that detachment took 5 days. Pearce (1981), in a study of cultural shock on the part of island tourists in Australia, identified that negative moods decreased after the third day, hastened by self-initiated activities. The detachment process is a complex issue but an important one for experience designers. Intuitively, the faster consumers can detach themselves from their daily lives, the faster they will be available to fully enjoy their holiday. However, even if holiday-makers start enjoying their holiday as soon as they arrive at the destination, it seems to take at least 3 days to truly settle into the holiday spirit. Outstanding experiences, powerful emotional encounters, and in fact any fulfilling experience might help to reduce this lengthy entry into the experience. But immersion is also a physical and mental process, and regardless of the experience, it also takes time for tourists to gradually let go of their daily lives and the stresses and burdens that might stay with them for the first few days of the holiday.

If the 3-day rule seems to apply to holidays of a certain length, it does not give a clear insight into what takes place on shorter holidays. For example, if tourists take a city break, for instance an extended 4-day weekend in London or Amsterdam, they seem to be able to engage rapidly with the destination even though the holiday is rather short. In this instance, immersion seems to happen more quickly. More studies are needed to explore how immersion unfolds in shorter holidays. These holidays might not have the same immersive dimension, but yet they are enjoyable breaks, and some form of immersion does take place. It is more probable that consumer agency plays a key role in those instances; if consumers know that they only have a few days at a destination, they will set their mind to enjoy it to the full even though they know that the immersion won't be as intense as on longer holidays.

2.3.6 Immersion and the disruptions to holiday immersion

If immersion in the holiday is an essential component of the experience, it is equally essential to understand what might produce immersion breaks (or emmersion). Immersion is a gradual process; the more tourists become immersed in their holiday, the more they will distance themselves from their daily lives. However, there might be occurrences where tourists "jump out" of this immersive process. One of those occurrences might arise from the work universe. The temptation to check emails or take an impromptu call from work are all intrusions that will limit consumers' ability to disconnect. It might send them straight back to the universe they aimed to leave behind when deciding to take a holiday, and it will take them some time to re-immerse themselves into the holiday universe. One might also wonder what is the place of digital intrusions into potential immersion. In this regard, one question that an experience designer might contemplate is the need, or not, to impose digital disconnection on their consumers.

First and foremost, the vacation world is one of freedom. Tourists must feel free in their choices and movements, and this is an essential condition to the holiday. Imposing digital and/or phone disconnection would be badly received by many tourists. First, the telephone is a tool widely used during tourist visits (to obtain information, to find directions, to take pictures and videos, etc.). Second, digital technology can also be an experience booster (using geocaching apps to localize heritage, identify plants, etc.). Finally, it is also a tool for connecting to one's social sphere directly and through social networks.

When digital connection turns out to be impossible due to poor network coverage, studies show that tourists accept the situation but need time to adapt. The first 2 or 3 days can be difficult, but then an adjustment occurs once tourists have identified the benefits of this unwanted but ultimately appreciated disconnection.

Cai, McKenna and Waizenegger (2020) studied a group of tourists who voluntarily chose to cut themselves off from their digital connections while on vacation. Their study identified that those tourists first experienced withdrawal symptoms related to anxiety. They also expressed frustration at the difficulties they experienced in finding their way and getting around the destination. These tourists also spoke of their feeling of loneliness linked to their inability to communicate and exchange on their social networks with their families and friends.

Analysing digital-free holidays is also interesting because it points at the same time to the difficulties experienced by contemporary consumers in disconnecting from their lives. Paradoxically, disconnectivity creates a whole range of opportunities that can lead to more fulfilling experiences. Indeed, the recurring intrusion of the digital into the holiday experience creates a distraction that cuts tourists off from the present moment and distances them from the physical, visual, auditory and sensory experiences. Digital intrusion, as useful as it might be, brings a distance that is not always beneficial to tourists' stays.

In existing studies, customers who agree to disconnect make it possible to identify to what extent digital technology can be a hindrance to vacations. Cai et al. (2020) analysed the benefits felt by tourists who experienced digital disconnection. The tourists interviewed clearly identified their newfound and regained attention capacity, their more relaxed approach to travel, a certain experience of getting back to basics, and opportunities for engaging with other tourists or locals that would probably never have been possible if they had used their cell phones (especially for finding their way around the destination). Leaving digital tools aside during the trip also allows a reconnection to a certain feeling of freedom, and the capacity to regain a form of control over the holiday.

Digital detox products have been available for several years now, which allow tourists to enjoy a tourist vacation without being connected to the Internet. For these offers, disconnection is desired and assumed right from the purchase of the holiday. One tour operator, Voyageurs du Monde, illustrates this vision in its communication strategy:

> How long has it been since you turned off your cell phone for a whole day? Your first instinct when arriving at a vacation spot is to track down the wifi … What if happiness was elsewhere? What if the real break was to cut out everything else to focus on the essentials: chatting with friends or loved ones, feeling the wind on your skin, listening to the birds tweeting, reading a real paper novel, meditating by the ocean? Forget about the wifi network (by the way, the nearest one is miles away). On this island, on this mountain, in this oasis, in this medieval hamlet, or in this house that has such great character, you can finally recharge your batteries.
> (https://www.voyageursdumonde.fr/voyage-sur-mesure/idees-voyage/
> sejour-detox-numerique-vacances-deconnectees/151)

These digital-detox products are far from representing the majority of tourist offers, but they are interesting because they ask tourists to question their own behaviour and invite them to consider their active role in the holiday they are going to experience.

Should a destination encourage its consumers to disconnect from their digital devices?

By connecting to the digital sphere, tourists will also communicate about their vacations and their experiences and share the most beautiful Instagrammable views, and these actions translate into advertising that the destinations and tourism actors would be wrong to miss out on.

Digital identity is also an extension of oneself through one's visibility on social networks. The tourists are their own storytellers, and through the narration of their trip, they communicate information about their identity, their image and their activities. Sharing live on social networks will also engage tourists to renegotiate the experiences they are living, resulting in a positive reassessment of their holiday. Kim and Fesenmaier (2017) have shown that sharing experiences on social media improves and reinforces positive vacation evaluations. Sharing one's vacation experiences is part of maintaining visibility and display on social networks but is also a way to give more meaning to lived experiences, and potentially to reduce cognitive dissonance (discrepancy between pre-experience expectations and the lived reality of the stay). Wong, Wai and Tao (2019) have shown that the renegotiated social media experience has more impact on future purchases than the evaluation of the experience itself. Digital connection can therefore also be considered as an essential asset in the negotiation of vacation memories and their dissemination on social networks, and it has an impact on repurchase behaviour.

All in all, the dependence on digital tools is relatively recent. But its intrusion into the vacation world has been very rapid, and one cannot ignore its pervasiveness throughout the tourist experience (and beyond). We can consider that learning mechanisms are still at work for contemporary tourists and that digital practices will continue to evolve. The hypermodern traveller is therefore an experienced traveller who is coming to understand better and better the uses and limits of digital tools: "ICTs are no longer added to a pre-existing reality: they are mixed with it, combined with it and articulate to plunge us into a new hybrid environment where it is now difficult to think one without the other, and in which the very notions of separation, estrangement and distance are modified" (Jauréguiberry and Lachance, 2011, page 27).

In this dynamic, tourism providers have a role to play. Offering helpful guidance on moderating the use of new technologies or designing temporarily disconnected micro-experiences can be particularly beneficial to the customer experience.

We can observe also that tourists are gaining experience; they know how to identify the disruptive dimension of digital tools in their vacation experience and are increasingly developing their own strategies to limit this impact. In a study on mountain resort vacations, Frochot, Ellliot and Kreziak (2017) studied the immersion mechanisms in a tourist stay. Their study indicates that tourists, especially when they are on a family holiday, develop different strategies to preserve quality family time. Internal family habits are thus temporarily erected to regulate the use of digital technology: refusing to turn the television on, limiting the use of tablets in the evening and resorting to traditional games are all elements which undoubtedly reinforce the quality of the exchanges.

All the elements presented in this chapter are the results of years of research and consultancy that have gradually contributed to the development of a rich background of knowledge to understand the consumer experience in a tourism context. This consumer intelligence has also been produced by developing different research techniques that allow researchers and consultants to investigate in a detailed way the various dimensions of experiences. The final section of this chapter presents some of those instruments. It does not aim to be exhaustive but to point to some of the relevant techniques that can assist experience designers in gaining more strategic intelligence. The last chapter of this book will also present other techniques that can assist experience designers.

2.3.7 Investigating the experience

Consumer intelligence is a key factor underpinning all marketing processes. Understanding consumers' needs, profiles, behaviour online or offline, habits, etc. is an essential component of all marketing decisions. We live in an era where more consumer information is available than ever before. Tourism businesses and destinations can question, observe, follow, trace offline and online, collect detailed information, target their products and communication strategies more precisely and promote their experiential offer more efficiently. Yet, consumers evolve fast and need constant and precise monitoring. Yet, despite this existing and extensive knowledge and intelligence, the understanding of the experience itself is still somehow in its infancy. First and foremost, this field is comparatively new, emerging in the early 1980s and attracting real interest from the 2000s onwards. Secondly, the experience touches different fields and it is a complex task to integrate all this extensive knowledge. For instance, psychologists, sociologists, human geographers, marketers, neuropsychologists and medical researchers can all contribute to the understanding of the experience. Being able to concentrate, digest and understand the complementary knowledge gained throughout those fields is a complex and cumbersome task. Thirdly, experiences touch emotions, feelings, and subconscious elements that are intricate and difficult for researchers to grasp using traditional market intelligence techniques.

2.3.7.1 Qualitative and quantitative research techniques

Whilst most market research still uses traditional qualitative and quantitative techniques, new approaches are also emerging. These research methods can be divided into two large families: quantitative and qualitative approaches. In a nutshell, quantitative approaches include surveys of fairly large samples of consumers, administrated onsite or online/mailed after the experience. Quantitative techniques are powerful at measuring phenomena, variables and profiles, including their evolution through time. Qualitative approaches are developed on smaller samples of visitors who are interviewed (on their own or in groups) onsite or after an experience. Qualitative techniques bring detailed and rich results which might not be generalisable (due to the sample size and representativeness) but are extremely useful to experience designers.

2.3.7.2 A lack of research providing a vision from within the experience

Within the broad range of research conducted on tourist experiences, what takes place during the experience itself has been comparatively less researched. The majority of existing studies often investigate the experience by interviewing or surveying visitors after their holiday. Even if those results are very rich, they can be limited because they lack scope on the day-to-day experience as it unfolds.

Questioning consumers after a holiday might lose the richness of what actually takes place during a holiday, and that is constructed of multiple encounters. Those various encounters get lost in translation if consumers are interviewed or surveyed after the holiday in a snapshot data collection. Experience designers can also gain extremely rich data by investigating the experience as it evolves, by developing techniques that immerse them in the holiday process itself as it unfolds. To achieve this type of data collection, several qualitative approaches can be adopted; we shall present some of them in this section, and specific tools developed in the experience design field will be presented in Chapter 6 (Section 6.5).

2.3.7.3 Observation

Observation is a technique that has been used by tourism researchers for some time. This technique involves observing participants engaging an activity, and recording their actions. The observation might be unstructured, in which case any of the events taking place will be noted down by the observer. Observation is an unobstructive approach that can be useful to experience designers – observing how tourists move around a resort/destination/national park, how they behave, how they interact or not with other individuals, etc. Observation provides the great advantage of observing situated behaviour: behaviour that is set within a specific environment and conditions. Participant observation means that the researcher becomes involved with the group of tourists, the observant choosing to be identified to the observers or not (overt or covert observation). The observer will take various notes about the experience observed, and he/she might also take pictures, record participants, count flows, time experiences, etc. This necessarily involves some privacy and ethical issues that need to be addressed.

The major drawback of observation lies in its inability, on its own, to determine for certain the real motivations behind observed behaviours. The generalisability of the results is limited. There might also be some contextual elements impacting the observed behaviour that might be difficult to appreciate. Nonetheless, observations might allow the observer to identify elements not discovered previously, or to open new avenues of experience investigation; it is a rich technique that should not be disregarded.

2.3.7.4 Photo safaris

Tourists' intimate insight into their experience can also be achieved by the production of pictures taken during a holiday. Using photographs as primary research material is an appealing feature in visual methodologies. This approach usually involves researchers giving out a camera to consumers and collecting the pictures that tourists have chosen to take during their holiday activity (with or without instructions). The range of pictures collected and associated comments or, in the best case scenario, the opportunity to interview tourists to let them comment on the pictures they took (photo elicitation), brings a valuable insight into their daily experience. This approach also has its own limitations, and Markwell (1997) notes that the photographs tourists choose to take tend to reinforce the idea of a perfect holiday, and therefore some mundane and unattractive elements get to be left out in those choices. The risk of subjective interpretation of the photographic material (collected by tourists, on Instagram, etc.) does exist and it is vital to be careful not to over-interpret the material collected. Photo-elicitation (inviting participants to comments the pictures taken) is commonly an interesting approach to ensure that the meaning of those pictures is correctly expressed and thereby interpreted.

2.3.7.5 Netnography

Alternatively, social medias provide rich insights into consumers' restitutions of their holidays. Kozinets (2009) developed an approach to studying online communities in his book *Netnography: Doing Ethnographic Research Online*. Netnography is a contraction of "networks" and "ethnography" and involves observing and analysing communication among members of a virtual community. In this approach, consumers are observed through the textual information they produce online, the various multimedia contents posted and the timing of those dynamics. Netnography is a less obstructive approach and allows the experience designer to access information available online and to gain access to a large amount of data.

2.3.7.6 Travel diaries

Traditionally the closest approach that researchers have developed to studying the experience as it unfolds has been to use diaries. Diaries are given to consumers with some specific instructions, and then visitors fill in the information as they go through their holiday.

With diaries, researchers collect rich information about consumers' activities, practices and whereabouts, and how they perceive their encounters and experiences. The information is collected in a sequential approach and provides a good insight into daily experiences and their evolution throughout a holiday. Spatial locations can also be recorded, thereby providing the researchers with an interesting insight into the sequence of events throughout a consumer's experience.

2.3.7.7 Videos

Requesting consumers to create videos of their experiences is too complex a command, even though consumers might take snapshot videos of their experience (see Section 6.5). However, videos have been used in various academic fields to investigate consumers. The CCT field is one that has used videos extensively to document various consumption phenomenon. Some of those videos have been referenced in this book (the video on the Burning Man Festival in Section 2.1.2, for instance, or that on Tomorrowland festival goers in Section 4.9). Those videos might not as such provide a detailed approach of the service delivery as some of the tools presented in Chapter 6. However, videos are extremely rich because they allow experience designers to understand consumer cultures more clearly.

2.3.7.8 The need for longitudinal studies

One last element to consider is that experiences evolve through time, and what takes place on the first day of a holiday might be perceived differently to what takes place later on in that same holiday. More studies are needed to identify how the experience unfolds over several days and how experience designers can integrate into their thinking the rhythm and gradual evolution of the consumer experience through the holiday.

Conclusion

This chapter aimed to gain an insight into the holiday experience itself. The dynamics of holidays are fascinating and complex. They encapsulate a broad range of elements that need to be fully understood for experiences to be efficiently designed. Through this chapter, the holiday experience was analysed from the consumer perspective. The roots of the whole tourism experience need to be understood in relation to the feeling of and need for escape from everyday life, an escape that opens doors onto various processes that are essential to experiences' structure and design. In this process, immersion, with all its processes and rhythms, is an essential component to master for an efficient experience design. This observation calls for specific research methods, especially those that allow experience designers to gain an intimate knowledge of the experience as it unfolds and its resonance on digital media.

Whilst this process is at the heart of experiences, it does not provide a full vision of the holiday experience. Visitors have come to collect experiences that will lead to deep memories and transformations. The next chapter will investigate those experiences under the general banner of deep experiences in order to understand how those "peaks" bring the true essence of experiences.

Chapter 3

Deep experiences

Introduction

The previous chapter investigated the experience itself and how consumers get away from the everyday to enter the holiday period, where different practices take place and where they can immerse themselves in a new environment, take on a new identity and develop social connections. These elements are important to include in the experience design process. However, they are not the only dimension that contributes to successful experiences. For an experience to truly touch consumers and become memorable, it needs to provoke in consumers some deeper engagement that we will address in this chapter. Deep episodes are particularly interesting elements of the tourist experience because they are able to create intense emotions and long-lasting memories. Moreover, they clearly boost the disconnection from everyday life, so they can help consumers to immerse themselves even more into the holiday context and spirit. Finally, deep experiences can lead consumers to experience transformation. Deep experiences create a positive "shock to the system" that helps consumers disconnect even more. The world of academia has used different terms to describe those experiences, ranging from *extraordinary* to *peak, optimal* or *transcendent* experiences, etc. It is not the aim of this chapter to represent this diversity in its entirety, but rather to offer a global vision of those intense experiences. For the sake of simplicity, we will refer to these experiences under the general banner of *deep* experiences. We will first look at the different types of deep experiences

DOI: 10.4324/9781003019237-4

that can impact consumers. The chapter will then investigate the concept of transformation, which means the extent to which an experience has impacted consumers. Finally, we will investigate the notion of memory, how it forms from an experience and how it evolves.

3.1 A broad range of deep experiences

Experiences that can impact consumers have been investigated for a long time in different disciplines. Each of those reflections bring a very interesting insight into the processes at stake and why some experiences are more impactful than others. In this first section, and under the general banner of deep experiences, we shall address different academic works that have investigated those elements.

3.1.1 Peak experiences

As early as 1964, Maslow identified a concept named the peak experience, which relates to experiences of greatest happiness and fulfilment. Those peaks translate into an altered state of consciousness that is ecstatic and euphoric and creates deep happiness and fulfilment (Maslow, 1964). Peak experiences can be achieved through the consumption of activities such as art, intellectual insight, aesthetic perceptions, nature experiences and so forth. If religious experiences and exotic travel can produce peak experiences, Maslow also suggested that peak experiences may be created by ordinary people under quite common circumstances. Peak experiences are not so much described by the activity itself but by the ecstatic feeling that is experienced while doing it.

For the experience designer, peak experiences are very interesting to understand because they are clearly episodes, within the holiday, that create intense enjoyment and contribute to creating a distance from the everyday. They might be perceived as complex to understand because their occurrence and how they unfold might not involve complex service provision. While some researchers argue that consumers need an extraordinary event to create an intense and unforgettable experience (Arnould and Price, 1993; Pine, Pine and Gilmore, 1999), others indicate that not all experiences need to be extraordinary to procure a pleasurable experience (Carù and Cova, 2006; Maslow 1964). This aspect is worthwhile mentioning since, in the case of tourism, some intense experiences might occur in very simple circumstances. It is their personal meaning, their intensity, the emotions they evoke that make those moments special. They might involve extraordinary encounters, landscapes, or activities, or they might emerge in more simpler circumstances. In other words, some intense holiday experiences are not always extraordinary in the purest sense of the word. For instance, connecting with one's children by building a sandcastle and defending it against the rising tide for hours might be lived as a key experience and a strong connecting moment. A rich encounter with a local inhabitant who welcomed the family to his farm and taught them to make blueberry jam might also be an extremely fulfilling experience. It is out of the ordinary but probably not extraordinary in the purest sense of the term, as it is commonly understood. Those experiences develop deep feelings of joy, togetherness and strong emotions, but in fact they are quite banal. It is what emanates from them that makes them extraordinary.

Designers should not forget also that tourists consume holidays to come back home refreshed and rested. They might be seeking intense moments, but they are equally in need of calm and relaxing episodes; therefore, peak experiences are not the only feature that will structure their holiday. Tourists would probably experience tiredness if intense experiences took place over a long period and on a very recurrent basis (this might not apply to mountaineers aiming to reach Mount Everest, but it would apply to more ordinary holidays). It is therefore more interesting to consider that peak experiences occur only at some points during the holiday. In order to understand this process more clearly, the notion of optimal experiences offers some interesting pointers.

3.1.2 Optimal experiences

Optimal experiences is a term often used for flow experiences, but it might be more accurate to say that flow is one specific type of optimal experience, and we shall present this in Section 3.1.4.

There is clearly an important distinction to be made between short-lived pleasures and those that impact consumers more deeply. Csikszentmihalyi (1991) differentiates between the notions of pleasure and enjoyment. Enjoyment is usually conceived as an optimal experience. Pleasure, on the other end, is considered as a reflex response genetically embedded in human beings. For instance, a human being will experience an instant pleasure from relieving his hunger by eating some food, feeling warmer by lighting a fire, etc. This type of pleasure is considered as evanescent: one might experience great pleasure from relieving hunger with a good meal, but this pleasure will be short lived. Enjoyment seems to be related much more vividly to optimal experiences and is more interesting because it is longer lasting and impacts memories more deeply. If the tourist relieved his hunger but this was done with a nine-course dinner, tasting different wines and with dishes cooked by an outstanding chef, then this experience would have created enjoyment.

Campbell (1987) indicates that pleasure can transform itself into enjoyment only under certain conditions. Campbell argues that this process happens if:

- intensity of attention is produced by the experience;
- consumers develop a sense of achievement;
- consumers gain psychological growth from the experience.

In other words, experiences that touch consumers are those that are able to create a sense of achievement and/or growth. The attention a consumer pays to an experience is a central criterion that contributes to the success of the experience: the more attentive a consumer is, the more they will immerse themselves in the experience and the more the consumer is likely to develop satisfaction and memories.

We mentioned earlier that not all experiences have to be totally extraordinary to be impactful. This explains that what might appear to be mundane experiences might actually impact visitors more than expected. A nice encounter with a local inhabitant relating about his life in the destination, a long chat with one's teenage children on a ski lift when this clearly has not happened for several months, the discovery and taste of wild food on a foraging trip; these are all deep experiences. None of these experiences have anything spectacular about them, but they all touch deeply the consumers experiencing them, catch their attention and create a feeling of growth and/or achievement. The following case study displays an analysis of a group of consumers, identifying key optimal experiences in a 5-day stay and providing an interesting insight into the elements contributing to the experience.

ANALYSING OPTIMAL EXPERIENCES ON A TOURIST HOLIDAY

This study investigated how the consumer experience evolved over the course of a 5-day holiday. This study was conducted with ten tourists who were interviewed every evening of their stay. With this research protocol, the researchers wanted to investigate how a consumer experience evolved and changed as the holiday unfolded, and what were the contributing components to this change. Presented here are the results focussing specifically on optimal experiences.

The holiday involved skiing as the main activity, and the group stayed in rented accommodation (apartments) in a high-altitude modern resort. One of the notable experiences that impacted them was associated with a snowshoeing activity on the second day. The results showed that the snow-shoeing experience was a key highlight to the holiday since, first and foremost, all the participants in the group could take part in it without any major difficulties. The important dimension of this experience was the fact that participants were in a different setting: a field of powder snow, away from the resort. Participants could finally see what they called "real snow". Whilst they were surrounded by snow at the resort, in the snowshoeing experience, the fact that they could touch powder snow and make their own prints in the snow created intense emotions. There was a strong element of magic (and even discovery) associated with powder snow. The social dimension of group bonding was also evident in this experience.

On day three, a new episode of optimal experience took place, when the weather cleared up. Whilst good weather was an evident feature of this enjoyment, it was in fact a means to an end, and what mattered for the experience was what the good weather invited. The quality of the skiing was identified as an important component but, more importantly, participants formed smaller groups and enjoyed deep camaraderie and true connections with each other. Another key highlight of this experience was the outstanding view (which participants finally discovered on that day) and it became the main component of their enjoyment: "When I arrived at the top of the resort and suddenly discovered the view, I got taken over by the magnitude of the landscape, its sheer beauty and magnitude, it just took over me" (Marie-Charlotte, day 3). This episode created intense emotions and pleasure (the sheer joy of looking at a beautiful and overwhelming landscape (Figure 3.1).

It is essential for experience designers to understand the dynamics of such key experiences. They were clearly the highlight of the holiday; they created a deep sense of enjoyment, and, when living those experiences, participants were attentive and expressed feelings of growth that originated in various dynamics. Most interestingly, but unsurprisingly, when those consumers were interviewed one year later, only those two experiences stood out in their memory. If those optimal experiences had not taken place, the holiday would have probably been satisfactory but not necessarily memorable.

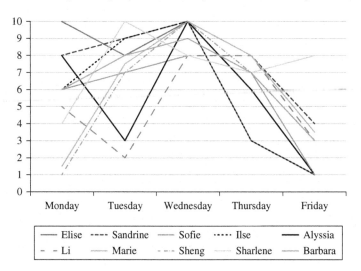

Figure 3.1 The evolution of optimal experiences in a tourist stay. Source: Author.

The occurrence of those types of experiences also created a deeper feeling of engagement with the holiday and a stronger distancing from everyday life. Such episodes necessarily feed memories but, depending on their orchestration, they might also create a deep attachment to the place where they occur. As a result, notions of loyalty and e-word of mouth (eWOM) are equally outcomes that are worth considering.

For the experience provider, it means that in order to achieve these outcomes, the experience needs to provide the opportunity to live such intense episodes from times to time throughout the holiday. Whilst a destination cannot predict the weather, it can magnify the experience opportunities that take place when the weather finally improves. For instance, a destination can improve engagement with the view by designing viewing platforms at the right locations. The destination might also provide a phone app that allows participants to geolocalize each other on the slopes and meet with other groups of friends from time to time (localizing oneself on ski slopes can be particularly difficult). If the snow-shoeing experience is not a common feature in skiers' holidays, one snow-shoeing outing could be included for free in the price of weekly ski-lift tickets, etc.

Source: Frochot I., Elliot S. & Kreziak D. (2017)

3.1.3 The teachings of positive psychology for the understanding of experiences

The sense of achievement and growth is not new in itself. In fact, the field of positive psychology can bring some interesting insights into what makes a tourist experience impactful.

The theories developed in positive psychology are particularly interesting since they offer pointers to the mechanisms that can help individuals increase their sense of deep satisfaction.

Earlier in this chapter, the different notions of pleasure and enjoyment were briefly explained; these notions echo more profoundly with the Aristotelian conceptualization of eudaimonia and hedonia. Eudaimonia is a contraction of *eu* (good) and *daimon* (spirit or self). It implies achieving a fulfilling life in various domains such as virtue, morality, happiness and meaning. Whilst this implies excelling in the various tasks of our lives, it also implies sticking to some personal virtues, achieving a form of balance and developing wisdom. As such eudaimonia might not be best translated by the word happiness but rather by the notions of fulfilment or flourishing. For many, hedonia refers rather to a pleasurable feeling, one of enjoyment and comfort. Both elements are important in tourism experiences, but we shall focus rather on eudaimonia, since this notion offers an interesting insight into impactful experiences.

In positive psychology, two prevailing models can offer some interesting leads to help developers enhance the impact of their tourism experiences:

- PERMA model: Seligman (2018) developed mechanisms and exercises that help individuals naturally fight depression without reverting to medical assistance. The PERMA model stipulates that to achieve a deep feeling of satisfaction with life, individuals need to cultivate positive emotions, engagement, relationships, meaning and achievement.

- Another model also used is DRAMMA (Newman, Tay, and Diener, 2014), which lists characteristics of subjective well-being as follows: autonomy, mastery, meaning, affiliation and detachment-recovery (detachment from everyday life and work and the opportunity to recuperate).

Other approaches exist, and studies on subjective well-being (SWB) also bring an interesting insight into experiences. For instance, in a review of the SWB concept, Laing and Frost (2017) list the key qualities of well-being as including personal growth, authenticity (being true to oneself), positive relationships, environmental mastery (identifying an environment that suits one's personal needs and abilities) and excellence.

Many different theories and concepts have been developed to help identify the key triggers to a successful experience. It is impossible to relate the richness of those concepts in this book, but collectively they point to some key elements: achievement, engagement, meaningfulness, relationships and personal growth.

Inspired by those approaches, the following example shows how a tourist destination might use some of those mechanics to increase tourists' well-being while at the destination.

POSITIVE TOURISM – *MY SERENITY* AT THE VAL THORENS SKI RESORT

The resort of Val Thorens has chosen to develop an approach inspired by positive psychology as part of their experiential marketing strategy. Their concept is to use and simplify some key mechanics developed in the positive psychology field and redeploy a simplified version in the holiday context.

The resort has produced a small booklet that first introduces how happiness can be achieved in everyday life, what the origins of stress are and how to identify them, and some simple exercises that tourists can use to help them unwind during their stay. The booklet also explains in simple terms how some experiences can reduce stress and improve happiness – for instance, contemplating a mountainous landscape reduces heartbeat and stress, etc.

Then the booklet encourages visitors to learn to take a step back and appreciate what they are living. On one page of the booklet, consumers are encouraged to write in one column what did not go well during the day and what stood out positively. The tourist singles out three key positive experiences during the day and think about them before they go to sleep, thereby improving sleep quality and decreasing stress levels (a simpler version would be simply to write down the three outstanding experiences of the day, similar to what is encouraged in the PERMA approach). Then another section of the page is dedicated to improving tourists' feelings of personal efficacy in order to boost their self-confidence. Tourists are encouraged to write down the parts of their day where they feel they improved themselves/gained new competences.

Source: http://www.valthorens.com/presse/h2018/My_Serenity_Fr.pdf

Earlier in this chapter, we mentioned that flow was a form of optimal experience. Flow is being treated separately in this chapter because it is an interesting concept and one that relates to some specific experiences.

3.1.4 Flow as a key experiential component

The concept of flow was developed by a Hungarian sociologist, Csíkszentmihályi (1991), who identified a state of being that could be observed in artists during their artistic creative process.

The state of flow is an optimal mental state of intense concentration in which the individual feels completely absorbed in what he/she is doing. The activity is then seen as very rewarding and the productivity is described as maximum. The individual experiences a feeling of hyper-concentration which makes them feel good, and which brings them spontaneous energy. Activity can be maintained for a long time without effort. The worries of everyday life are temporarily erased, which leads to what is termed a constructive escape, that is to say, it induces a posteriori positive emotion. There is a loss of self-awareness; people act but do not watch themselves acting at the same time, and the lack of reflexivity is seen as a factor of well-being. The individual is totally immersed in the present moment, with a distortion of the perception of time.

The main characteristics of flow have been defined as follows (Csíkszentmihályi, 1991):

- Intrinsic enjoyment;
- Loss of self-consciousness;

- Skill/challenge balance (notion of optimum level);

- Intense focused attention;

- Immersion in the activity;

- Clear goals;

- Immediate but not necessarily ambitious feedbacks;

- Sense of control over the environment and actions;

- Momentary loss of anxiety and constraints;

- Enjoyment and pleasure.

This state has been studied in the field of sports, games (especially video games), reading, recreation, Internet browsing, education and tourism.

One of the prime elements that condition the occurrence of flow is the congruence between an activity, one's level of skill and the perception of the challenge of the activity. The challenges experienced in an activity must also be high for flow to occur. For instance, cooking a plate of pasta will rarely create flow (although it is probably at the skill level of the domestic cook); however skiing in powder snow will create intense feelings of flow (as long as it matches the skier's level of skill). If a consumer experiences an activity but it requires less than his/her level of competence, boredom might set in. If, on the other hand, the activity is above the participant's capability level, it is likely to create stress.

Activities are seen as being conducive of flow if they have been designed to make accessing this state easier: "they have rules that require the learning of skills, they set up goals, they provide feedback, they make control possible" (Csíkszentmihályi, 1991, p. 72). The intensity of such an experience leads people to forget totally about their surrounding environment, and the intrinsic reward of the activity could lead people to seek experiences at great cost, for the simple objective of doing it. The notion of the intensity of the experience is important, though: "flow is likely to occur when a context exists that pushes individuals to near their physical and mental limits, without overwhelming them" (Celsi, Rose and Leigh, 1993, p.12).

In summary, flow is a type of optimal experience, but it does carry a separate status because it involves the notion of goals and skills. Flow can be experienced in activities that require some form of competence, which is not the case in the optimal experiences we addressed earlier. Flow is a very interesting concept, because it describes an experience in which the total absorption in the activity leads individuals to distance themselves further from their everyday lives. Flow episodes are experience boosters, an important component of the disconnection process, and an accelerator of immersion in the experience. It is explicitly mobilized to accelerate and guarantee the immersion and the well-being that results from it, and which permeates the entire stay. From this perspective, skiing, seen as an accelerator of this process, is particularly interesting to study. For example, in winter sports consumption, the concentration necessary for skiing means that when tourists put on their skis, they almost instantly forget the daily life which they have just left; the cut-off is instantaneous. This separation is also accelerated by the environment (clean air, light, change of scenery, etc.). Flow can be overpowering; consumers will experience, ideally, several episodes of flow, but they will not experience flow on a continuous basis.

FLOW IN OUTDOOR ACTIVITIES: MOUNTAIN BIKING

Would an experience of mountain biking create a flow experience? Let's imagine that Mr Taylor has booked a long weekend in Loch Lomond National Park in Scotland with two friends who also practice mountain biking. The group of three friends has been mountain biking for some years and have similar levels of competence. As soon as they start, a combination of the effort needed to power the bike, pacing that effort and making sure the bike does not leave the path means that the biker will be fully absorbed in his activity. This focused attention will mean that Mr Taylor will be completely immersed in this activity and will no longer think about either work or personal problems. Mr Taylor does not necessarily want to undertake this activity in a competitive spirit – there is no reward, it is not a race; he might want to challenge his friends from time to time, but the element of competition is out of his experience. His goals are clear; they had already studied the park's paths and had determined the roads they would take during their long weekend. He has enough experience to feel in control of his bike, and he is satisfied that the group of friends has chosen a level of difficulty in line with his level of skill. The flow magnifies itself through a feeling of deep enjoyment and pleasure. Obviously, the activity contributes heavily to this feeling, but the company of his friends plus the amazing surrounding of the National Park also contribute to it.

If Mr Taylor had been an unexperienced cyclist, however, he would have been left behind by the group; he might have felt anxiety (not feeling in control, fear of falling, not being fit enough, etc.) or frustration that he was slowing his friends down, and this negative feeling will have been overwhelming. Equally, if the paths taken were clearly below his level, he would have still enjoyed it (due to the cycling, friends' company and surroundings), but he would have experienced few flow episodes.

Does this example mean that flow is directly associated with competencies? According to the definition of flow provided by Csíkszentmihályi (1991), it is indeed a prerequisite condition.

However, providers can develop strategies to bypass this difficulty. They can provide training for their consumers, but they can also use technology to ease this process. Indeed, technological advances have allowed the development of electric bikes. With these bikes, consumers, even those who are inexperienced, are able to reach, master and conquer paths and hills they would previously have been unable to tackle. The advent of electric bikes is a real boost to the experience and a technological advance that is able to make cycling available to a wider range of tourists, those who currently do not necessarily consider cycling as a tourist transport mode or activity (seniors, some women, families with children, etc.). It can also be an even bigger provider of flow episodes for those consumers since some of them might consider cycling again and feel very satisfied with their achievement.

3.1.5 Awe

Another optimal experience category is that of awe, the root of the term *awesome*. This type of experience can be treated separately from optimal experiences or flow since it appears to federate different types of experience processes. "As a self-transcendent emotion, awe arises when people encounter perceptually vast stimuli that overwhelm their existing knowledge and mental structures, and, meanwhile, this also elicits a need for accommodation" (Wang, Zhang, Shi, Lu & Song, 2019, page 1). Awe translates into a feeling of positive powerlessness when confronting an object that is vast, magnificent and immense. Awe can be inspired by encounters of various types, for instance a beautiful landscape, a wonderful work of art, a beautiful natural phenomenon, a vast historical site, etc.

Awe designates an experience where tourists are confronted with an outstanding destination feature, one that leaves them powerless and overwhelmed by their emotions. Keltner and Haidt (2003) have identified two major features in awe experiences. They indicate that the object of awe should be vast, and that this vastness should be different from tourists' usual spheres of life. For instance, a tourist accustomed to living in a modern urban centre will experience awe when watching whales on a boating trip in Canada. The beauty of the mammals, their grace, their unthreatening approach and how they live will most probably create instant awe.

The second aspect Keltner and Haidt identify is the fact that tourists need to adapt to this encounter and might need to change their existing beliefs in order to make sense of it. Using again the whale example, tourists might reflect on their own lifestyle and integrate the fact that these mammals leave a peaceful life without the constant stress and complexities faced by human beings. They might also reflect on the beauty of nature and on their own unsustainable behaviour, which needs to be changed. Shiota, Keltner, and Mossman (2007) identified that awe triggers feelings of rapture, love and contentment along with surprise, pride and excitement. Shiota et al. (2007) also identified that awe creates a feeling of humility through the connection it creates with the surrounding world, the presence of something greater than self and a feeling of being small and insignificant. As a result, participants do not want the experience to end, and feel more connected with their values and culture. Awe is therefore another form of experience that is worth investigating because it occurs often in tourism encounters. It is a dimension of experiences that is also very connected to the notion of transformation that we will address later on in this chapter.

EXAMPLE FEATURING A MOUNTAIN HUT EXPERIENCE

Mountain huts are a very specific product in the array of tourist service provision. Mountains have a long history of providing shelter for walkers and mountaineers, with a range of huts of different capacities and service delivery spread across mountains throughout the world. The huts are often run by mountaineering associations and they require some major investments (building the huts in different locations, managing the huts, bringing the food in by helicopter, etc.). They don't necessarily have hot water; they have limited electricity supply, and the sleeping arrangements are mostly in the form of dormitories. Some huts are not staffed while others provide a full-board service with the provision of breakfast and dinner (set menu).

Mountain huts are most often located in remote areas and have no road access. As such, they offer tourists an experience in the midst of nature, in direct contact with mountains' wild and preserved environments. This type of tourist experience is interesting to investigate because it provides an insight into the place of wilderness and simplicity in potentially transforming experiences. The verbatims listed underneath come from a study on mountain hut users conducted in the Ecrin National Park in France and funded by Labex ITTEM.

When walking from mountain hut to mountain hut, tourists will quite rapidly adopt a very different rhythm from everyday life. They will wake up early, whereas in normal life this might be a struggle. The rhythm is different, and they will walk slowly; they will be dependent on the time it takes them to reach the next hut. Once at the hut, there is often no wifi connection so they will experience idleness. Upon arrival, they might take a nap, rest, read a book or engage in conversation with other tourists, all in a very relaxed atmosphere:

I experience a rhythm that is completely different from my everyday life. It is a different rhythm because I wake up much earlier than I would normally do, and I participate in different activities. Once I reach the hut, I just stop, and I don't ask myself any questions; I have time to myself until dinner is served. There is a freedom in my head, because I have no obligations, no imposed rhythm, and time goes slowly, time expands.

(Anna, 55)

The emotion of awe is present in this type of experience: "When I am in the mountains, it is calm, I experience silence; and the open landscape, its sheer vastness is breath-taking. It creates a form of vibration, I become much more at one with nature, the smells, the sounds" (Matthieu, 40).

This encounter with nature has a strong impact upon tourists, inviting them to reconsider their own place in the universe: Frédéric (42), a keen rambler indicates that "the space is so vast, we just want to take full advantage of it, dive in it so to speak, and nature has a very imposing dimension which calls for respect". Another rambler, Natacha (62), indicates that "When I am in the mountains, I realize how small we are, us human beings, we are confronted

Figure 3.2 Picturing a memorable experience, indulging in a beautiful mountain landscape. Source: Author.

with the sheer magnitude and beauty of the mountains, it gives us a different perspective on our place on this planet".

These types of experiences also provoke a change in behaviour and a different relation to oneself: "Afterwards, we also feel, I don't know how to put it ... more attentive to everything? In fact, in the mountains, I suddenly become much more aware of the things around me, other people, myself, my feelings, my emotions" (Jean, 32).

In summary, walking in high-altitude mountain ranges and staying in huts are deeply moving experiences. They are totally out of the ordinary, connecting people with "true nature" and the beauty of the mountains which provokes a rethinking of oneself, perhaps leading to a different outlook on one's life. In these types of experiences, the activities undertaken, the contexts and the encounters all contribute to a transformation (Figure 3.2).

3.2 Transformation

To conclude, one of the outcomes of deep experiences is the impact that they can have on human beings. The references to positive psychology in the previous section and eudemonic experiences are intimately associated with the notion of transformation.

The notion of transformation can be used to investigate the extent to which a tourist experience might impact consumers at different levels (physically, mentally, etc.). Whilst most marketing literature in previous decades has focussed on satisfaction, quality and loyalty, experiential marketing is more interested in understanding how some experiences transform visitors. In this line of thinking, marketers contemplate looking beyond producing satisfactory holidays and focus on creating vacations where consumers can experience a deep sense of change and a transformation that will stay with them beyond the holiday. In a study on life-changing vacations, Kirillova, Lehto and Cai (2017) demonstrated how "a transformative tourist experience necessarily implies a greater awareness of existential concerns and heightened sensitivity to existential anxiety, which encourages a tourist to seek a more authentic lifestyle" (2017, page 11).

Because tourism experiences are episodic and take place within set period of time away from the usual structures and control, it is a period that can liberate individuals and therefore open up potential opportunities for transformation.

When investigating the concept of escape, various studies have aimed to understand the extent to which holidays can bring change in individuals' lives. Some studies point to existential transformation, which brings in tourists the feeling of being someone else and being able to live a different identity (Oh, Fiore and Jeoung, 2007; Hosany and Witham, 2010). The various studies reviewed on positive psychology point to the fact that by offering growth and learning, many experiences intuitively will bring transformation to holiday consumers (the encounters during the holiday might lead to deep changes in individuals during and beyond the holiday). Transformation can also be experienced by adopting a completely different lifestyle to what an individual is accustomed to. Holidays can be seen as temporary periods where individuals will experience transformation and might learn new skills that they go on to pursue beyond the holiday. They might also take the opportunity of a holiday to experience a different lifestyle, one that might transform their perspective on the world (see the example on slow tourism).

SLOW TOURISM AND THE RECONSIDERATION OF TIME

Slow tourism belongs to the broad family of sustainable tourism practices. It is a form of tourism that exists in many ways in opposition to mass tourism. The objective of slow tourism is to reposition tourism consumption within a more localised approach: staying in small-scale accommodation closer to local inhabitants, buying local products, relying on organically and locally produced food, living authentic experiences, etc.

Slow tourism also includes mobilities and integrates the fact that the journey is part of the holiday. For instance, a journey from Paris to Berlin can be operated by an airline company. The flight itself reaches Berlin fairly quickly, but the waiting times before and after the flight are long. More importantly, this type of mobility does not allow the traveller to fully enjoy the journey, to take into account the evolving landscapes, to sit and rest during the journey, etc. If that same journey was undertaken by train, it might take longer but it would allow the participant to take in the changing landscapes, to sit and enjoy the journey, perhaps read a book, listen to music, meet other passengers, etc. The journey will also provide the consumer with a nice smooth entry into the holiday, a period where he/she can gradually unwind and make himself/herself available for the holiday.

Beyond those "practical" considerations, slow tourism has developed in response to contemporary citizens who feel that their lifestyles put an increasing pressure on time and create a stress that they want to escape from when holidaying.

Whilst time can be considered in terms of fastness or slowness, in slow tourism, the notion goes beyond the simple perception of time; it is also an opportunity to step away from the time pressures consumers experience in daily life. While on holiday, the fact that time pressure will ease off creates a new universe where time regains its value; consumers finally "find the time" to engage into various pursuits, and it also allows them to spend quality time with loved ones, step away from restrictive schedules, etc. In other words: "consumers' temporal experiences do not exclusively result from performing practices, but also from immersing into, or escaping from, the broader social temporal logics that emphasise slowness and fastness" (Huseman and Eckhardt, 2019, page 1145).

Can slowness be a key and valuable characteristic of tourism experiences? Hartmut Rosa (2013) identified territorial niches that form pockets of resistance against the acceleration of society. Those niches respond to different temporal logic and provide consumers with the opportunity to slow down, enjoy, recharge themselves and come home rested. The experience described earlier in this section on mountain huts describes one of those niches. Huseman and Eckhardt (2019) indicate that full consumer deceleration can only occur if three forms of deceleration take place: embodied, technical and episodic. In their work, embodied deceleration refers to the engagement into slow forms of transport, leading to the body slowing down; technical deceleration refers to reducing the presence of technology during the holiday; and episodic deceleration implies a reduction in choices and a simplification of experiences.

Echoing this work, Chapter 2 of this book investigated the intrusion of digital devices into holiday dynamics, and in the next chapter, the section on simplicity will further address those elements.

Another dimension of transformation can be captured through the studies that have investigated the impact of holidays on life satisfaction. Various studies have been conducted in this area, and the results seem to lead to varied conclusions. Richards (1999) identifies that vacations contribute to quality of life through their capacity to generate social interactions, facilitate personal development and improve individual identity. Gilbert and Abdullah (2004) demonstrate that having taken recently a vacation was clearly associated with a greater sense of well-being, not just after the holiday but also before. Hence, the holiday anticipation phase is also conductive to a sense of well-being. Weastman and Eden (1997) demonstrated the impact of vacations on the reduction of burnout syndrome, whilst Strauss-Blasche (2000) confirmed an improvement in mood and sleep quality during a vacation. Whether holidays impact long-term happiness remains to be further investigated. Nawijn et al. (2010), among other researchers, have failed to identify the long-term impact of holidays on happiness. More research needs to be developed to identify the scope and length of improvements in well-being associated with holidays and the scope of transformation.

3.3 Memory formation, retention and renegotiation

Memory is a complex mechanism, a process involved in capturing, storing and retrieving information. Its complexity lies in the fact that memories evolve differently; some events will stay in the memory while others will disappear. Memories will also evolve through time and might be distorted. Every time a memory is recalled, it will be changed and stored in a modified version, one that might change again on the next recall process.

As we have stated from the outset of this book, memory is the outcome of experiential marketing; the "success" of an experience can be measured through the intensity of the lasting memories that it leaves consumers with. Evaluating memories is an interesting process that allows for a better understanding of the most important elements that "stick" in the memory. In other words, memory can be conceived as a pertinent variable that allows experience designers to evaluate the outstanding components of their experience. The study developed earlier on deep experiences (the mountain resort experience in Section 3.2) identified the key components that remained in participants' memory one year later. Overall, it appears that optimal experiences, flow and awe, are good predictors of outstanding experiences that will stay in the memory.

3.3.1 Memorable tourism experiences

Since the 2010s, several studies have investigated the role and dimensionality of memory in the tourist experience. The most famous scale aiming to identify the different memory dimensions was produced by Kim, Ritchie and McCormick in 2012. Their scale identified that memorable experiences share some key characteristics that can be divided according to seven dimensions: hedonism (excitement and enjoyment), novelty, local culture, refreshment (revitalization and sense of freedom), meaningfulness, involvement (places and activities one really wanted to do) and knowledge. Those scales are useful and they also confirm the notion that the characteristics of optimal experiences seem to create the most memorable episodes. For instance, elements such as meaningfulness and knowledge are key pointers in deep experiences. Kim and Fesenmaier's scale also exemplifies the true nature of tourism experiences: a sense of freedom, hedonism, involvement, etc.

Since the production of these memorable tourism experience scales, other studies have investigated the dimensions of memorable experiences in other contexts. As is often the case, there is no one scale that is identified as being the definite answer. However, altogether, these scales identify components that are in line with the findings on optimal experiences coupled with knowledge gained in experiential marketing studies, as we will identify in the next chapter.

3.3.2 The rosy view

Memories, however, are complex since they are not static. The field of tourism experiences still lacks sufficient longitudinal studies that allow experience designers to understand how memories evolve over time. Some elements are forgotten, others are renegotiated and memories get recomposed through time. For instance, the rosy view is an interesting phenomenon that investigates the extent to which tourists renegotiate positively a memory over time. According to the rosy view, tourists will tend to have memories of an event than are more positive than it actually was. In other terms, over time, tourists will renegotiate their memory by overemphasizing positive elements. This is a known phenomenon in tourist experiences, whereby an experience that might have had some negative components when it happened is remembered as a positive experience.

THE ROSY VIEW: HOW A NEGATIVE EXPERIENCE TURNS INTO A POSITIVE MEMORY

A group of tourists has decided to organize a cycling trip across southern Norway over 7 days. They have rented bikes locally; they have organised their itinerary and have already booked their accommodation. During the cycling trip, on day 3, participants experienced a rainy day, cycling against the rain and wind, and ending up being completely soaked and cold. While it happened, this experience was not a pleasant one, and rather one of discomfort. But as soon as the experience was over, when the participants had reached their accommodation, and when they felt safe, warm and in a new set of dry clothes, they were most likely to remember this cycling trip as a positive memory. There were indeed no major negative elements in this experience. There was some discomfort, but no-one got injured and the participants were not impacted financially. They are also aware that they undertook this trip of their own free will, and they knew that rain could invite itself along for the journey. They will also have developed a feeling of success and transcendence from what they have achieved that day. As a result, the negative episode will most certainly translate into a positive memory.

Mitchell, Thompson, Peterson and Cronk (1997) identified that the rosy view occurs because participants do not wish to remember minor components of their experience, even if those are negative. This is a very interesting aspect of experiences of the hedonic type – interesting because it questions the ways in which consumers appreciate their experience and thereby interrogates the notions of quality and satisfaction. Indeed, decades of research on service quality has encouraged service providers to evaluate their consumers' experiences based on lists (scales) evaluating different components of their experience. For instance, quality scales of the SERVQUAL type (Parasuraman, A., Zeithaml, V. A., & Berry, L., 2002) are very useful in identifying the key components that are central in the evaluation of the quality of an experience. However, those scales tend to focus their evaluation mostly on the service provision itself according to a very functional logic. These scales are useful and necessary because they allow service deliverers to evaluate the standard of their service and correct areas that need to be improved. Considering also the power of e-word of mouth, service providers need to monitor their quality in order to avoid any negative echo that consumers might diffuse over the Internet (Tripadvisor, Google advise, etc.). However, the impact that those negative evaluations might have on the formation of the memory of an experience remains unclear.

3.3.3 The experiential CV

A very interesting study conducted by Keinan and Kivetz (2011) demonstrated that "some consumers choose novel experiences not for the sake of immediate pleasure but rather for the opportunity to add experiences to their experiential CV" (page 948). Keinan and Kivetz's experiments identify that for the sake of collecting experiences (most commonly known as the "bucket list" phenomenon), consumers are willing to absorb some elements of discomfort as long as the experience is worthwhile. Their study identifies that the "race" for collectable (and sharable) memories is driving a range of consumption choices and practices, and might modify how consumers evaluate their experience. Beyond the bucket-list dimension, this study points to the capacity that consumers might have in absorbing some form of discomfort for the sake of a sought-after hedonic experience. In summary, both the rosy view and the concept of the experiential CV encourage experience designers and researchers to consider carefully which elements stand out in experiences.

There is, in the understanding of tourism experiences, more studies and experiments needed to clearly understand how and why consumers negotiate their memories and how both functional and experiential elements together impact memorable experiences (Figure 3.3).

3.3.4 The peak-end rule

Another interesting insight into memories was produced by Kahneman, Fredrickson, Schreiber, and Redelmeier in 1993. According to their work, individuals tend to remember an experience according to its best intense point

Figure 3.3 Having fun as a family unit in an outstanding landscape. Source: Photo by Juan Cruz Mountford on Unsplash.

(peak) and its final one (end), but not on an average evaluation of the different components of the experience. The authors also identified that the duration of the experience seems to have little impact on the evaluation (referred to as the duration effect). In the tourism sphere, Kemp, Burt and Furneaux (2008) investigated the peak-end rule on the perceived happiness on vacations. Their results showed that, for a vacation, it is the most memorable or unusual 24 hours that has the most impact on consumers' happiness. They also identified that the duration of the holiday seemed to have little impact on its memorability. Whilst Kahneman et al.'s study (1993) is concerned with the memory of pain in hospital examinations, there is not enough research on hedonic consumption to identify if the same dynamics characterize a tourist experience. There is a need for more studies that clearly investigate the evolution of memory, the renegotiation process and the extent to which negative experiences during a holiday might be recalled positively.

Conclusion

This chapter has aimed to present a more detailed vision of the characteristics of the deep experiences that impact consumers most. Peak, optimal, extraordinary experiences along with awe and flow provide some guidance on the elements that impact most consumers. Those models can also assist experience designers in understanding the processes that can explain why some experiences are more impactful than others. This strategic knowledge can find its inspiration in theories and models that have been developed for some time, especially in the fields of consumer behaviour and positive psychology. Whilst some of those notions might seem remote from the preoccupations of tourism managers, they bring a very interesting, detailed and analytical vision of the components that trigger deep experiences. The notion of deep experiences is particularly important since those key experiences accelerate tourists' disconnection and fuel memories. Beyond those experiences, the more general knowledge brought about by studies on well-being and quality of life and the general approach taken in positive psychology are equally important since they offer some interesting pointers on mechanisms, elements and exercises that can be redeveloped within tourist experiences to boost their impact. The knowledge gained in the study of deep experiences will be reintegrated in Chapter 5 when investigating the six cues to developing impactful experiences. However, before looking at the construction of the experience, the next chapter will investigate the key consumer trends that can also assist experience designers in positioning their experience within current influences.

Chapter **4**

Major tourism trends

Introduction

This new chapter investigates the different trends that are characteristic of tourism demand. Some of these trends are a reflection of the evolution of consumer behaviour in society at large, while others are specifically associated with tourism. The ten trends presented in this chapter will be developed to give readers pointers to the different elements that can be integrated into experience design in order to produce memorable experiences. The chapter will present and illustrate each trend: playfulness, well-being, unique experiences, nature, sustainability, authenticity, localhood, simplicity, fantasy and, finally, package holidays. Those trends are not just ephemeral fashion fads; they are emerging or strengthening trends that represent the backbone of current consumer demand and that fuel successful experiences. This chapter gives pointers and inspirational elements from which experience creators can create new experiences.

4.1 Playfulness

Whilst play is often associated with childhood, it can be present at any stage in life and is a core component of experiences. It is generally understood that play is freely undertaken; it has to be unconstrained in the sense that it is a leisure activity and therefore defined by freedom and enjoyment. There is no notion of profit in play (although in competitive games some price might be an outcome); in most cases, play is usually undertaken for intrinsic rewards. Play in adulthood

DOI: 10.4324/9781003019237-5

allows participants to experience simplicity and innocence by stepping out of reality (Figure 4.1):

> Summing up the formal characteristic of play, we might call it a free activity standing quite consciously outside "ordinary" life as being "not serious" but at the same time absorbing the player intensely and utterly. It is an activity connected with no material interest, and no profit can be gained by it. It proceeds within its own proper boundaries of time and space according to fixed rules and in an orderly manner. It promotes the formation of social groupings that tend to surround themselves with secrecy and to stress the difference from the common world by disguise or other means.
>
> (Ackermann, 2011, page 13)

We mentioned the notion of immersion in Chapter 2, and play fits well within this dynamic. Play creates a bubble with its own settings, rules and organization, a bubble where players can act and think differently. In other words, play can be an opportunity for consumers to immerse themselves in an experience. Because play takes place outside the usual constrictive boundaries of everyday life, it reinforces the feeling of escapism. Play can contribute to cognitive learning but can also create strong social connections. The range of activities that fall into the realm of play are rather broad. In the tourism context, play can involve very creative activities, games, role-play, improvization, acting, etc.

Figure 4.1 Entering the dream of Disneyland. Source: Photo by Quick PS on Unsplash.

Educational games have also gained popularity in the world of education, especially serious games that allow students and professionals to engage into a game-based approach to solving managerial issues and developing creative answers to innovation challenges. Play can therefore also be considered as an interesting option when a destination wants to train staff, seasonal workers, trainees, etc.

To some extent edutainment (education and entertainment) falls in this category as a way to attract interest and keep consumer attention in cultural experiences. Edutainment mixes together the educative component and the entertaining dimension, and has been used in museums and more generally in theme parks such as the EPCOT centre or Puy du Fou (see example).

LE PUY DU FOU: AN EXPERIENCE ENTIRELY FOCUSED ON EMOTIONS

The Puy du Fou park is undoubtedly one of the most emblematic and unique tourist sites in the panorama of French theme parks. In 2022, the Cinéscénie show will be performed for the 45th year; this is a great show that retraces the history of the Vendée region with the help of numerous sets and pyrotechnic effects. The show lasts 1 hour 40 minutes, and welcomes nearly 400,000 spectators every year. The show is performed by 3,200 volunteer actors and dancers, with more than 24,000 costumes and a 23-hectare stage.

Since 1989, the Puy du Fou has hosted "Le Grand Parc", a park made up of various performance stages which retrace different themes and eras (Roman times, the Vikings, the Renaissance, etc.), and also visually astonishing shows such as the *Bal des Oiseaux Fantômes* (a performance with birds flying over and between spectators) or the *Orgues de Feu* (a night-time musical show on water). Unlike a traditional theme park, the Puy du Fou does not really play on sensations or adrenaline to attract consumers; it has rather centred its offering much more on emotions.

The Puy du Fou is a clever mix of a spectacular performances (which fits well with current expectations), amazing sets and costumes. The theme park value is developed on the basis of a very elaborate script and a skilful acting that positions the shows somewhere between history and fantasy, and immerse visitors in a different world. Unlike a traditional theme park, the consumer does not move between different attractions that are often short and highly adrenaline-pumping. The Park has rather invested in an innovative concept: to offer spectators a set of spectacular performances which take place at different times during the day and which last from 20 to 40 minutes each. Visitors plan their day by themselves by choosing different shows. A total of six large shows are offered as well as other smaller activities (not necessarily involving actors), as well as reconstructed period villages and natural areas so that children can play in peace. This is clearly a family product; all shows are accessible to all audiences.

The success and originality of this concept, unique in the world, earned the park the prize for best theme park in the world in 2012 (the Thea Award from the Themed Entertainment Association).

The park is a great success with 2.1 million visitors welcomed in 2019 (including 9% foreigners). On average, the shows run for 8–10 years, and they are constantly evolving. Of the park's clientele, 65% is made up of repeat visitors, and on average a client revisits the park every 2–3 years. The renewal of the shows has kept up consumer interest in the park over the years (The Puy du Fou creates its own attractions thanks to its artistic team, which designs and renews the shows). On average, a third of visitors stay on site for more than a day. The Park has also invested in themed hotels, and the park now has a capacity of more than 1,500 beds. The Puy du Fou park invests between 10 and 20 million euros per year in its offerings and has set up a reservation centre which allows its products to be marketed efficiently (the large park, the Cinéscénie, hotels and a specific offer for business customers).

From a commercial point of view, the pricing policy aims to price the park at a very affordable level especially because it is primarily targeting families. It is indeed the cheapest of the large parks in France that welcome more than 1 million visitors.

4.2 Well-being as an evolving trend

Well-being includes various forms of services and activities dedicated to health and leisure and tourism consumption. Well-being encompasses both the physical condition of an individual and his/her mental/psychological state. Well-being has often been associated with medical spas where specific waters were recognized to be good for healing specific health conditions. Those medical spas have a long historical legitimacy; emerging in Greece in the 6th century BC, they were later on developed by the Romans. In Europe, thermal spas became hugely popular in the 19th and 20th centuries and led to the development of spa resorts. However, as the popularity of other forms of tourism increased (the seaside, for instance, in the mid-20th century), spas resorts decreased in popularity.

Over the last 30 years, a gradual renewal of spa resorts has taken place, and spas, including the most ancient European ones, have invested in new technologies to provide top-class services. To rejuvenate their product, most spas have also enlarged their positioning, keeping their medical dimension but, at the same time, developing a secondary market aimed at relaxation and well-being in the general sense. This second market has allowed many spas to keep afloat and has led to the opening of new offers based on the benefits of mineral or sea waters and even grapes. More generally, the spa offer has become a common feature within hotels.

THE WELLNESS AND SPA MARKET

The Global Wellness Economy Monitor (2018) estimates that the spa industry is worth $119 billion, the thermal/mineral springs industry is worth $56 billion, and altogether the wellness industry is worth $4.2 trillion. The monitor has identified that the wellness economy keeps on growing rapidly, at a healthy rate of 6.4% per year (twice the global economic growth). Despite the various crises the world has recently experienced, this rise can be explained by various factors, among which are population ageing, stressful and sedentary modern living conditions, lack of health prevention, widespread prosperity in developed and emerging countries and the increased popularity of wellness lifestyles. Wellness trips are most popular in Europe, while North America remains in a strong position on the wellness market (highest average spending per trip), and Asia is the fastest growing market due to economic expansion and the rising middle classes.

> The wellness tourism market includes two types of travelers: those who are motivated by wellness to take the trip or choose the destination (primary wellness travelers) and those who seek to maintain wellness or engage in wellness activities during travel (secondary wellness travelers). The bulk of wellness travel is done by secondary wellness travelers, who account for 89% of wellness tourism trips and 86% of expenditures in 2017. Wellness tourism is also high-yield tourism. The Global Wellness Institute estimates that international wellness travelers spend at a 53% premium (over the average international tourist), while domestic wellness travelers spend at a 178% premium (over the average domestic tourist).
>
> (Global Economic Wellness Monitor (2018) Global Wellness Institute, https://globalwellnessinstitute.org/industry-research/2018-global-wellness-economy-monitor/#)

On top of spa provision, whether it is undertaken for medical or leisure purposes, leisure services have developed based on water's inherent playful quality. For instance, spas and swimming-pools have merged into new types of aquatic leisure centres (aquaparks), where the water is given a more playful touch by adding slides, wave machines, lagoons, waterfalls and all sorts of spa effects (jacuzzis, showers, different types of sauna, etc.). Those aquaparks become a main outing for half a day to a day. They add to the fun of the water by providing facilities that either play on the resting and soothing dimensions of water (the spa side) or on its playful dimensions (waves, etc.). Across the world these aquaparks are expanding rapidly, ranging from those offering purely aquatic fun (Disney Typhoon Lagoons, for example) to parks that also include a more wellness-oriented dimension (Széchenyi Thermal Bath and Swimming Pools in Hungary).

Beyond the historical spa industry, the notion of well-being has grown to integrate broader spheres of well-being such as of the mind and spirit. Therefore, beyond spas, the wellness sphere, especially in continental Europe, has reintegrated practices taking their inspiration in Asian culture. Qi Gong, yoga and feng chui have become familiar practices in sports clubs, local classes and on holidays as well. Most resorts nowadays offer these practices among their range of activities. Those practices echo the need felt by contemporary consumers to turn their focus inward on the body and mind and regain some form of well-being in a world that is fast-paced and stressful.

One of the latest trends in this area has been to reconsider the need for and power of mindfulness to bring consumers back to a full engagement with their life and distance themselves from various stress and pressures (including digital distractions). Those various wellness dimensions are becoming a common feature of activities in destinations, resorts, cruise ships, etc. Some resorts have also developed apps or initiatives to engage consumers in mindfulness at a time when they have available time to invest in this practice. For example, the *My Serenity* program in Val Thorens involves the distribution of a guide that invites tourists, through several steps, to achieve mindfulness. The resort has also created a *My Serenity* label that validates different tourism providers within the resort who have developed various practices to encourage mindfulness practices in their consumers (see Chapter 3).

4.3 The once-in-a-lifetime experience

Contemporary tourists are seasoned travellers who have inherited, from their parents and grandparents, various travelling experiences and a fairly deep understanding of what holidays bring to one's life. They represent the fourth generation of mass tourists and they have accumulated a broad range of holiday experiences. The holiday booking process has now also become vastly easier. Contemporary consumers can, in a few clicks, book their flights, find a hotel (and its evaluations by other consumers), identify the best places to see, etc. The fact that traveling is now so easy also explains why holidays are a big part of contemporary consumers' lives, with millennials planning on average four to five holidays a year. Holidays are taken more often but are not as long as in previous generations.

This cumulated experience has led consumers to understand what constitutes memorable experiences. They have come to recognize the value of holidays as periods where they live exceptional experiences and "buy" souvenirs that they will cherish in the long term. This thirst has also been boosted for some by the selfie craze and the bucket-list obsession. Tourists are increasingly looking for evidence of exceptional and outstanding episodes in their lives that they can proudly display on their social networks. For certain categories of consumers, it is part of their identity and visibility, and a strong motivation to live some experiences. Experiential marketing has also played a role in this trend by boosting the offer of unusual, atypical and extraordinary tourism products. Across the world, various innovations in this domain have popped up. From ice hotels in Sweden and bunker rooms in Russia to igloo hotels in Finland or snow groomers in the Alps, the range seems to be endless.

AN AIRY SWISS HOTEL ROOM: "NULL STERN – THE ONLY STAR IS YOU"

The zero-star Swiss hotel concept was created in 2008 in a nuclear bunker in the municipality of Sevelen, St Gallen, and developed further in 2009 in Teufen with the brand "Null Stern – the only star is you".

The product is, as such, rather simple but particularly innovative: a wood and concrete base serves as the floor for the room, which is arranged as a hotel room (a comfortable bed, two side tables and bed lamps, hygiene facilities a 5-minute walk away and a local butler providing room service on demand). As for the rest, there are no walls, simply the natural surroundings, a 360-degree panoramic wallpaper, with the starry sky acting as the ceiling. Due to its outdoor location, this seasonal room is commercialized in the summer months only.

Of course, for mountain enthusiasts, this might look like a strange concept. Mountaineers accustomed to sleeping in bivouacs have all the necessary competence and equipment to engage in this experience at no cost. But, precisely because not every consumer has this equipment and skills, the room is attractive to consumers who want to buy an exceptional experience, one that is prepackaged for them and offers them the dream of a night in nature with reassuring comfort.

The project has been a real success with the room being booked as far as a year and a half in advance. The room is priced at 270 euros a night. After two successful seasons and over 4,500 reservation requests, concept artists Frank and Patrik Riklin and hotel expert Daniel Charbonnier launched the *Zero Real Estate* project in 2018 and have already developed seven new rooms in Eastern Switzerland, and another one, in the Principality of

Liechtenstein, which joined the project in 2020. The waiting list of 9,000 potential customers is living proof of the success of this concept.

There is no hotelier in the classical sense since the local community is the hotelier. The *Null Stern* Modern Butlers are local residents and promote a culture of hosting, sharing and experience. The butlers that run the rooms have to conform to a strict dress code: white shirt, black bow tie, and white gloves. However, the clothing "below the belt" is personalised by the butler – whether farm trousers with rubber boots, business trousers with patent leather shoes or a skirt with high heels. This unusual visual identification is also part of the originality of the concept.

Null Stern Modern Butler training assures the quality of services in the outdoors: carrying a serving tray over steep slopes, climbing over a fence while holding two cups of coffee or transporting mattresses up to the summit. The butler's responsibilities include welcoming guests upon arrival, check-in, escorting guests to the suite, answering guests' questions about the area and serving a breakfast of coffee, bread, cheese and Pantli (local sausage) bed-side.

A "TV-Direct" option translates into an old recycled TV frame with one exclusive channel where the Modern Butler delivers the day's news headlines, weather forecast and local anecdotes face-to-face.

Figure 4.2 Nullstern's outdoor hotel room. Source: Zero Real Estate Null Stern Spin-off Säntis.

Figure 4.3 Modern butler outfit in Null Stern. Source: ©Patrik Riklin AfS 2016.

Figure 4.4 The butler and the hotel room at Null Stern. Source: ©Caroline Krajcir Thurgau Tourism Switzerland 2020.

This unusual experience has received several awards over the years. Necessarily, it has benefited the image of the company and it has also broadcasted an image of Switzerland as a modern and creative destination (Figures 4.2, 4.3, 4.4).

Source: https//nullsternhotel.ch

The other reason for the demand for this type of experience is associated with the fact that, has we discussed in Chapter 2, travelling first and foremost fulfils a need to get away from routines and everyday life. The more this everyday life is anchored in frustrating routines, the more consumers will hope to find in their holidays opportunities to live experiences that are totally different from their daily reality. In their eyes, those experiences need to bring them some element of novelty and make them experience intense emotions, different from what they are accustomed to.

Whilst this frantic thirst for unusual tourism experiences was temporarily tempered by the Covid crisis, it has pushed consumers to reconsider where they can live those experiences. While for many, unusual experiences were located in "exotic" destinations, they have revised their perception of "exoticism" to redefine it more locally, often within their own countries. In this line of thought, consumers have rediscovered experiences in domestic destinations, experiences that cut them loose from the ordinary, and create memorable experiences. In many ways, extraordinary experiences do not necessarily need to be located at the far end of the Earth to provide excitement and extraordinariness (see the example on glamping).

TREE HOUSES AND THE ART OF GLAMPING

The recent phenomenon of glamping (a conflation of glamourous and camping) is particularly interesting because by re-conceptualizing products in the camping sphere and by riding the environmental wave, operators have succeeded in attracting new consumers who would never have purchased these products previously. Indeed, even if there have been huge innovations in camping over the years, it still carries for many the connotation of an uncomfortable and rudimentary product. But by creating new products (trailers, tree houses, yurts, igloos, etc.), tourist operators have succeeded in attracting a new category of clientele: urban dwellers chasing dreams of nature. This category of guests are from the middle upper classes and seek the romantic dimension of nature, and they can temporarily accommodate themselves to limited comfort, provided the experience is exceptional. These products combine the sensations and the innovative and unusual dimensions of the product offered but retain a certain level of comfort. All products are turnkey, removing the burden of bringing heavy, bulky equipment and having to pitch a tent.

Houses can be located at different heights from the ground. The product is very attractive to a range of consumers, especially families, since it provides them with the opportunity to experience and relive childhood dreams.

Tree houses are usually fully integrated into site landscapes and are in total harmony with their surroundings. Tree houses should have limited impact on their direct environment. When being built, tree roots can be protected, no material is screwed or implanted into the tree trunks and wooden planks protect the trunk from the structures. The houses can be suspended by a system of pulleys which are adjusted to respect the growth of the trees.

Tree houses offer an intense environmental experience: the houses usually do not have running water, they are equipped with dry toilets and they are without electricity (consumers can light the space with candles and dynamo lamps). Customers appreciate this break from everyday life and also see it as an interesting way to introduce their children to simple living principles close to nature.

This return to a simple life offers customers an experience totally out of the ordinary and in total opposition to their daily life, allowing them a much-appreciated return to their roots. This experience revives various emotions and sensations. Tree houses offer an experience of calmness and closeness to nature; consumers live a total immersion in the sights, smells and sounds of nature (the rustling of leaves in the trees, owls hooting at night, waking up to birdsong, etc.). The beds are often protected with a mosquito net which adds to the sense of adventure of the experience. Breakfast might be served at the bottom of the tree and lifted up with a pulley.

Are 21st-century consumers able to adapt to this radical change in lifestyle? Overall, satisfaction with this product is very high. The originality of the experience, the total disconnection from the everyday environment, the total immersion in nature is a great success and leaves strong and lasting memories. It goes without saying that the intensity of the experience makes consumers forget the lack of comfort, which is only temporary (these consumers could not accept this lifestyle on a long-term basis).

4.4 The love of nature

Nature has always been a prime attraction in the tourism sphere; the landscape is the most sought-after resource when traveling and it is most often interrelated with natural elements. Nature offers spontaneous sources of positive emotions, its beauty having been celebrated in various literary works, among which the romantic movement played a key role in recognizing its value.

Beyond its aesthetic values, nature is first and foremost a context that favours disconnection and restoration, and it can therefore play a central role in creating impactful experiences.

Connections with the natural world are becoming increasingly important because those contacts are scarcer in contemporary societies. It is commonly estimated that 70% of the world's population will live in urban areas by 2030. This urbanization has reduced the possibilities of contact with nature. Citizens who have lived in urban locations for several generations are often disconnected from nature and have lost both the knowledge and competencies to appreciate nature to its full.

Contacts with nature have long been established as carrying various health benefits (Williams, 2017). Time spent in nature can reduce the stress hormone (cortisol), reduce blood pressure and boost the immune system. In 1985, Kellert and Wilson elaborated the biophilia hypothesis – the belief that humans are genetically predisposed to feel attracted to nature. In their vision, human beings are intuitively and inherently in love with the natural world.

Nature encapsulates various experience opportunities with fauna and flora and some specific contexts appear to have particularly strong evocations and impacts. For instance, forests have been identified for their specific capacities in restoring attention as identified by various Japanese researchers who have promoted the benefits of forest bathing (*shinrin-yoku*). Experiences in the wilderness have also been identified as boosters of humility and oneness (Borrie & Roggenbuck, 2001).

EXAMPLE: FINLAND FOREST BATHING

A long way away from the Japanese-based tradition in shinrin-yoku, Finland has developed a range of tourism experiences based on forest bathing. The country has a vast range of forests (almost 70% of the land area is covered by forest) and natural areas that can serve as a base from which to develop experiences for tourists. Various operators have developed products to guide tourists through an experience of bathing in pine forests. Some of those experiences might involve some form of foraging for local mushrooms and berries. Meditation techniques might be passed on to visitors to increase the benefits of the experience. Tree hugging is another practice that increases oxytocin levels and contributes to calmness and bonding emotions.

Forests can be intimidating for visitors who are not accustomed to them, and there is always the fear of getting lost or having an undesired encounter with a wild animal. Therefore, forest experiences need some form of guidance. Path maintenance and signage is a basic service, and the presence of a guide will greatly enhance the experience as well as reassuring visitors.

The relationship with nature can be experienced at different levels. As expressed at the beginning of this section, consumers' relationships with nature can take various forms. A large proportion of visitors come from urban areas and often have limited experiences and previous connections with natural spaces. Those visitors will need special attention since they will need to be accompanied in making connections with the natural world. Beyond this need for intermediation, major tourism actors have also understood this demand. Contemporary consumers are attracted to nature and the sustainability discourse (which we will address in the next section), and the Covid crisis has boosted demand for nature-based experiences even more. For a contemporary unexperienced consumer, operators have developed products that surf on the dream of nature but with the comfort and access that respects consumers' uneasiness and expectations. This is the case with Disney, which has developed a new park in Marne-la-Vallée (France), the Villages Nature, by combining its expertise with that of CenterParks. The village developed by Disney is an attempt to target contemporary consumers who are keen to live an experience closer to nature and in line with sustainability principles. To surf on the feeling of being in nature, the park offers various forms of accommodation, from traditional apartments to tree houses. Areas have been closed to car traffic and the site is landscaped with a broad range of trees and bushes. Some electric buses along with small electric vehicles and bikes are the preferred modes of transport. A central lagoon offers bathing opportunities, and the water is heated naturally by underground thermal waters. A farm and an outdoor nature activity park offer another immersion into nature. Restaurants are themed, either with local food or veggie/vegan menus. The park has an ambitious plan for recycling, reusing the warm water from other amenities, and privileges local producers and fair trade.

Whilst this product might not be attractive for the pure nature enthusiast, it does provide an interesting product for visitors, especially families, who want to live an experience as close as possible to nature without giving up the comfort and holiday amenities they are used to (Figure 4.5).

4.5 A sustainable consumer?

Whilst the previous section addressed consumers' relationship to nature, this section treats a related but broader topic, that of the consideration of sustainable issues within tourism consumption. The notion of sustainability is

Figure 4.5 Investigating the canopy. Source: Photo by Josh Hild on Unsplash.

unavoidable in the development of new products. This section provides some indications of the complexities of sustainable consumer behaviours.

The UNWTO defines sustainable tourism as "Tourism that takes full account of its current and future economic, social and environmental impacts, addressing the needs of visitors, the industry, the environment and host communities" (https://www.unwto.org/EU-guidebook-on-sustainable-tourism-for-development). The impacts of tourism have long been identified and analyzed, and they include social, economic and environmental dimensions. Each of them have led to the integration of new set of practices in the tourism industry, whether those aim to integrate more fully local communities and genuine contacts with tourists (social impacts), to integrate local employees within the tourism industry (economic impacts) or to reduce environmental impacts.

The increasing number of diverse sources of pollution and the threat of global warming need no demonstration. Considerations for the environment are necessarily an essential component of the tourism offer, including experience design. In this short paragraph it is impossible to detail the diversity of issues related to sustainable tourism, and so we will focus mostly on its behavioural and experiential dimensions from consumers' point of view.

One subject of interest is to clarify the extent to which 21st-century consumers are capable or not of adopting sustainable behaviour. The openness of urban-based consumers to accepting sustainable products can in fact be limited. We have seen that urban consumers often need a packaged product, as in the Disney initiative with the *Villages Nature*.

However, does the consumption of sustainable holiday products lead to the adoption of sustainable behaviour beyond the holiday? This is a particularly thorny question since various studies have pointed to the difficulty in engaging behavioural change. As a start, numerous studies focus on consumers' intentions without validating whether those intentions translate into actual behaviour. Secondly, the notion of taking responsibility and having control are key determinants. For instance, Juvan and Dolnicar (2014) identified that tourists often feel powerless in the face of environmental issues; they perceive that they have little control over this situation and somehow expect the tourism industry to take responsibility for sustainability initiatives and solutions. In their study, Juvan and Dolnicar (2014) followed a group of tourists who were involved in pro-environmental actions in their daily professional activities. The study broadly indicates that, when on holiday, even those consumers disregard sustainable issues if they conflict with their travel behaviour. In simple terms, it means that those supposedly eco-sensitive consumers took a plane or engaged into environmentally unfriendly behaviour despite their beliefs. Because holidays are inherently associated with pleasure and freedom, feeling constrained by sustainable principles still remains difficult to integrate for a lot of consumers.

We mentioned earlier that contacts with nature can create intense emotional connections and might lead to transformative experiences. This is an interesting avenue to contemplate: by creating emotional and sensual experiences within nature (connecting consumers to flora, fauna, landscape beauty, etc.), one might hope to engage consumers in more sustainable behaviour beyond the holiday. For instance, Cheng and Wu (2015) have identified a link between environmental knowledge and environmentally responsible behaviour.

Environmental sensitivity and place attachment are also elements that can lead to more responsible behaviour. Direct experience with nature appears to be a key element leading to pro-environmental behaviour because it connects cognition and emotions to nature preservation (Duerden & Witt, 2010).

This field of research is extremely complex. So far, the majority of studies tend to point to the fact that tourists do not necessarily keep up their sustainable behaviour beyond their holiday. It does not imply that such a transfer is impossible but it means perhaps that a better understanding needs to be developed to appreciate better how some specific experiences might lead to transferable behaviour beyond the holiday.

4.6 Authenticity

Authenticity is a complex notion that has always been intimately intertwined with tourism consumption. This short paragraph cannot encapsulate the complexity of this notion, but will briefly summarize the key knowledge that has been acquired in this area over the years.

By definition, authenticity refers to what is pure and genuine in any form of consumption. Whilst it is at the root of tourism (i.e. discovering a destination in its true nature), the advent of mass tourism and the development of tourism on the scale that we know nowadays has led to various interpretations of the notion of authenticity.

In this domain, academics have produced various analyses and perspectives. Boorstin (1964) underlined the importance of taking into account how tourists perceive authenticity. In his view, tourists are mostly seeking an entertaining vision of the destination, and can be very disregarding about the true nature of its authenticity. It is for instance the case in many destinations where what is presented as authentic is partially false, either because it is a re-enactment of some culture, an adaptation to suit tourists' needs or even a completely fake experience. MacCannell (2013) examined the notion of staged authenticity, implying that many destinations will put on staged local culture for tourists in order to create an impression of authenticity. The example and video on authenticity of mountain resorts illustrate this dynamic in the box below (Figure 4.6 and example underneath on "Staged authenticity in Val Thorens").

Contemporary societies have cut individuals from their roots and alienated them from the "simple life" that previous generations often experienced. Therefore, authenticity is most often idealized as a fantasy version of the past (Goulding, 2001, Wang, 1999). Contemporary inhabitants are seeking evidence of their roots and are looking for true connections with the rural landscape, nature and agriculture. In other words, they are seeking connections with an idealized past where life is perceived as having been simpler and better. Nostalgia is therefore a strong component of this fantasy perception of authenticity. This implies that tourists bring with them preconceived ideas of what authenticity should be like or, at least, that they pick the images that they intend to see while at the destination. The roots of those images are extremely varied. They can be found

Figure 4.6 Teamlab Borderless' digital art museum. Source: Photo by Egor Myznik on Unsplash.

in early childhood (books, tales, recurring images, school programs, etc.), movies or a national culture that promotes specific images, national and regional stereotypes, etc. Urry (1990) demonstrated that tourists might even aim to adapt the reality to their preconceived images. Tourists would tend to make sure that they don't encounter cognitive dissonance (i.e. purchasing a tourist service that might not correspond to what they initially expected). As a result, once at the destination, tourists will identify in the surrounding landscape elements that will confirm that the destination matches their preconceived images. This idea that tourists will have a limited discerned perception of their holiday environment is of course not true of all tourists. The degree of perception will be dependent on preacquired knowledge, level of education and willingness (or not) to discover the destination as it really is.

STAGED AUTHENTICITY IN VAL THORENS

This video was filmed in the ski resort of Val Thorens, which is located in the French Alps at an altitude of 2,300 meters. Val Thorens is a renowned resort, with a vast ski area and state-of-the-art facilities. This resort was built in the early 1970s on a grazing field. Therefore, this resort has no original buildings, not even an old barn or a church. All the buildings were built from the early 1970s onwards, so there are no heritage sites as such that can provide a solid basis for purely authentic experiences. Nonetheless, consumers demand the authentic alpine style. The video identifies how consumers perceive authenticity and where they expect to find it. The video also shows tourism providers who explain how they have integrated the notion of authenticity in their service delivery and why it is important to do so. Overall, the video demonstrates how authenticity can be developed in a modern premises and can be done with professionalism.

Video link: https://www.youtube.com/watch?v=phQcjkhdggY

4.7 Localhood

Localhood is a more recent trend that responds to the need for tourist experiences that provide a more genuine and meaningful contact with locals. Whilst this trend is part of authenticity, it is being addressed in a separate section because it relates to different forms of connections and experiences.

Connecting with local inhabitants has always been a strong component of tourism service provision. Guest houses and bed-and-breakfasts provide a genuine and direct contact with locals and have successfully done so for decades. Beyond providing a service, these forms of contact also allow tourists to be a party to privileged to "in-house" information, gaining some intimate knowledge about the destination. This type of information goes beyond offering knowledge about local sites and attractions; it also offers visitors information that is often considered as minor but that can be absent from formal sources of information. Indications about the best local coffee shop, the best markets, the best times to visit specific places, a very local event are also what spices up tourists' experiences. All this intimate information can tremendously enhance tourists' experience; it brings a feeling of intimacy with the destination, opens up opportunities that tourists might have never discovered otherwise, and gives them access to other dimensions of the destination culture. In localhood, the local elements of culture opened to tourists are often more mundane, those that are not the object of interpretation. Localhood is important because it humanizes destinations, and it helps tourists to feel closer to them. Contemporary tourists represent the fourth generation of modern tourists; they have grown to understand fully the tourism industry, and some tourists have increasingly become tired of the usual mass-tourism products. They are also interested in discovering a destination as it is – its usual customs, habits and ways of being. They want to really delve into the destination and discover how local inhabitants live their lives on a daily basis, and uncover local habits that are different. Those experiences are another learning curve for tourists, allowing them to contrast their own lifestyles with that of the destination and to learn from this encounter.

Localhood has been boosted by the advent of the sharing economy, which has opened new opportunities for connections between tourists and locals. The demand for this type of information became more apparent with the emergence of Couchsurfing, whose main positioning relies on true encounters with locals: "We envision a world made better by travel and travel made richer by connection. Couchsurfers share their lives with the people they encounter, fostering cultural exchange and mutual respect. With Couchsurfing, you can stay with locals in every country on earth. Travel like a local, stay in someone's home and experience the world in a way money can't buy". (https://about.couchsurfing .com/about/about-us/).

AirBnB, another key player in the universe of localhood, also promotes the feeling of community belonging by offering experiences of belonging and closeness with local communities. AirBnB has also created an "experience" section that allows visitors to book activities to learn a local trade. For instance, in Paris, tourists can learn to make croissants, baguettes, choux pastry, macarons or crêpes. Other local creative activities might involve making a unique hat, joining a calligraphy workshop or learning graffiti painting.

This range of activities had previously already been developed with the Greeters networks. This network groups locals who volunteer to welcome tourists to allow them to discover local activities that tourists often fail to discover. The first Greeter initiative emerged in New York in 1992 to give a different image of this city to visitors. Many greeter associations now exist across the world. If we take the earlier example of Paris, the greeters.paris network offers encounters with locals who offer to take visitors around different areas. Their objective is to offer free walks around Paris and the surrounding districts: "Each encounter is a unique experience: sharing the world, discovering someone else and a different culture. It is the opportunity to see Paris as its locals know it, to discover neighbourhoods that one would not have imagined or dared to visit" (https://greeters.paris/en/)

EXAMPLE: LOCALHOOD AS A DESTINATION STRATEGY WITH WONDERFUL COPENHAGEN (WOCO)

Localhood has even become an integral part of destinations' strategies. As an example, Wonderful Copenhagen has launched a new strategy for its tourism developments:

Localhood is a long-term vision that supports the inclusive co-creation of our future destination. A future destination where human relations are the focal point. Where locals and visitors not only co-exist, but interact around shared experiences of localhood. Where our global competitiveness is underpinned by our very own localhood. And where tourism growth is co-created responsibly across industries and geographies, between new and existing stakeholders, with localhood as our shared identity and common starting point.

(http://localhood.wonderfulcopenhagen.dk/)

Part of this strategy involves using data and visitor insights to first identify the weakest points in the destination. The objective is not necessarily to focus on visitor satisfaction but most importantly to create value, inspire visitors to stay longer and increase the number of returning visitors. One of the avenues WOCO is following is to increase quality contacts with local inhabitants, and thereby reduce overtourism-related resistance from local inhabitants. In other words, the notion of value is applied to locals' quality of life as much as to that of visitors.

Their localhood strategy involves enhancing experiences that develop a true sense of immersion in local culture with a true and authentic value making the destination unique. WOCO considers that locals are the destination, and they are the element providing emotional and personal connections to the destination. WOCO considers that it is their responsibility to ensure that tourists' connections with locals are as harmonious as possible. Their strategy also questions traditional marketing and branding functions, moving away from traditional brand messages and evolving towards a brand that is co-constructed with local businesses and inhabitants, and where storytelling will have an important place.

Full details about the WOCO strategy can be found at: http://localhood. wonderfulcopenhagen.dk/wonderful-copenhagen-strategy-2020.pdf

To finish with localhood, it is worth mentioning that several destinations have also developed new guiding experiences co-constructed with local inhabitants, ones that are usually totally left out of tourism encounters. For instance, various neighbourhood visits are led by homeless inhabitants, and Copenhagen has developed guided tours with ex-drug addicts or prostitutes. These are not the usual guided tours. They are emotionally weighty, and, most importantly, they allow tourists to access a societal universe that they never would encounter otherwise (on holidays or at home). These visits provide insight into destinations, most often in areas that tourists rarely visit. They allow for deep connections with the guides, and it creates empathy towards them, their situation and their personal history.

4.8 Less is more

For many, the idea of downsizing is an appealing objective and certainly a concept that has been fairly fashionable in recent years. This need has most probably been reinforced by the Covid crisis, with lockdowns across the world which kept people indoors, confronting the accumulation of goods within their private homes. With the advent of capitalism, easy credit, and the thirst for consumption, human beings in developed economies have accumulated far more than they need. The terms related to downsizing – less is more, declutter, simplicity – have all been the subject of various documentaries, self-help articles, blogs and books and have led to the new-found profession of "life coach". The basic premise of those methods is that clutter is associated with anxiety, an overwhelming feeling of stress and a feeling of unfinished work, which are necessarily detrimental to human beings' equilibrium (Figure 4.7).

Whilst decluttering is not really something that is directly exploited in the construction of tourism, it is somehow related to some types of experiences that are becoming increasingly popular. Any experience that involves a reliance on a minimal use of items is an experience that engages visitors in considering simplicity as an experience component and benefit. With a frugal experience, tourists engage in an experience that helps them to disconnect further from their everyday lives (see Chapter 2 for the concept of escape). A frugal experience might be undertaken for environmental reasons, but it might also simply be a way to distance oneself from everyday life. By embarking on a frugal experience, consumers can shake off their everyday identity. Going back to basics also helps them to gain a clearer vision of their lives and the world around them. Ultimately, simplicity is a key contributor in helping people reunite with their authentic selves. Frugal experiences such as hiking along an itinerary or cyclotourism are experiences that invite tourists to enter a universe where their own body will be the source of their mobility (cycling, walking), and they will have to rely on very sparse resources (a backpack as light as possible, minimum clothing, etc.). Food and water might become an important element since, not being able to carry much food with them, the tourists will need to rely on what is available when it is available. The return to bare necessities is a challenge that tourists will need to face, but one that is rich in bringing a real rethink of oneself.

Beyond those very intense examples, it might be possible for tourism providers to develop frugal experiences in totality or as subparts of an experience. Not all consumers are willing to engage in those experiences, which they might consider as too extreme. However, they might be receptive to taking part in a more frugal experience for a day or two within their holiday.

Lately, survival courses have become increasingly popular. Tourists might engage in a day or up to a week's holiday where they will learn various survival

Figure 4.7 The Swiss mountains' hut experience. Source: Photo by Fine Line on Unsplash.

skills and apply them in the outdoors. Those skills might involve building a boat from wood found in the forest, learning how to light a fire, filtering water, making temporary equipment, etc.

With such a holiday, consumers not only learn new skills but also gain a sense of achievement, a feeling of having survived the challenge and of being able to survive in natural conditions. For a contemporary consumer, such an experience sends him/her back to basics, like Neanderthals did when they needed to survive without modern necessities. The experience provides them with competencies that they will be able to use beyond the holiday. The experience also teaches participants what is actually needed to survive and will help them to reflect on the unnecessary clutter that is awaiting them upon their return home.

On a gentler note, other experiences might produce less intense but similar effects. For instance, camping or mountain huts provide a no-frills universe where participants will adopt a very frugal lifestyle. Camping covers a wide range of consumption practices, from heavily equipped camping to camping with very basic "facilities". When looking at the less equipped camping options, bivouacking is an activity that has drastically increased in the Alps over the summer 2020, following the first series of lockdowns. For example, in Les Orres, in the French Alps, a new product offers visitors the opportunity to walk up to meet a shepherd and his animals. The participants will then sleep overnight in tents put up far away from signs of civilization. The experience will be enhanced with a barbecue providing a nice earthy dinner, followed by a reading of the starry sky. In the Alps throughout Alpine European countries, summer 2020 witnessed a revived demand for mountain activities and outdoor sports. It will be interesting to observe to what extent this change will create a sustained demand for those products that will last beyond the Covid crisis.

4.9 Fantasy, science fiction and the digital world

The notion of fantasy refers to a universe of fiction that belongs not just to early childhood but has now penetrated realms of adult life. Fantasy often refers to a work of literature (a play, a book or a cartoon) where supernatural situations occur outside the bounds of reality but often with some connections or learning in relation to the contemporary world. Fantasy might involve magical elements and will take the viewer/reader far away from his/her daily life. In this sense, fantasy is a pertinent theme for tourism consumption since it fuels the desire to get away from reality and escape temporarily into a totally different universe. Science fiction evolves in the same sphere, but using technological advances or a jump through time that allow for the construction of a new world where technology is prevalent.

The development of fantasy and science fiction in contemporary societies has accelerated over the last decades, and the increasing popularity of books and films (from *Harry Potter* to *The Hobbit*) or television series such as *Game of Thrones* needs no explanation. Fan conventions have become increasingly popular, and attendees, regardless of their everyday identities, will dress as their favourite character and indulge in this fantasy world, collecting and buying items, meeting with stars, sharing filming secrets, etc.

Fantasy might be seen as being very distant from tourism destinations, which are indeed set in real-world situations. Nonetheless, the huge popularity of fantasy productions has led some destinations to reconsider this theme as a new tourism product and even a boost to their image (see the example in this chapter on New Zealand). Many destinations have surfed on the back of a movie. For instance, The *Harry Potter* movies have fuelled the creation of products based on its real sets (Warner Bros. Studios in London) and its filming locations (platform 9¾ in Kings Cross station). It has also inspired visitors to travel across the United Kingdom to see its various filming locations (from the University of Oxford to the Jacobite Steam Train in Scotland).

MIDDLE EARTH – HOW *THE HOBBIT* BOOSTED TOURISM IN NEW ZEALAND

The Lord of the Rings trilogy and *The Hobbit* movies, directed by Peter Jackson, not only celebrated the novels of J. R. R Tolkien but also embraced the beauty of New Zealand. Because the films were filmed across both islands and displayed some of the country's best natural features, it served as a rich platform to promote the destination. New Zealand has very strong natural and cultural features and had already developed a creative destination marketing strategy. With the movies, New Zealand also became Middle Earth. The films have had a tremendous impact on the number of visitors coming to New Zealand. They have encouraged visitors to visit different locations across the country and have proved a real success in showcasing the natural beauty of this country.

Hobbiton is the original filming location of the Hobbit Village, which has been kept in its original format and provides a surprising and rich experience, allowing visitors to enter the universe of the movie. The site has been managed so that visitors can only visit in small groups and with a guide. The whole village has been managed so that visitors have the feeling that hobbits will come out of the houses at any minute: smoke machines are used for the chimneys, several full-time gardeners look after the gardens and allotments and leave in baskets what they have grown, a fisherman's rods are in the water ready to catch a fish, announcements for a local fair are on the village noticeboard, etc. Hobbiton is pure fantasy, emanating from Tolkien's novels and from Peter Jackson's movies. Visiting Hobbiton is a magical experience, allowing tourists to dive into the novel and the atmosphere of the movie. Overall, the movie connects different parts of New Zealand to the magic of the story.

Beyond fantasy, technologies have also opened human beings to a new world of artistic production. Whether it is electronic music or works of art entirely composed on computers, it has become an indisputably rich artistic sphere. In February 2021, Christie's auction house sold a work of digital art by the artist

Beeple for $ 69 million. In Japan (Odaiba, Tokyo), Teamlab is an art collective made up of artists and experts of various competences. The Teamlab Borderless Museum (a digital art museum) has met with huge success and its attraction is based solely on digital art. Over 10,000 square meters, the museum offers visitors a unique experience, allowing them to immerse themselves in and interact with digital art projects. The works of art have no boundaries and visitors can move through them and enter different artistic universes. The museum brings together hundreds of computers and floodlights to create several rooms (universes) where visitors can immerse themselves in an otherworld of beauty. The works presented are fairly large and, through a convenient play on lights and creativity, visitors can stroll through the work of art, interact with it, influence the light colours with their own movements, etc. This museum definitely has a magic dimension that not many other museums can claim to have. In the first year of opening, the museum welcomed 2.5 million visitors, and it has collaborated on temporary exhibitions around the world (Figure 4.8).

Other sites have also invested in immersive experiences based on projected images and music. In Provence, the *Carrière des Lumières* is an old stone mining cave that has been converted into a virtual museum. The site renews its shows to portray renowned artists and combines each show with a musical soundtrack. There is no voice guidance, and the sheer magnitude of the place, the feeling of immersion (the images are projected from floor to celling) and the clever combination of music and art create a unique atmosphere which has proved to be a real success with visitors. For instance, the exhibition of artwork by Salvador

Figure 4.8 Immersing into digital art. Source: Photo by Note Thanun on Unsplash.

Dali combined with a Pink Floyd soundtrack attracted a lot of attention. This project is not digital art as such, as the work of art projected is by a contemporary artist (Gaudi, Van Gogh, etc.), but its portrayal offers a different perspective which allows visitors to appreciate this art "in a different light".

On a different level, sites have opened over the world which depict unusual and imaginary worlds. The Museum of Ice Cream in New York offers a child-like experience, a sweet universe where visitors can indulge in sweet treats, harking back to a world of childhood with its pink and pastel colours. This is definitively an unusual museum and one which develops visitors' taste for this type of universe.

TOMORROWLAND FESTIVAL

This festival takes place in Belgium every year and focuses on electronic dance music. Thanks to various extremely creative sets, amazing lighting, costumed crowds and electronic music, this is clearly a unique festival. The festival transports consumers to a magical land in total contrast to their everyday lives. A video produced by Masset and Decrop (2017) provides a very interesting insight into Tomorrowland consumers. The video identifies different segments of consumers, their identification practices and the rich communautas between festival goers. The video analyses the dynamics of transgression, regression, cathartic experience and heterotopia, all of which are particularly pertinent for the understanding of tourism experiences.

Source: https://vimeo.com/222471926.

To finish with, the digital world is also creating a new relationship to reality. Some museums have heavily invested in virtual reality (Philadelphia's Franklin Institute, the VR experience offered at the Louvre in Paris to explore the Mona Lisa painting, or that presented at the National Museum of Finland to investigate one of R.W. Ekman's paintings).

4.10 All-inclusive holidays

Package holidays are by no means a new feature in the tourism industry. Whilst package holidays certainly cannot be qualified as a new trend, they remain a strong feature of contemporary demand and one that is likely to remain so because it answers the needs of some tourists.

The first packaged holiday was created by Thomas Cook in 1841 with a trip organized to Loughborough and a world tour of Egypt in 1872. Even if some form of organized travel, or at least travel habits, were formed with the "Grand Tour", which served the British aristocratic elite back in the 17th and

18th centuries, it was only from the 1950s onwards that the package industry took off in earnest. In this period, the package holiday was fairly basic and involved a combination of no-frills flights, accommodation and transfers to the resort and back. It fuelled the rapid development of resorts, especially in Mediterranean destinations. The construction of these resorts had little regard for local building styles, and they were built rapidly, with little consideration for planning. Nonetheless, at the time, they were seen as life savers in some Mediterranean destinations that were suffering economically.

Over the years, the package industry has had its up and downs, with the emergence and disappearance of various companies. It lost trust in the mid-1970s with the collapse of Court Line Holidays and other tour operators such as Horizon Holidays, which saw UK consumers being stranded abroad. From the 2000s onwards, the package holiday took a new turn. The advent of low-cost airlines drastically reduced the price of air travel and allowed consumers to book and organize their holiday directly, and therefore independently (the Internet providing major help in this regard). But the package industry had not said its last word and, seen as providing some form of financial security and having improved its service delivery, it has regained some of its appeal since the 2010s. Major holiday companies have also been aware of changing consumer needs and, while there will always be a place for cheap and basic packages to Mediterranean resorts, there is also a broad range of consumers that can be tempted by package options, if resorts reposition their holiday concept.

Resorts have reconceived their delivery by integrating contemporary trends. They have integrated more local components in their premises' design and have also developed better connections with local tourist providers, especially for the design of their excursions.

Beyond the design of the resort experience, packages, and especially all-inclusive packages, have gained momentum because they increasingly answer contemporary consumers' needs. The all-inclusive package is not new in itself. They first appeared with the advent of holiday camps back in the 1950s and were first internationalized by the Club Med group. Whilst the first Club Med resorts were fairly basic and aimed at mixing consumers from various social origins, it has now developed into a worldwide premium company, aided by a Fosun takeover in 2015.

The reasons why all-inclusive holidays have grown in popularity are multiple. First and foremost, as we addressed in Chapter 2, the need to leave everyday life and responsibilities is a prime booster to holiday demand. The all-inclusive offer has developed expertise in responding to this need. The convenience of package holidays and all-inclusive resorts respond to the demand for a hassle-free holiday where everything is taken care of. Whilst everyday life is governed by various obligations and choice decisions, the all-inclusive package offers a wide choice of activities and never imposes their offerings, thereby guaranteeing the freedom that consumers long for on holidays. Resorts have also been clever at understanding that imposed schedules (characteristic of everyday lives) have to be removed from holidays. Resorts might offer all-day snacking, a late breakfast and a large choice of activities that remove schedule constraints. They have also understood the dynamics of the family unit by providing activities for children of similar ages, activities for adults and activities for family units. They might also provide free childcare services in the evening to allow parents to have quality time to themselves. Beyond these offers, package holidays offer hassle-free choice (because everything is paid for in advance), and large tour operators guarantee relocation in case of a major crisis at destinations.

The package industry has now reached a mature understanding of their consumers and has developed positioning for specific consumers' targets: from seniors to millennials, and across various classes. Cooks Club Hotels and the TUI Blue brand are concrete examples of the new generation of resorts which have integrated new consumer needs into their design (Dixon, 2018).

Package holidays do not dominate the holiday industry, but in some countries, such as Great Britain, they have been a key contributor to the holiday evolution. Independent travel also remains a strong component of holiday demand, but with package holidays modernizing their act and integrating new consumer trends, the future will most probably see consumers consuming both types of holidays because, on different occasions, they answer different experience needs.

Conclusion

This chapter has presented ten key trends representative of contemporary tourist demand. Those trends are probably not exhaustive of all the influences that can be identified in tourism nowadays. Elements such as digitalization, increased independence in purchasing modes, the advent of the millennial market, etc. were not addressed as they are considered ongoing evolutions of consumer demand. The trends refer rather to themes and directions that can inspire experience designers in developing innovative experiences that will meet their markets. These trends will keep on evolving but they are a good basis to start from when contemplating experiences, and they will be reintegrated in the experience generator model in the last chapter of this book.

Chapter **5**

Generating the experience

Introduction

In this chapter, we aim to understand how the experiential approach can developed into managerial principles in order to deal with the key components of experiential marketing. The six experiential cues detailed in this chapter have been inspired by the work of other scholars and consultants that have developed their own experience models. The first part of the chapter presents those models and resituates the diversity of experiential approaches. The second part of the chapter summarizes the key components and processes that have been identified as contributors to successful experiences. Each of these six cues will be presented, and an exercise and an experience generator guide will be provided to explain in detail each of the cues.

5.1 Why was experiential marketing created?

Experiential marketing has developed intensively over the past few decades, especially in the tourism industry. This is a fundamental development, involving a reconsideration of the basics of service delivery, the mechanics of satisfaction and consumer behaviour more generally. Experiential marketing is also a testament to changing consumer demand. Tired of services perceived as insipid,

DOI: 10.4324/9781003019237-6

21st-century tourists are turning to offers that offer a change from the ordinary, that disconnect them from realities and immerse them in new consumption universes. They long for a reenchantment of their consumption universe and are increasingly in search of unusual and outstanding experiences.

5.1.1 Holbrook and Hirschman, pioneers in experiential marketing

Experiential marketing is not in itself a recent phenomenon, since it appeared in the early 1980s with the work of two American researchers, Holbrook and Hirschman. These two authors questioned traditional marketing models, which were based on the conception of rational consumers who sought to maximize their utility through their consumption choices. These so-called traditional models were not really capable of explaining consumption phenomena such as emotional response, sensory pleasure, the playful dimension of consumption, etc. The experiential approach does not propose rejecting categorically traditional models but recommends that, in certain consumption contexts, the observed behaviour responds to different mechanisms. Those specific contexts include leisure, art consumption and tourism. Holbrook and Hirschman (1982) indicated that in those instances, consumers had different patterns of consumption that necessitated the development of new models more appropriate to those dynamics.

COMPARING A TRADITIONAL CONSUMPTION APPROACH WITH AN EXPERIENTIAL ONE

We shall take as an example a consumer choosing a food product, such as a packet of salt, in a supermarket. This consumer is likely to take a rational decision when making their choice. The consumer will base their choice on a limited set of criteria (the price, origin, recipe, salt format, whether it is organic or not and its packaging). According to their expectations, the consumer will add different weights to those attributes (multi-attribute choice). The product will be evaluated on the basis of the sum of those various components. By making their choice, consumers will aim to maximize their utility (getting the best value, according to their criteria, for the price paid). The objectives of the purchase are extrinsic; the consumer will achieve the objective of buying usable salt for cooking, and the criteria used can be qualified as utilitarian. The evaluation of the purchase will lead to either satisfaction or dissatisfaction with the product purchased. Overall, this context is one of a purchase decision.

If we investigate now the context of an experience purchase, the whole framework of this consumption phenomena is very different.

For instance, let's take the example of this same consumer taking part in an experiential activity such as bungy jumping. The decision to bungy jump is in many ways not rational; the whole body reacts with fear to the idea of jumping into emptiness, and indeed, some would-be jumpers might never take the plunge. Consumers like to take part in these activities for the adrenaline that they procure and for the challenge that they set themselves. If questioned about their choice, the consumer might find it difficult to explain clearly why they chose to do the experience and how they felt (the experience is often ineffable).

Contrary to the purchase of salt, the experience evaluation is not likely to be based on the sum of well-defined elements; consumers will form a holistic evaluation of the experience, a global appreciation that will sum up how they felt after having jumped. The objectives are different also; the consumer will not take home a physical element, neither will the experience be useful in the same way that the salt will be. The consumer will take home a bundle of feelings: the pride of having found the courage to jump, the deep sensations felt during the jump, the relief at the end of the jump, etc. This is not concrete; at best there might be a video taken of the jump, but the feelings stay with the consumer and are only understood by themselves (or by other jumpers). The objectives for consuming the bungy jump are very much intrinsic; the consumer took the jump for themselves. The criteria used to evaluate the jump are most probably of a deeply emotional and sensational nature, it might carry some symbolic meanings as well.

While the purchase of salt was based on perfectly identifiable utilitarian elements (usability, taste, etc.), in the case of an experience, the evaluation is quite different. The notion of satisfaction might also be present but it will translate into different elements than in the salt purchase experience. Rather than investigating satisfaction, experiences might be best evaluated by the pleasure felt while undertaking the experience and the intensity of the memories the consumers leave with.

The brief and basic example above gives some pointers to the rationale behind experiential marketing. Whether it refers to paying a high price for a modern art painting, attending an opera at the Teatro alla Scala in Milan, travelling to Rovaniemi to hug father Christmas or enjoying the Burning Man Festival, all these experiences are not just services. Each of them is a form of experiential marketing where the lack of rationality, the predominance of emotions and senses, the symbolical and esthetical experience value and the extrinsic objectives are clearly at stake. These experiences have no utility per se, but they bring intense pleasure and memories, and this is where their outstanding value lies.

In their original work, Holbrook and Hirschman (1982) did not reject traditional marketing models altogether. They rather advocated that these models were efficient, but mostly in the consumption context of utilitarian consumption. Booking a car service, shopping in a basic supermarket or visiting a DIY store are all useful experiences that can bring some form of pleasure. But these experiences are driven by needs that are led by utility. In those consumption contexts, the traditional vision of marketing remains useful and efficient in understanding the behaviour at stake. Necessarily, since Holbrook and Hirschman's articles were originally written, society has evolved, and nowadays, many products, even those of a utilitarian nature, aim to bring more experience in their delivery since it has been identified as a satisfaction booster and an opportunity to give a new dimension to the consumption of those products.

The experiential approach makes it possible to explain better the behaviours observed in certain spheres of consumption such as art, leisure, entertainment, etc. Among these activities, tourism represents a context in which experiential consumption is also at work. Tourism researchers and consultants, without necessarily referring to the term "experiential", have in fact been studying this phenomenon for decades, and consequently, knowledge in this area is highly developed. One might even consider that all the studies devoted to the analysis of tourist behaviour bring a deeper understanding of experiential marketing in their own way. This chapter will primarily refer to the work produced by researchers and consultants on experiential marketing, but it will also make reference to work produced in other spheres in order to enrich the understanding of the scope of experiences.

5.2 Various approaches to experiential marketing

Whilst Holbrook and Hirschman's articles on experiences and hedonic consumption received wide recognition, they were ahead of their time when they were produced in 1982, and it took several years for researchers and consultants to grasp their theory and understand its managerial implications. In this chapter, we will investigate other models that have been developed since their original articles.

In the late 1990s, several books were produced which provided a better understanding of experiential marketing managerial implications. These works did not exist in isolation; they also based their reasoning on various studies produced in different fields of research and that have provided a solid theoretical background to support those visions. We will present in the first part of this section the work of three scholars and consultants, since their models have been well acknowledged and constitute solid building blocks in the understanding of experiential marketing. We will then present the model that constitutes the basis of this book.

5.2.1 Pine and Gilmore's approach

Pine and Gilmore's approach (1999) has been widely used and recognized and was communicated in *The Experience Economy*. In this book, the authors consider that economies have evolved from the production of goods to the production of services and must now develop experiences as a supplementary asset to their delivery. In this line of thinking, experiences allow companies to differentiate themselves from their competitors (creating a competitive advantage) and also allow them to charge premium prices. In Pine and Gilmore's vision, an experience is produced when a business intentionally uses the service as a stage and the goods as a prop to involve consumers in a memorable experience.

According to Pine and Gilmore, five key principles govern a good experience:

- **Thematization**: This helps organize the impressions that consumers form when they arrive at the premises of a company. The purpose of theming is to unify the different elements to provide a cohesive story for consumers.

- **Align impressions with positive elements**: It is important to produce indelible impressions that consumers can take away with them.

- **Avoid negative elements**: Eliminate negative elements and anything that could reduce the quality of the experience.

- **Incorporate souvenirs**: These are goods that consumers can take with them and that will remind them of the experience.

- **Engage all five senses**: The more the senses are engaged, the more memorable experience consumers will have.

Pine and Gilmore's approach was also based on other models that we shall not examine in detail in this book. But their other approach has been to divide experiences according to the degree of immersion/absorption in the experience, and whether consumers were actively or passively involved in the experience. In this model, consumers were seen as living an entertainment experience (absorbed and passive) or an educational one (absorbed and active). On the other hand, immersive experiences were seen as being of an esthetical nature (if passive) or of an escapist nature (if active). The experience economy approach has a lot of value since it offers an interesting framework for understanding how experiences can be impactful and links those principles to different types of situations and managerial strategies. The five elements identified by Pine and Gilmore are pertinent but might not be sufficient to address the complexity and richness of tourism experiences. Their model can be enriched by other visions such as Schmitt's approach, which proposes other components to develop experiences.

5.2.2 Schmitt's vision of experiential marketing

Among the authors that have contributed valuable work to the understanding of experiences, Schmitt (2000) produced a book in which he identified another five characteristics to take into account when designing experiences. According to Schmitt, experiences should bring together five characteristics:

- **Senses**: Schmitt argues that the five senses contribute, together, to a satisfactory and memorable sensory experience.

- **Feeling**: Schmitt argues that affective connections are important to integrate in experience design.

- **Thinking**: According to Schmitt, experiences should also be conceived from the perspective of human beings' creative and intellectual minds. In this line of thinking, experiences need to stimulate consumers on those levels in order to be impactful.

- **Action**: Schmitt also argued that experiences need to be able to surprise consumers by offering opportunities whereby consumers will experience physical, behavioural and/or lifestyle challenges.

- The last dimension, *relate*, refers to consumers' social-identity experiences. In Schmitt's vision, experiences need to offer the opportunity for consumers to better themselves, be perceived more positively by others and encounter new cultures.

Schmitt's model is complementary to Pine and Gilmore's model. It is a particularly interesting model for tourism experiences because it integrates components that are particularly relevant to tourism consumption. Tourism experiences are episodes in which consumers are engaged with what they are doing, where they are and whom they are sharing their holiday with. This engagement might be passive or active, but it remains a central component of tourism experiences.

Lastly, another model was developed by Hetzel in the early 2000s, a model which brings another set of elements to contemplate when designing experiences.

5.2.3 Experiential marketing according to Hetzel

Hetzel (1992) worked on other components for an impactful experience, some of which were complementary to Pine and Gilmore's and Schmitt's models. Hetzel (1992) identified five components:

- Create a **surprise for consumers**: The tourist experience aims to create a break from consumers' disenchanted routinized lives.

- Design **extraordinary experiences**: Whether it is through hyper-reality or authenticity, the idea here was to develop experiences that would allow consumers to experience a completely different world.

- Stimulate the **five senses**: In common with other experiential models, sensorial marketing remains an integral part of experiential marketing.

- Create **links with consumers**: Complicity, personalization, ethical engagements or localized identity are all strategies that contribute to reinforcing linkages.

- Cultivate **brands' symbolical positioning**: How consumers relate to the brand spirit, the love relationship with brands or brand rituals can all contribute to experiential marketing.

This third model shares some commonalities with the ones previously presented. The new element that Hetzel introduced was the connection between the experience and the brand and the extraordinary experiences.

The model used in this book is a combination of some of the findings identified in the literature on experiential marketing, the models presented so far and the work conducted by the author on various experiential contexts.

5.3 The tourist experience dynamics

The model contains six dimensions that can be taken into consideration when developing experiences. Those six dimensions group components pertaining to the five senses, the need to create surprises, the need to involve consumers, the creation of souvenir opportunities, contextualizing the experience and emphasizing relatedness between tourists, locals and providers. Not all experiences will display all those elements at once, but it might be a safe rule to consider that an experience should display at least two of those elements. We will develop the experience structure in Chapter 6. In this chapter, we will focus on the six elements, and for each of them, readers will be offered some exercises that can assist them in cultivating each of the components in a tourism experience (Figure 5.1).

5.3.1 The five senses

Sensorial marketing is necessarily a central component in tourism experiences. Tourism is about smelling the air, tasting local products, hearing new sounds, seeing new landscapes, touching new substances. As such, tourists experience destinations through their five senses, whether this is a conscious process or not. It is the combination of those five senses that contribute to creating an identity for a brand or a destination, an identity that helps position the product in consumers' minds and feed memories.

The objective of sensory marketing is to engage one or more of the five senses in order to improve the consumption experience and influence consumers' purchasing behaviour. For instance, modulating elements such as the smell or the rhythm of background music in a store will impact sales volume, satisfaction and customer loyalty. It is also recognised that a sensory strategy will allow brand strengthening by creating an olfactive brand signature and a distinctive and unifying identity across different sales premises. For example, travel agencies have a rather functional role, that of selling a holiday in a destination. However, they do not sell just any product, and it is important for them to entice consumers,

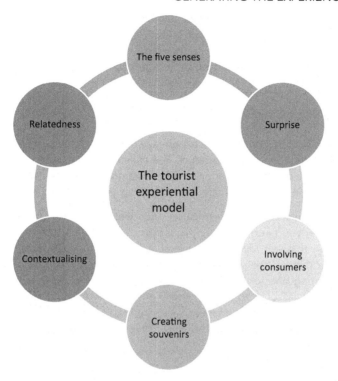

Figure 5.1 The Experience Generator. Source: Author.

especially when they are making their purchase choice. Agencies have evolved over the years, from a functional counter-agency concept to current concepts that are much more open, spacious and less "rigid". To support the promotion of a destination, agencies can accompany their sales context with music and the diffusion of scents. For example, Havas Voyages has opted for the distribution of scents that vary according to the seasons: a smell of hay in spring, of lily of the valley on May 1, of the scent of Coca-Cola during American fortnight, etc. Havas Voyages has also developed an olfactory signature for its brand. The chosen fragrance, "marine floral", is a blend of jasmine, rose and cyclamen. This fragrance illustrates the well-being of travel, the calmness of a distant destination, a flagrance which is both exotic and reassuring (Guivarc'h, 2002).

Sensorial marketing at the scale of a destination follows the same reasoning, but on a wider scale. We shall take the example of a consumer visiting Tunisia. This destination exists through the five senses, for example through the smell of jasmine, the taste of mint tea, the feel of hand-crafted copper plates, the colours of the locally made pottery and the ongoing noise in the souk market. Those senses create a sensorial identity for the destination, one that someone will reencounter with pleasure when visiting the destination again on their next holiday in Tunisia. The senses might also be used in a promotional strategy or by a travel agent wishing to promote Tunisian holidays. Smelling a souvenir brought back from the holiday might also reignite memories. Those senses might also be cultivated in souvenirs that consumers will take home.

THE SENSES GENERATOR

This exercise aims to encourage experience designers to cultivate the depth of senses in relation to their product. This exercise can be undertaken with a tourism product or a destination in mind. As a guide, we shall use the example of a destination in the same line of thinking as the Tunisian example.

Once you have chosen a destination upon which you wish to develop an experience, you need to list all the senses that can be attached to it. It is most likely that you will identify several possibilities for each sense. Smell is the sense that has the strongest connections to memory, and it is therefore an interesting one to use. From the perspective of the destination, which smells can be associated with its natural environments, local trades, culinary specialities, local productions, etc.? As a start, you should identify three different components of each of the senses (three different smells, three different tastes, etc.) (Figure 5.2).

Once those senses have been listed, you need to think how you can use some of those senses to market your destination. For example, you could choose the smell of mulled wine. It is an interesting smell to use in winter; it has strong emotional evocations, it is a nice comforting smell and it is especially associated with the Christmas season. To capitalize on this smell, the most evident option would be to provide (sell) mulled wine at different times of the day and at various locations. Selling mulled wine outdoors will diffuse

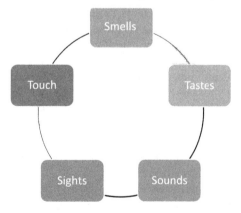

Figure 5.2 The Senses Generator. Source: Author.

the smell nicely, warm hands and bodies and immerse visitors in a soothing Christmas feeling. Other options might be to use some of the ingredients (dried slices of orange, cinnamon sticks and a few branches of fir tree on a steamer placed in the streets). It could equally be developed into souvenirs (provide a recipe, even organize a cooking class); the ingredients could also be combined into a small cotton bag that will diffuse the smell in tourists' houses once they are back home.

In the same line of thinking as this simple example, you are invited to develop a strategic approach to the five senses for your destination. Among all the options that you have listed for each of the five senses, choose one of them. You should have therefore one smell, one taste, one sound, one sight and one touch. For each of them, develop an experience or a product that will make the best use of each sense. You might find that an experience develops more than one sense; this is not a problem as long as it is not too overwhelming for visitors and does not detract from the core experience.

This exercise was detailed for destinations but you could engage the same form of reasoning for a museum: take an example of a museum that you wish to "experientialize". From the main museum theme, identify the range of the five senses and develop five experiences that cultivate each of the senses.

In summary, sensory marketing can act on different levels in order to be able to influence behaviour, contribute to experiences and impact memories. It also has the advantage of being able to elicit sensations in individuals which, associated with other experience components (such as theming, which we will address later), will create a powerful immersive experience and leave an unforgettable memory. The link between these different elements might also be accentuated by the storytelling that will unite the different components of the experiential universe. Pine and Gilmore mention the need to unify the experience universe. This is an important element to keep in mind. An experience will be successful if it capitalizes on the elements we are addressing in this chapter, but also because those elements are woven together to produce a coherent and unified experience universe.

5.3.2 Creating surprises

Surprise has been identified as a key component of satisfaction (Oliver, 1980). Surprise is an emotion, a response to an event that was unexpected. Surprise can be of different intensity, ranging from a small event that might create a positive, but probably short-lived emotion, to more intense surprises that might feed a stronger emotional response and thereby more intense memories. Beyond feeding memories, surprises allow providers to redirect consumers' attention towards a new object/event and create interest.

As we mentioned in the introduction, gaining consumers' attention is a particularly useful dynamic when one considers that contemporary consumers are exposed to various stimuli and tourism actors are competing for this attention. In the light of digital intrusions into tourists' experiences, surprise might be another way to draw consumers' attention away from digital devices (typically a mobile phone and all its attractive features) and refocus the consumer on the experience at stake.

The major difficulty with the orchestration of surprise lies with the fact that it cannot be produced twice with the same consumer. Neither can a surprise be announced in advance. Various components can be developed to create a surprise; the only rule is that it has to be unplanned and unexpected in the eyes of the consumer.

THE SURPRISE GENERATOR

Considering the inherent limits in generating a surprise, some pointers can be helpful in assisting tourism providers in developing their creativity and remodelling their experiences to integrate surprises. This section does not give an exhaustive account of the ways in which surprises can be developed but it indicates four different ways to develop surprises, giving an example for each of these approaches. Readers can use these examples to develop surprises within their destinations or with their products.

We can engage the discussion on surprise with a very simple example. A holiday resort might decide to redesign its aperitif experience in order to integrate an element of surprise. For instance, in early evening, when the consumers like to come to the bar for an aperitif, the resort might decide to delocalize the aperitif to the beach (= change the experience context). The resort will only announce the delocalization to the beach when the consumers are about to order at the bar. There will be no obligation; consumers will be free to take their drinks at the bar, but they will be informed of a new opportunity to have them on the beach (= create the unexpected). The beach aperitif will be planned so that it makes the most of a beautiful sunset (= time the surprise). The beach aperitif experience might be accompanied that night by a band of local musicians creating a soft and localized atmosphere (= cultivate a magical moment). Another example could be to apply the exact same reasoning to breakfast (Figure 5.3).

The example provided is fairly simple, giving an indication of the types of reasoning that can be applied to develop surprises and can be expanded to any type of service provision. The following other examples give more pointers to cultivate surprise.

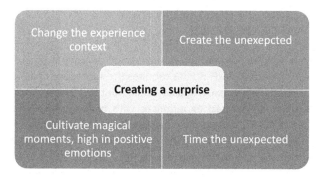

Figure 5.3 The Surprise Generator. Source: Author.

- **Change an experience context**: This is a way to create a surprise by simply moving an existing product or service to a completely different context. For instance, the sleeping experience can be redesigned by changing the location of the bedroom: outdoors, such as in the Null Star hotel that we presented in the previous chapter; in a snow groomer alone at the top of the mountain such as in the La Plagne Ski resort (France); or in a zoo such as in Jamala Wildlife Lodge (Australia).

- A true surprise arises **when it is least expected**: Surprises don't have to be overwhelmingly outstanding and creative; they might simply involve an unexpected service delivered. Necessarily, the most powerful effect will come if it is unannounced.

- A surprise will also want to **cultivate an element of magic and positive emotions**. Eliciting unexpected emotions might also be another dimension; for instance, the connection with childhood experiences is a powerful mechanism. Whilst providing experiences for children has always been a common feature in tourism experiences, sending adults back to childhood emotions might equally create positive emotions and a surprising effect. For instance, playing a geo-caching game, attaching wishes to a wish tree, participating in treasure hunts or sledging on snow are all activities engrained in childhood that many adults will enjoy again, and share with their children.

- **Timing the surprise**: Managing a surprise effect might also come from the strategic timing of experiences. After a strenuous experience, one that has required physical effort or that might have taken place in difficult conditions (windy, dry or cold conditions), the provider might want to orchestrate a nice, unexpected and surprising relief (see the following example of truffle hunting in Italy).

EXAMPLE: TRUFFLE HUNTING IN ITALY AS A TOURIST EXPERIENCE

Truffles are a very expensive and sought-after delicacy across the world. They are also difficult to find and this requires the assistance of a pig or, more commonly, a dog, and an experienced truffle hunter. Truffle-producing areas have increasingly developed experiences with truffle hunters. The hunter takes groups of 10–15 tourists into a wooded area accompanied by his/her dog. The participants then follow the hunter wherever the dog takes them to, and witness the soil digging to finally find the truffles. It is an exciting experience; the dog leads the group, and his eagerness in finding the truffle is palatable. The hunter "teaches" the group how to recognize when the dog is only sniffing and when he has identified the smell of a truffle. The relationship between the hunter and his dog is very moving, and the hunter needs to find the truffle before the dog (or the dog might eat it). Every time the dog finds a truffle, it is a new surprise to add to the experience.

After two hours hunting for truffles in the woods in the cold winter, the hunter takes the participants back to a chalet in the middle of the forest. This part of the visit is unannounced and will create a nice surprise. A wood fire has been lit in advance, and the participants sit around a wooden table and warm up quickly. The truffle hunter cleans a few truffles and butters sliced fresh bread; a participant is invited to open a nice bottle of local wine, while another one puts a few logs on the fire, and the hunter starts grating the truffles over the buttered bread. This is a simple experience, but

Figure 5.4 The precious treasure: a truffle found during the hunt. Source: Photo by Amirali Mirhashemian on Unsplash.

the combination of the precious truffle hunt (not a hunt people can usually participate in), the encounter with the hunter and his/her dog, the warmth of the chalet and the delicious tasting, all done with the assistance of the participants, is most likely to create an unforgettable experience. This experience mixes elements of surprise, novelty and engagement.

Truffle hunting usually takes place in winter, although there are also opportunities in summer. It is an opportunity for destinations to identify activities that will be attractive in the off-season period (Figure 5.4).

5.3.3 Consumer engagement

Getting consumers' attention is at the heart of successful experiences. By engaging, consumers in the experience, providers can guarantee that they will be more attentive and focused on the experience. By being engaged, consumers will also absorb more information. An engaged consumer is a consumer that is more likely to remember the experience and to produce positive word-of-mouth, loyalty and behavioural intentions (Taheri, Hosany & Altinay, 2019). Beyond achieving more positive attention from consumers, engagement creates value for consumers and a sense of personal growth, on top of feeling valued by the service provider.

According to Huang and Choi (2019, page 6) "Tourist engagement is defined as a psychological state incurred by interactive, co-creative, tourist experiences with a focal agent/object (people/attraction/activities/encounters)". Engagement is a two-way process whereby tourists can bring skills, knowledge and practices to the tourism experience. On the other hand, tourism providers also have competencies that they can share and engage consumers with.

In tourism experiences, the possibilities for engagement are diverse and multiple, and the destination itself, through all its facets, can foster engagement opportunities through encounters with local inhabitants, providers, tourism resources and other tourists.

Consumers' motivations play a key role in their capacity to be receptive to engagement opportunities (depending on their motivations, tourists will choose to engage with some specific service deliveries and not others). Engagement can be undertaken freely under the tourist's control (engaging with other consumers on-site, sharing advice online, choosing to participate in specific activities, etc.). Engagement might also be part of a formal destination/provider strategy to engage consumers (guided tours, interactive devices in museums, workshops, etc.) (Figure 5.5).

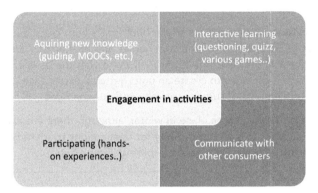

Figure 5.5 The Engagement Generator. Source: Author.

There are many opportunities to create engagement, and Figure 5.5 differentiates four of them. Again, readers might want to develop these opportunities for engagement for their destination or product.

- **Acquiring new knowledge** (guiding, etc.): In Chapter 3, we have already established that the feeling of growth and achievement which often comes from learning was a key component of deep experiences and a powerful source of satisfaction and memories. Learning new knowledge brings a deep sense of growth, of not only having learned new elements, but also of understanding better a destination and creating more connections with its culture and inhabitants.

- **Interactive learning:** This has been developed extensively in museums for some time. Interactive learning allows visitors to stay more attentive to the exhibits on display and the information given. It might be a simple quiz where visitors will be able to test their newly acquired knowledge (for example recognizing different birds after a visit to the ornithology section in a natural history museum). Interactive learning might also take the form of a game where the visitor has to solve puzzles with the knowledge acquired within the museum, etc. In this domain, the possibilities are endless.

- **Interacting with other consumers:** New technologies have boosted the capacity that consumers have, nowadays, to communicate with each other. Many websites exist that allow visitors to share information and inform each other beyond traditional modes of communication (guide books, traditional advertising and communication strategies, etc.). Considering that word-of-mouth is the most influential source of information on decision making, and that consumers have developed a parallel world bypassing more traditional marketing strategies, this dimension is important for tourism providers. Many travel agents and guide books have now developed options on their websites to allow visitors to communicate with each other, share advice and give personal tips about destinations.

- **Hands-on experiences** or learning by doing is a similar approach but is even more direct because visitors are engaged in learning how to do something. Learning by doing helps to make more sense of a practice, how it fits into an environment and increases memory retention. This approach empowers consumers not only with new knowledge but also with the capacity to reuse newly acquired skills in different contexts beyond the tourist experience.

For example, on a foraging trip, tourists will learn how to recognize edible wild plants and can even be given some recipes to preserve them. If they live in similar areas, they will be able to reuse some of those skills when undertaking nature trips once back home. In this sense, the experience has been very fulfilling but will also accompany the tourist in their daily leisure life well beyond the experience (and nourish souvenirs).

EXAMPLE – THE GUINNESS STORE HOUSE

Guinness beer is undoubtedly an integral part of Irish heritage; it is unique, recognized across the world and instantly associated with Ireland.

The Guinness Storehouse is located right in the centre of Dublin, where beer is produced, and its visitor attraction has been developed over seven floors. The attraction provides consumers with insights into the beer's history, manufacture, transportation and advertising strategy.

Presentations of the different pieces of information are made through interactive tables, videos, etc. In relation to the beer itself, all the stages in the creation of the beer are presented; however, exhibits tend to leave visitors rather static, taking in the information with little interaction. In order to engage consumers further in the Guinness experience, the Storehouse has developed one experience that has proven to be very successful.

This experience involves teaching consumers the art of serving a pint of Guinness. Groups of ten visitors are supported by a coach who teaches them the basics steps to pour a perfect pint of Guinness (tilt of the glass, speed of flow, resting the beer, etc.). The coach shows the different steps and consumers can then, in turn, pour their own pint. Visitors then have the right to taste their pint and receive the "Guinness perfect pint pourer" certificate.

Originally, partnerships had been established with several pubs across Ireland, and a certificate holder was allowed to step behind the bar to pour his/her own pint.

Engagement is not a new approach and has always been a strategic component of tourism providers' strategies. The knowledge gained in education research has long established how students can become more involved and attentive to their studies. Museum studies and heritage management is also a key field which has addressed the relationships with consumers and has investigated how to foster engagement. Whether it refers to interactive devices, live classes, workshops or gaining new practices, engagement brings rich and valuable dimensions to the experience.

5.3.4 Creating souvenirs

By definition, creating valuable memories is the outcome of experiential marketing; a fulfilling experience is one that will leave long-lasting memories. Memory and its evolution has been addressed in detail in Chapter 3, but the dimension of souvenirs, especially those taken home after a holiday, has already been highlighted by Pine and Gilmore in their model (1999) and has also been the object of various research activity in tourism academia. Memorabilia has long existed in our world of consumption and more particularly in the tourist experience. In tourism consumption, souvenirs act as reminders, a way to prolong a valuable experience (Gordon 1986), and a proof of one's travel. Masset and Decrop (2020) provide a detailed and particularly interesting study of the roles and place of souvenirs in consumers' everyday lives. They demonstrate that souvenirs might or might not find their place back into tourists' homes depending on the decontextualization effect and potential negative perceptions. They also show that souvenirs are placed in different rooms depending on their legitimization, and their meaningfulness can be reactivated or dismissed over time.

When a destination wishes to develop souvenirs for its visitors, inspiration can be fuelled by different elements that can be used as ingredients or themes to create souvenirs. Objects designed for tourists, souvenirs have been around for as long as humans have been travelling. Any destination has a large range of souvenirs. Those souvenirs might be made abroad, not use sustainable materials or might not be the production of a local craft. Even though they can be attractive to tourists, they are often not the best representations of a destination (they might provide a cheap, tacky and commodified version of local culture). In the 21st century, consumers expect souvenirs that have deeper meanings and that have their roots in local productions and resources. To generate new ideas for souvenirs, it can be interesting to revisit the conception and positioning of souvenirs. It is important that souvenirs convey images of sustainability, modernity and creativity, and are in line with the destination positioning.

THE SOUVENIR GENERATOR

Souvenirs can take different forms, as summarized in Figure 5.6. This exercise encourages you to develop four different forms of souvenirs from your destination, and it might also be interesting to envisage those souvenirs from a sustainable perspective.

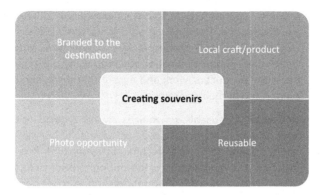

Figure 5.6 The Souvenir Generator. Source: Author.

In this generator exercise, we will work on a destination as an exercise.

- First list the various resources that you have within your destination: physical or natural elements, local trades that require a certain know-how, local crafts, etc.

- From this range of elements, identify two souvenirs that should have at least two of the four characteristics:

  - **Locally made**: Necessarily, local crafts can be used to feed tourists' hunger for souvenirs. In this perspective, an interesting option is to use local productions. The souvenir will then both create a memorable item and encourage local production. Food items spring to mind, but other products can also be used. In Scotland, on the Outer Hebrides, Harris Tweed has come back into the limelight with a label protecting this trade and a thirst for new colours, designs and products. Beyond the traditional use of tweeds in clothing and upholstery, a new range of items has been designed such as purses and bags. Smaller and more affordable, those items have become a common feature in souvenirs shops across Scotland and a nice change from the more common tartan souvenirs commonly found. Those items are produced from a sustainable resource (wool) and they are woven in the Outer Hebrides. It is a local, reusable and culturally engrained souvenir.

  - **Branded to the destination**: In the best case scenario, souvenirs can be packaged to reinforce the destination's brand strategy. Local products can be branded under the destination brand, which includes a logo, but also a colour and graphical charter, at least for the product packaging. Achieving some form of uniformity in terms of the destination brand by using the same graphical components in souvenirs provides a coherent vision of the destination. The products sold as souvenirs under this banner might also use local producers and know-how. In order to assist the producers, the destination can fund some designers' costs to assist the producers' work and ensure that the brand is correctly embedded in their packaging.

- **Reusable**: A reusable souvenir is always a good option; it will have the benefit of having a use in the longer term and will communicate about the destination every time it is used. For instance, a bag might be a good option to print an iconic feature of the destination with a modern design. A toilet bag or a purse might also be another option. With the world moving away from plastic bags to cotton bags, those give the opportunity to print a picture or an old representation of a destination on items that will be reused. It is both a subtle tourist souvenir and a useful object.

- Identify **the best photo opportunity**: Beyond physical souvenirs, the opportunity to take the best picture is another option. Souvenirs have taken on a new meaning with the advent of the digital world. The picture-taking tradition has always been present in tourism consumption, but the advent of mobile devices, the ease with which pictures can be taken with a phone and their other life on social networks have all contributed to the advent of the selfie and holiday picture sharing. For a tourism provider such as a hotel or a museum, and for a destination, it is essential to identify specific locations where pictures can be taken.

5.3.5 Contextualizing

First and foremost, an experience takes place in what is termed a serviscape (Bitner, 1992), which refers to the space within which the service experience takes place. In services, consumers are present in the servicescape during the delivery, and the servicescape encompasses all the physical elements that convey cues to consumers about the firm (or destination). The servicescape is made up of three dimensions: the ambient conditions (temperature, music, noise, air quality, etc.); the spatial and functional dimensions (furniture, structuring of the space, etc.); and the signs and symbols (signage, style, decor, etc.). This space conveys cues about the positioning of the tourism actor, its ethics, and, in tourism particularly, contributes to the immersion in a new environment. The servicescape can be managed in different ways to create a memorable experience.

Tourism providers can act on the servicescape at different levels, not only at the sensory level but also at the level of the organization and thematization of the service universe. In tourism experiences, the servicescape takes on a broader definition, encapsulating the geographical, physical and symbolical dimensions of a destination that can also be managed to an extent.

Contextualizing involves creating a universe that confers a unified environment where consumers can immerse themselves during the experience. Thematizing this universe is essential to creating this feeling of entering a new space that makes sense through all its references and contributes to taking consumers away from their everyday universe.

5.3.5.1 Thematization of tourist resorts and premises

Theming is an essential element which also helps to encourage the consumers' immersion in the consumption experience. Through a play of colours, materials, design and layout, it allows a place to have its own unity, which will position it within a well-defined theme. For example, Léon de Bruxelles restaurants, Hard Rock Cafés or, more simply, Irish pubs are institutions that have cultivated a theme that gives them a unique image and atmosphere that has created their success. The theming thus makes it possible to unify a place of consumption and to provide a coherent universe to the consumer. This consistency is not only reassuring; it also makes it possible to clearly identify a supplier or a brand.

This unifying action is also particularly interesting in the context of tourist resorts where architectural and stylistic unity remains problematic. The notion of theming a tourist resort remains interesting because it allows consumers to be transported into a world of consumption that will free them from their daily lives and which will greatly contribute to their immersion in the consumption experience (see the example on mountain resorts).

THEMING ALTITUDE MOUNTAIN RESORTS

Most French mountain resorts have their origin in the snow plan, a development program through which the government has appropriated large tracts of land to build ski resorts. This plan began in 1946 in Courchevel, and was then followed by the construction of many other resorts. Each resort originally had a functional and architectural unit established from the design stage, and the designer architects applied their own stylistic touch to each resort concept. Most of the resorts have been designed with the idea of having ski-to-door access so that consumers do not need to use their cars. In their conceptualization, these resorts have cultivated a theme that reinforces the feeling of being in the mountains for the tourists who come to stay there. This theming is based on several pillars: wood, snow, fir trees and key references to the mountain universe.

Wood

In terms of theming, all these resorts have taken on an alpine theme without necessarily sticking to local styles. For example, wood has been used as cladding in the majority of projects but not necessarily in the form of chalets; some resorts have been very modern and visionary in their architectural design. Consumers who come mainly from urban areas have preconceived images of alpine villages that they will project on resorts. It's quite a general image, which explains why consumers can adapt it when they encounter different styles. In fact, a large part of the resorts was built with concrete buildings (the massification of skiing required it), which were then covered with wood. Even if these buildings are only covered with wooden cladding, this meets at least the expectations of customers, and the mountain image is recognizable.

This mountain theme is also found inside the accommodation. If in the 1970s, resort accommodation had a very sober interior with little theming, current accommodation freely cultivates the mountain theme indoors (fabrics, wood and slate cladding, old paintings on skiing, themed crockery, etc.). Even if these elements have nothing old about them and do not necessarily respect the local particularities, they have the merit of corresponding to tourists' mental image who want to be constantly immersed in the mountain world during their stay.

Snow

Snow is an element highly prized by customers, and beyond the skiing possibilities it offers, it is an element that thrills tourists: it is white, luminous, and has a magical dimension that few other natural elements have. The presence of snow, like the accommodation covered with wood, contributes to this feeling of being far from everyday life. The snow offers a striking contrast: in a few hours, tourists pass through a wintery urban universe, plunged into darkness and polluted, into a sudden bright, pure, white and invigorating universe, all "packaged" in a grandiose panorama. Unlike architecture, designers cannot cultivate snow (at least within resorts), but they can nevertheless stage it. For example, the Avoriaz station has taken the approach of relegating cars to underground outdoor car parks to have a completely car-free resort. This design is a real success; when a tourist arrives in Avoriaz, they are sure to be entirely cut off from the negative elements that could send them back to the urban universe they have just left: noise, pollution, and danger associated with cars. Another detail to note is that with the ban on the circulation of gasoline vehicles, the snow remains white and tourists can therefore feel totally immersed in the white mountain universe during their stay. Snow is also highlighted in non-skiing activities (it is estimated that one in five skiers in a resort does not ski). The resorts have thus created (even if this commitment is still rather timid) altitude trails, which allow non-skiers to walk in the cottony softness of the snow, to take in the fresh air to the full and appreciate the beautiful scenery that surrounds them.

Fir trees

Fir trees are a highly sought-after element in the mountain world; they refer to the magic and emotions of Christmas, and represent the only plant that does not hibernate. Fir trees are naturally present (at resorts which are not at too high an altitude) but they can also be integrated into the design of resorts.

Mountain essentials

Other elements are cultivated to reinforce a mountain atmosphere: carriages with horses (and their bells tinkling), mulled wine served outside to tempt the taste buds, the traditional shared gastronomy (raclettes, fondues, grolle, etc.) and outdoor markets that sell local products (cheese, sausages, local crafts, etc.).

5.3.5.2 Thematization and the extended serviscape

One of the peculiarities of tourist services is to sell just as much in situ services but also to sell these services in a landscape which is also part of the service. Therefore, in the tourism context, the natural environment is considered as an extended servicescape. Tourists behave like contemplators (Urry, 1990) and seek above all to absorb the landscapes through their eyes but also through other senses. The view is therefore a commodity that can come at a high price; for example, "rooms with a view" are sold at a much higher price than rooms without a view. This view is protected by planning laws (coastal law, mountain law, for example) by local planning rules, by regional/national park regulations, etc.

Theming is perhaps not the most appropriate term when referring to the extended servicescape. In this section we do not suggest that the surroundings and the landscape should be redesigned or tampered with in order to suit tourists' idealized images. However, the landscape is a key resource that needs to be preserved in order to keep its value.

Some countries have even taken measures to limit the impact of new economic activities on their tourist attractiveness. This is for example the case in Ireland, whose Ministry of Agriculture (2015) has produced a guide on forest and land-scape management which aims to establish guidelines for planning and manag-ing forests so that biodiversity is respected and landscapes can be enhanced. The objective is to obtain a balance between the forest cover on the ground compared to the characteristics of a landscape: to better integrate forests to preserve the integrity of the landscape, minimize the visual conflict between the forest and the landscape, maintain the natural diversity and minimize the negative impacts of forest cutting (in visual terms in particular). Likewise, one can wonder about the impact of the development of wind turbines on the tourist attractiveness of a territory (see the following example).

TO WHAT EXTENT DO WIND TURBINES IMPACT THE TOURIST ATTRACTIVENESS OF LANDSCAPES?

Opponents of wind turbines consider that these constructions help to create an industrial landscape in areas of great natural beauty. There is therefore a movement against the construction of wind farms in highly attractive areas (Grouse Mountain in Vancouver or near Mont St. Michel, for example).

Wind turbines as tourist attractions?

For others, wind turbines are symbols of sustainable development and are valuable because they produce clean energy. Advocates therefore con-sider them to be part of modern heritage and argue that windmills, when they appeared in the 12th century, also met their share of opposition. In Holland, windmills are now part of the national heritage, and in Quebec some are open to the public as tourist attractions (Île Perrot and Île aux Coudres).

Wind turbines are unlikely to become a major attraction, especially as their exponential development has made them commonplace. However, they can be developed into a tourist attraction. For example, in Cap Chat on the Gaspé Peninsula in Canada, an interpretation centre describes and explains the operation of the tallest wind turbine in the world. Other guided tours of wind turbines have been developed in Denmark: near Copenhagen, guided boat tours provide visits of wind turbines in the open sea in Middelgrunden.

Visitor expectations

A Scottish report has reviewed a number of studies assessing the impact of wind turbines on landscapes and indicates that this impact is generally not negative, although tourists prefer wind farms to be located far from their accommodation, historical sites and natural areas. However, tourists who categorically oppose the installation of wind turbines near areas of tourist interest represent a minority. For example, a study carried out in France showed that only 22% of the population believes that wind turbines have a negative impact on tourism activity in a region. A survey in Languedoc-Roussillon also indicated that 16% of visitors consider that wind turbines degrade the landscape and a study in Scotland puts this proportion at 25% of tourists. We can therefore assume that approximately a quarter of the tourist population is affected by the presence of wind turbines. Another study, in the Gaspé region of Quebec, reports that more than half of tourists prefer concentrated wind turbines (more than 12 turbines) on a few sites rather than in multiple locations.

Economic impact of the installation of wind turbines

Very few quantitative studies have established empirical links between wind turbines and their economic impact on local tourism activity. However, some studies have used hypothetical scenarios to assess tourist preferences. The results indicate that tourists do not intend to change their visit intentions if the destination has installed wind turbines (study in the South West of England). In the end, there aren't really any studies showing a seriously negative impact on visitation intentions.

A Scottish report assessed the combined effect of the drop in visitors and their spending in an area where wind turbines have been sited, and their willingness to pay or not for a "room with a view" if the accommodation is affected by the construction of wind turbines. The study looked at four distinct areas that account for 12% of its economic activity and identified that, ultimately, 81%–98% of tourists visiting these four areas would be affected.

This study also assessed the proportion of accommodation establishments in these regions for which the integration of wind farms would have consequences; it was between 9.83% and 32.40%. Of the tourists polled in this study, 63% said they preferred a view without wind turbines from their hotel room, while 28% were indifferent and 9% were in favour. The authors suggest that visitors' perceptions of wind farms vary depending on where they are located. Thus, opinions about wind turbines change depending on whether you see them for a few seconds while moving along the road, or whether you see them for longer, without moving, from your hotel room. For establishments whose views are compromised, the study found a reduction in attendance from 4.9% to 16.20% and estimates the net decrease in their income as being between 0.48% and 1.59% respectively. Finally, the study found that the construction of a wind farm could result in a loss of 2.5% of income due to the fact that fewer tourists would return to visit the area.

In conclusion, in most places there is a large set of laws and planning tools that keep the social and environmental impact of wind farms as low as possible. In addition to the resulting visual consequences, the establishment of wind farms continues to be opposed for various reasons related to planning, management, operational control and the equitable redistribution of profits. From a tourism point of view, the impacts are undoubtedly less strong than one would have imagined; the fact that wind turbines produce renewable energy confers on them a legitimacy which increases their acceptance with the tourist population. However, as often, the reaction "not in my backyard" remains relevant, and wind turbines are accepted as long as they do not directly affect the visual comfort of a tourist (the impact in fact is only really felt if the wind turbine is placed very close to accommodation).

Source: Adapted from Priskin J. (2009) Do wind farms affect tourism? Tourism Intelligence Network, Transat Chair in Tourism, School of Management Sciences, UQAM, https://veilletourisme.ca/2009/12/09/do-wind-farms-affect-tourism/?lang=en

Beyond the physical aspects of the servicescape, contextualizing is also transmitted through interpretation of a place's history and culture.

5.3.5.3 Interpretation

Visitor interpretation aims to provide information about a destination's nature, culture and/or heritage. It might also aim to provide information explaining ideologies and engaging attitude change (Cave & Jolliffe, 2012). In a nutshell, interpretation is the art of revealing and explaining a meaning from a heritage or natural resource through a communication process. The outcome of interpretation, beyond allowing visitors to acquire new knowledge, is also to engage visitors to develop a better understanding of the world around them, and ultimately to develop empathy and reflection and potentially change their attitude towards various subjects.

Interpretation involves a vast array of techniques, from the usual interpretative signage to leaflets, information boards, guiding, interactive exhibits, guidebooks, etc. Historically, guides have been the most prevalent form of interpretation, providing tourists with professional and localized knowledge of a site or destination. With the advent of technology, various devices now allow new non-human-based forms of interpretation (audio-guides, GPS, localized phone applications, augmented reality, etc.). Interpretation needs to create meaning for visitors; it makes sense of a place, places it in the context of local and global history, explains its role in a destination's cultural and social directions and can relate the object of interest to broader contemporary issues (relating older lifestyles to sustainability, learning from previous war sites in regard to contemporary conflicts, etc.). Ham (1992) is a key reference in the interpretation field, and his work identified that an interpretative experience should combine moving from the familiar to the unknown and use examples, metaphors, analogies and comparisons.

Interpretation needs to be targeted to the needs of the public, which can be varied. It needs to integrate the age of participants, from young children to teenagers to experienced adults. It also needs to integrate visitors' levels of interest into the topic in order to adapt the type and depth of the information provided. Visitors will also have different needs, and special needs also need to be integrated in interpretation planning.

5.3.5.4 Storytelling

In recent years, the topic of storytelling has emerged as a powerful mode of interpretation. Storytelling is a narrative-based method of communication which develops stories that will have a strong evocative power, and elicit emotions from consumers. When telling the story, the author will arouse emotions that will make the consumer more receptive to the message. The story will focus the consumer's attention, and the storytelling will increase the consumer's engagement with the narrative. The narrator will use anecdotes, entertaining stories and untold details, and incorporate historical elements (including legends, which are highly prized by tourists), all embedded in a story. The intensity of the elicited emotions will help nourish the memorability of the experience.

Storytelling can also emerge from the tourist angle. For instance, in promotional messages, the voices of tourists can be used to share their experience and tell the story of their holiday to other potential tourists. This technique was used by Travel Oregon, which produced a video representing the story of a father and his son sharing a special moment on a local golf course (Hallé, 2012). At the heart of this staging, emotions create a link between the destination and the viewer; any parent can relate to this connecting moment between a parent and a child and how it could take place in the destination portrayed.

Canada has used a similar approach to promote its ski offer by producing promotional videos, one of which features two skiers filming their descent with a camera mounted on their helmets. The video shows their descent on skis but in fact focuses mainly on the emotions of the present moment: the sound of skis screeching in the snow, the cries and laughter of the two skiers and the frank laughter when one of them falls, etc. Storytelling invites the viewer to be part of the experience being lived; it is an outside audience but the consumer needs to project himself/herself into the experience portrayed.

In November 2012, Tourisme Québec launched a communication campaign based on storytelling on the French, New York and New Jersey markets. The website followed six vacationing couples through their trip to Quebec. The couples were filmed on various occasions, and asked to describe how they felt at different stages of their journey. The videos showcased the different emotions experienced by the tourist couple, from attending a concert or fishing for trout in a lake, to their feeling of sadness as the vacation ended. These videos played on the emotion and the reality of what was evoked; the sincerity of the words gave the speech a strong credibility (Thellier, 2012).

THE CONTEXTUALIZING GENERATOR

As we have seen in this chapter, contextualizing encapsulates very different approaches, which all have their value in developing the tourist experience. Contextualizing anchors tourists in the destination visited or product and service consumed. When developing an experience, it is therefore essential to identify the possibilities that will allow destinations and enterprises to cultivate contextualization through various strategies.

In order to develop contextualization within an experience, the following exercise might provide a relevant starting point. Taking the example of a destination:

- First identify the key cultural elements that are characteristic of the destination. Those might be associated with its history, its local culture, special trades and know-how, singular architectural elements, local legends, etc.

- Once you have listed those elements, choose one of them and identify how it can be developed within one or several of the four options indicated in Figure 5.7.

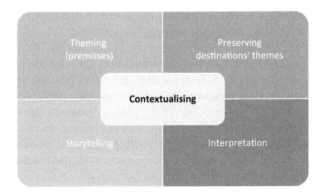

Figure 5.7 The Contextualization Generator. Source: Author.

For instance, if taking the example of a rural destination, the following reasoning might be developed:

- **Theming the premises:** This might be done at a village level by implementing local planning restrictions that will make sure that local style is encouraged throughout the village in relation to the buildings. This might be applicable when house owners restore their buildings and for new constructions. These regulations might concern roof shapes, wall coverings, shutter colours, etc. The rural theming might also be encouraged within tourist accommodation to cultivate this rural style with colours, cloths, antique agrarian tools, etc.

- **Theming destinations:** Planning restrictions will also be concerned with the public space and aim to achieve some form of continuity of the rural theme at the destination level. For instance, the upkeep of the village, materials used for roads and pavements, outdoor flowering, burying telephone lines, converting plastic shop signs to wood, etc. are all details which, together, achieve a unifying and contextualized vision of the destination. In this process, local style is the governing principle and it needs to be integrated in all the amenities.

- **Interpretation:** The rural theme is necessarily a rich topic that can serve as a basis for developing interpretation in various directions. It can be the object of interpretation in agro-museums depicting rural life, professions and activities in the past and present. It might be an open air museum with live guides guiding visitors, demonstrating rural skills or even running workshops to involve visitors (making old-fashioned sweets, simple lace making, etc.). Interpretation might also take place throughout the village with guides or phone apps.

- **Storytelling** can be used to enhance the depth and richness of rural heritage. Storytelling can revive the memories of famous local individuals who influenced the destination's history, or to tell the story of a local family. Legends can also offer a rich fund of stories to enchant tourists.

5.3.6 Relatedness

Needless to say, tourism is about connecting with other human beings and relatedness is an essential component of tourists' experiences: connecting with locals, connecting with loved ones, connecting with other tourists and/or connecting with providers. The Covid crisis has reminded consumers how much their lives depend on and are enriched by social connections. It is to be expected that relatedness will be reinforced further after the pandemic.

Huang and Choi (2019) developed a scale of consumer engagement and identified four engagement dimensions: social interactions (with loved ones and other tourists); interactions with employees (emotional, proximity and appreciative services rendered by employees); connecting through activity engagement; and relatedness (getting closer to travelling companions). This study is particularly interesting since it demonstrates the extent to which tourist engagement with other participants enhances value-creation. The strength and the quality of the human connections developed during the holiday is therefore a key element to integrate in experience design. To some extent, relatedness is transversal to the first five elements addressed in this chapter. We will concentrate in this section on how relatedness can be boosted through experience design.

THE RELATEDNESS GENERATOR

In order to integrate relatedness in an experience, it is important to take into consideration its various dynamics (Figure 5.8). Here are some examples of the dynamics that can be developed to boost relatedness in different circumstances:

- **Relatedness with loved ones:** Any experience that takes place within the intimacy of a group unit (a couple, a family) is by definition one that takes place away from the commercial spheres of the tourism delivery. However, group cohesion might find its roots in a co-creative processes that boosts relatedness. For example, larger groups (groups of friends, two families travelling together, three-generation families) will be receptive to large rented accommodation that can guarantee that the group can be together. This might be integrated into the design of rented accommodation such as large villas or *gîtes*. For resorts who

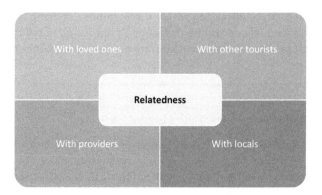

Figure 5.8 The Relatedness Generator. Source: Author.

have rented flats, this can be more challenging since flats are often of small capacity. In this situation, it might be interesting to develop a search engine that identifies flats that are close to each other, or ideally on the same landing, to guarantee closeness for the group. Playing board games is an old favourite but yet one that is still in demand because it creates genuine connections and fun times between loved ones. Board games also have the benefit of keeping the children away from screens. In a more organized approach, a destination can design playful occasions where all the members of the family play together (geo-caching, treasure hunts, escape games, etc.)

- **Relatedness with other tourists**: Again, this can be spontaneous, with tourists socializing on the beach, around a drink or during a walk. Nonetheless, this relatedness can be encouraged by providing items that can boost the possibilities for encounters. As an example, the Lux* company has created an interesting experience where a wooden truck is hidden in the resort premises' bushes. The tourist who finds the truck will discover a range of bottles and recipes to make cocktails and is invited to share those cocktails with another group of tourists. Resorts can develop games and competitions that increase encounters between tourists. Lately, some start-ups are creating new phone apps that allow tourists to meet while they are travelling.

- **Relatedness with locals**: In Chapter 4, we have already addressed the new trend "living like a local" which detailed various tourism provision-enhancing contacts with local inhabitants.

- **Relatedness with providers**: This form of relatedness is different from the previous ones. Often, when destinations aim to connect tourists with local inhabitants, they necessarily think of local people. However, providers, those that are local but often behind the scenes, can be an interesting resource to develop experiences. Tourists are increasingly eager to gain more knowledge about a destination from within, and this includes its tourism industry. Tourists might be interested to know how life evolves outside the main season, the personal history of some providers or how some technical facilities function. For instance, tourists are increasingly interested in visiting technical elements such as ski-lift machinery rooms or water dump electric platforms. In Paris, the Eiffel Tower commercializes tours that give access to areas that are usually closed to the public: the Champs de Mars Bunker, which used to be devoted to military communications; the engine room, which still controls the operation of the elevators, etc.

Conclusion

This chapter has taken the concept of experience design further by presenting the key components that allow tourism providers to design memorable experiences. The field of experiential marketing is rich and has accumulated over the years an extensive body of knowledge that can assist the design of experiences. The chapter presented six elements that can be developed in experiences and provided readers with exercises and indications that can assist designers in this process. Experiences are subtle, and their design might not need to deploy all six cues at once. The components of an experience need to fit together and provide a unified experience to the end consumer. However, creating experiences is only one part of the experiential process. Experiences need to be thought out with more strategic marketing and managerial objectives in mind. The following chapter addresses those issues with the aim of providing a comprehensive vision of the whole experience design process.

Chapter 6

The Experience Generator

Introduction

This last chapter aims to provide experience designers with a set of tools that will make sense of the various components addressed in this book. So far, the first chapter has reviewed the key behavioural principles that underpin the understanding of consumer behaviour. The following chapter looked at the dynamics of the experience as it unfolds, and the many implications in terms of service design. Chapter 3 investigated deep experiences and how they can help experience designers understand better experiences' impacts upon consumers. The next chapter then addressed ten major trends that can be taken into consideration when identifying and positioning an experience. Chapter 5 investigated the six key experiential components that can be integrated to develop impactful experiences. This final chapter aims to integrate the different learning from this book into a more managerial framework that can assist experience designers in organizing their strategy around the creation of an experience. The chapter will take the reader through several steps that will assist experience designers in understanding the different components that are strategically associated with the creation of an experience. The chapter will finish with a detailed example that illustrates those steps.

DOI: 10.4324/9781003019237-7

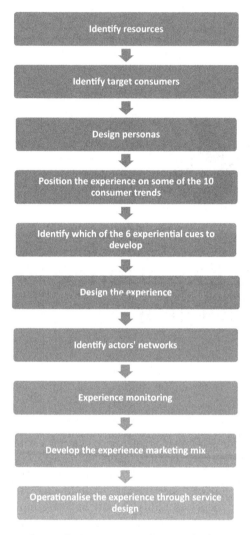

Figure 6.1 The experience design strategy. Source: Author.

6.1 Identifying tourism products/ destination resources

The objective of the resources identification stage is to engage providers in investigating all the potential components that they can use as resources in their service design. Destination resources are vast and can cover several elements. Resources represent what is inherent naturally in destinations, but they can also be man-made and can be related to specific competencies and activities provided at the destination. We shall present those resources in several categories: natural resources, cultural resources and activities (Figure 6.1).

6.1.1 Natural resources

Natural resources refer to features that are characteristic of a destination. They can be sourced in various components as long as they refer to its natural dimensions. Those resources might be exceptional and create a definitive advantage for the destination, or they might be seen as more mundane. If they are unique and outstanding, those resources will inherently create a competitive advantage (for example, Niagara Falls, the giant turtles of the Galapagos or active volcanoes in Iceland). Those unique resources can differentiate a destination from its competitors and create a clear unique experience proposition (UEP). Other natural elements can be perceived as more mundane (wild flowers in coastal areas, beavers in the Alps or bluebell fields in England), but nonetheless they can create some form of magic, and an emotionally laden experience. All those features can be constitutive of a memorable experience and can be sourced in different elements:

- Landscapes;

- Flora and fauna;

- Natural areas (protected or not);

- Geological or other specific features;

- Water-based elements, etc.

6.1.2 Cultural resources

Cultural resources are at the heart of the destination. They place the destination within its broad history and are intimately related to its multi-cultural facets. Cultural resources might refer to formal built architecture but they might also refer to local cultures, art or creative cultures. The scope of culture is therefore very broad and caters for different market needs. The sphere of culture opens up tremendous possibilities to develop experiences; it assigns meaning to the destinations, anchors consumers in a cultural universe and provides sources of enchantment and discovery. Cultural resources are broad and can be sourced in different spheres:

- Built heritage such as archaeological and historical sites, monuments, churches, etc.;

- Interpretation: museums, interpretation centres, etc.;

- Live culture (music, theatre);

- Creative culture;

- Immaterial and local culture.

6.1.3 Activities

Activities might not be conceived as resources as such since they are often developed from a natural or cultural resource. But we have chosen to treat them separately since they might be a source of experience in their own right. Activities refer to an action that tourists will undertake. Those actions can be of a very different nature, ranging from intense and physical activities (sports for instance) to more passive activities. Activities might focus purely on a creative component that relies on learned competencies, but they can also include an artistic dimension or a spiritual dimension. For simplicity, we will categorize activities as follows, and each of those categories opens onto a broad range of possibilities:

- Sports activities;
- Cultural activities;
- Creative activities;
- Local trade learning;
- Spiritual activities.

6.1.4 Service facilities

Finally, a destination or enterprise includes a range of options related to functional services that might be used by tourists. If these are functional elements, they are essential in the experience because they will support the organization of the holiday and contribute to consumer satisfaction. Some of those elements might be an experience in itself (a scenic route or a boutique hotel, for example), while others might only be a means to an end and provide only a functional and necessary service. Those components need to be aligned with the positioning of the experiences offered in order to have a cohesive offer.

- Accommodation;
- Catering;
- Travel operators;
- Transport;
- Entertainment;
- Information networks.

6.1.5 Identifying key resources

The range of resources that can be identified respond to a fairly vast universe. The first step in the resource identification process is essential because it will give direction to the conceptualization and positioning of the experiences developed by the destination. The objective is to focus on the elements that are outstanding (through their magnitude, their originality and/or their association with the destination). In other words, this is the destination DNA – this is the flesh and blood of a destination and can represent strong resources for tourists.

Identifying resources is not simply a marketing exercise; integrating the dimension of local resources into an experience-generating process is important because it will reflect the local population's pride in its destination. If the experiences valued allow local populations to feel proud of their own resources and heritage, they will be more inclined to be involved in the development of those experiences and respond positively to tourists' demands.

Various techniques can be used to identify those resources. In order to identify the key resources that can be developed in experience design, several tasks can be completed, and they require an understanding of which markets hold which strategic information, from consumers to professionals and local inhabitants (Figure 6.2).

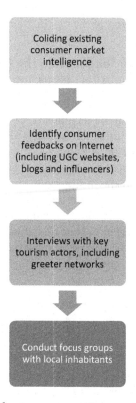

Figure 6.2 Resource identification process. Source: Author.

Destinations know their own strengths and weaknesses, but it might be worthwhile engaging into an introspection exercise that allows for the clarification of those elements.

6.1.5.1 Collating existing consumer market intelligence

The first step will involve collating previous market research and any survey data that will bring an insight into tourists' evaluations of the destination's strengths and weaknesses. Destinations and companies usually have a range of available data that give some interesting insights in terms of consumer intelligence. Satisfaction surveys, market research and data from different services or sectors all bring interesting insights into consumer perceptions of the existing offer. This analysis might also point to weaknesses: elements that create dissatisfaction among existing consumers, sites that have decreasing visitor numbers, suggestions identified in different surveys, etc. Various data collected in tourist sites (tourists flows and seasonality, for instance) might also represent another interesting source of information. Finally, destination branding strategies often involve rich consultancy work to establish destination profiles, which can also provide interesting information. This is a basic first step but a valuable one; destinations and enterprises often have hidden data that can be "dug out" and compiled into a first evaluation of the destination offer.

6.1.5.2 Identify consumer feedback on the Internet (including UGC websites, blogs and influencers)

Consumer intelligence can also be collected over the Internet by simply carrying out an overview of tourists' comments. In this regard, Google reviews, Tripadvisor, travel blogs and influencer websites all constitute an extremely rich and varied source of information. As simple as it might seem, they hold interesting and in-depth information about consumers' perceptions of the experiences and products already sold in the destination. An analysis of this feedback will rapidly allow experience designers to identify what the existing experiences already offer in terms of high levels of consumer satisfaction. It will also give them indications about experiences that are failing to meet customers' expectations. It might equally point to experiences that might not be reaching their full potential and could be redesigned to improve their desirability.

6.1.5.3 Interviews with key tourism actors, including greeter networks

When it comes to sourcing information from key tourism actors, the simplest approach might be to conduct interviews. The targeted professionals can include tourism officials at a destination and regional levels, tourist office directors along with tourist office front staff employees. This analysis can be supplemented with consultations with local guides (heritage, art and nature guides) and cultural resource managers (museum curators, etc.). Greeter networks are another source of strategic information; greeters encounter tourists on a regular basis and have gained some intelligence about their expectations and what interests them.

Interviews can be time consuming, and focus groups can be another way to efficiently consult larger groups (focus groups have a maximum of 10–12 participants and also yield rich results). Surveys can be an option, but they might be too reductive for this research step.

6.1.5.4 Conduct focus groups with local inhabitants

Finally, local inhabitants are another key strategic source and a very important one. Local inhabitants necessarily know about their local resources, whether natural or cultural. More interestingly, they also have an intimate knowledge of local habits and practices that are often not considered in experience design. For instance, they might undertake practices locally such as shore fishing, they might have specific practices, play a local card game, know where to spot migrating birds, forage specific resources from nature, etc. these practices are very rich and can be developed into experiences. They represent what happens "behind closed doors" or at weekends for local inhabitants – what is part of the very local culture. These components are extremely rich because they offer something different to tourists compared to traditional service provisions. They represent what local inhabitants share with each other or when welcoming friends and family. They are often not valued in tourism because they might be perceived as too mundane. However, they should not be disregarded since they are rich in emotions, constitute closeness with the destination and its inhabitants and might allow a destination to differentiate itself from competing destinations.

A supplementary approach to surveying local populations can be to conduct interviews or focus groups with inhabitants who have left a destination. For example, Irish people who live in London or Bretons who live in Paris are a resourceful source of information. Populations who have migrated to other areas of a country can clearly identify what they miss most about their original region and bring an interesting insight into its key features.

IDENTIFYING DESTINATION RESOURCES – WORKING WITH LOCAL INHABITANTS

This approach involves running a series of focus groups with local inhabitants of different age ranges to identify the key characteristics that fuel their local culture. It might be difficult to engage participants to discuss this question since they often perceive that some habits and practices in their culture are so banal that they are not worth mentioning. However, those elements are what also make the richness of a destination, its heart, where local people feel they belong, and they can be particularly interesting for tourists.

To understand clearly the objective of the focus group, participants can be shown some examples. For example, some short-term accommodation operators have a range of experiences on their website that give examples of other destinations' local experiences. It might be interesting to identify three or four experiences and show them to participants so that they can grasp the idea of a localized experience.

The focus groups might be better if organized with local people of similar age ranges (within a bracket of 20 years). The objective is to engage them to identify and discuss the local customs and practices that are unique to their destination. Participants might be motivated by discussing what are their fondest memories from their childhood, activities they did with their parents or grandparents (picking snails on a rainy day, shore-fishing at very low tide, cooking wild flower donuts, making elderberry lemonade, etc.). They can also be invited to discuss what they miss the most when they are away from home. They might also be invited to discuss what they show to visiting friends and relatives.

This is a fairly simple exercise but a very rich one. Its objective is to be able to identify a range of resources, those that pertain to the local, and often less formal, culture but that can be a valuable source for experiences.

In summary, this first step aims to list all the resources that a destination can use to develop experiences. Those can be more formal, the ones that are currently identified in tourism offerings (natural and cultural resources), or they can be more informal, based in local traditions and practices. Once this background work has been undertaken, the second step will identify customer segments that the destination or enterprise wishes to attract.

6.2 Identify target customers

As a preliminary task, destinations and enterprises will identify their key consumer market segments. Once those are identified, each of the experiences developed will be targeted at one or several of the segments.

Identifying consumer segments is based on segmentation strategies which can be diverse in nature (see Chapter 1, Section 1.6.1). Segmentation is a tool heavily used in marketing, and it encompasses a variety of techniques. The objective of segmentation is to identify variables that can be used to group consumers who display similar behaviours. They may be seeking similar types of experiences, they might be more sensitive to some specific components of the experience or they might behave very similarly. What is important with segmentation is to find the key variable or the combination of variables that best explain similar behaviour. Those similarities imply that customers belonging to each segment will respond similarly to the experiences on offer and to the marketing mix designed for that segment, and differently to other segments.

Segmentation is an important tool for becoming consumer-centric and designing services that will be able to answer customers' needs and thereby create value for them. Segmentation offers companies and destinations the opportunity to develop strategic advantages over their competitors since it encourages them to focus on one or several segments, understand fully the needs of those customers and serve them more efficiently than their direct competitors. However, segmentation is also a costly approach, and therefore several guiding principles need to be followed.

6.2.1 Segmentation principles

In order to conduct segmentation, the segments identified should respond to different categories:

- **Be identifiable**: Is it easy for the company to access the data necessary for the type of segmentation that is sought? Does the segmentation require new data collection? Which information needs to be collected to direct the future marketing mix?

- **Each segment should be measurable**: Each segment should be measured through specific variables such as purchasing power, shopping basket, size, profiles, etc.

- **Segments should be substantial**: If the company/destination is going to expend the effort to develop a different marketing mix for each segment, it needs to guarantee that the segment is large enough for the whole strategy to be profitable. Substantiality implies that each segment is evaluated both as a combination of size and spending (i.e. a smaller segment might still be of interest if it is made up of individuals ready to spend more than other segments, or who come to a destination at different times of the year, etc.).

- **Each segment must be reachable**: The company will investigate how each segment can be efficiently reached. For example, communication channels are essential to understand how to communicate with each segment.

On top of those principles, two other principles, which pertain to statistical procedures but which also have strategic implications, refer to the construction of the segments:

- **Internal cohesion**: If a new marketing mix is developed for the segment, it will necessarily be more costly, so the company has to make sure that the segments identified are close enough in needs to be receptive to this marketing mix. Statistical techniques used to segment data usually use this principle.

- **External differentiation**: For a segmentation strategy to be efficient, each segment has to be as different as possible from the other ones. In other words, if the company is to design a different marketing mix for each segment, it wants to make sure that this marketing mix will respond specifically to the needs of one specific segment. If it partially attracts several segments, then the segmentation strategy has not been efficient.

It is always possible to segment a market with various variables, so it is important to be careful that the segmentation is not just another interpretation of a market but that it provides a pertinent segmentation reflecting real differences in consumer behaviour.

6.2.2 Types of segmentation

Traditionally, segmentation was undertaken on the basis of different variables that could describe consumers (in socio-economic terms) rather than what they expected out of a product. As a result, traditional segmentation approaches would segment consumers on the basis of one or a combination of several variables such as age, life-cycle, generation, gender, household composition, nationality, etc. Consumers could also be segmented according to their type of usage of the product/service, with variables such as rate of use, (heavy/intermittent/low), loyalty, consumption timing, etc. Other socio-economic factors could also be used, such as level of education (which, in tourism consumption, is a key variable), social class, occupation, revenue, etc.

All these variables remain interesting and useful in explaining different behaviours and have always produced efficient segmentation strategies. However, if they are pertinent at decrypting some behavioural commonalities in segments, they remain very descriptive. They do not offer an explanation as to why and how some consumers perceive some products differently than others. For instance, consumers within the same age group, or social class, or revenue range might have very different expectations of a product. Experiential marketing theories also show that an experience is highly personal and needs to be understood with more subtle segmentation strategies than the traditional ones mentioned here.

Psychographic segmentation is a very different approach from traditional segmentation since it divides buyers into different groups based on either their lifestyle, psychological values or benefit-seeking objectives.

6.2.2.1 Lifestyle segmentation

Lifestyle segmentation is based on variables that collect information on how individuals choose to live their life. Typically, lifestyles are evaluated using a scale measuring activities, interests and opinions (AIO models). As such, the technique aims to understand how consumers envisage their life in terms of their place in society, what they do in terms of activities, which political opinions they have developed, what interests them, etc. AIO models give a global picture of individuals as one would see them in their daily lives and within their society. This approach is supposed to translate quite accurately consumers' expectations and preferences in terms of consumption. Lifestyle segmentation is relevant to tourism, especially if lifestyle segments have been designed in terms of tourism lifestyle.

6.2.2.2 Values as segmentation

Values were inspired by the work of Rokeach (1973): "A value is an enduring belief that a specific mode of conduct or end-state of existence is personally or socially preferable to an opposite or converse mode of conduct or end-state of experience" (p. 5). Rokeach associated deeply-rooted values with beliefs and attitudes. Values are influenced by culture, society and personality and are considered more stable over time than attitudes since they are more central to an individual's cognitive system.

Values were divided into two broad categories: instrumental and terminal values. The instrumental dimension grouped values such as courage, honesty, cheerfulness, forgiveness, responsibility, politeness and so forth. Terminal values were connected to the end states of existence, in other words the goals that one would want to achieve in life. Those end states of existence grouped values such as security, happiness, true friendship, inner harmony, freedom, wisdom, etc. Instrumental values refer to preferred modes of behaviour and can be considered as means to attain instrumental values.

The overall list of values was also named the Rokeach Value Survey (RVS) and was operationalized by asking respondents to rank each set of values in order of importance. Rokeach argued that, once learned, values were ordered hierarchically into a value system.

Since Rokeach's original article, various researchers have used values in segmentation strategies, and this is an interesting approach in the tourism context, although the segments remain fairly large.

6.2.2.3 Benefit segmentation

Benefit segmentation was primarily introduced in 1968 by Haley, who aimed to develop an instrument that would provide a better understanding and prediction of future buying behaviour than did traditional market segmentation techniques. As a practitioner, and having admitted the limits of traditional techniques such as geographic, demographic or volume-based segmentation for advertising purposes, Haley was mainly concerned with the development of new market segmentation tools.

Although he did not deny the advantages of traditional techniques in guiding promotional tools (media purchase, identification of users and non-users, geographical identification and so forth), he criticized their inability to predict behaviour. Haley introduced benefit segmentation as a market segmentation technique whereby market segments would be identified by causal factors: "The belief underlying this segmentation strategy is that the benefits which people are seeking in consuming a given product are the basic reasons for the existence of true market segments" (Haley, 1968, p. 31)

Although the concept in itself might not have been revolutionary, the main advancement brought by Haley was to motivate marketers to analyse their consumer markets from a different perspective and consider the benefits sought as a primary source of purchasing behaviour. Haley was also determined to develop a technique that would have practical implications; for instance, the benefits identified could be used directly as promotional messages.

While Haley studied benefits of a tangible nature, years later, the notion of benefits was expanded to integrate experiential benefits. This is particularly true in tourism research, where benefit segmentation has proved to be particularly well adapted to this consumption context. For a review of its applications in the tourism sector, see Frochot and Morrison (2000). Briefly, benefit segmentation can be considered as a segmentation that addresses experiences sought as the discerning variable between consumers. This segmentation technique partitions consumers according to what they are seeking out of a consumption. The example at the end of this chapter illustrates in detail how this technique can be used in a tourism context and identifies the strategic marketing offshoots.

Identifying segments does not mean that a destination or company will target all of them. Segmentation provides a range of consumer segments on the basis of which a destination can make choices in relation to its general positioning and in relation to the experiences that will be developed.

6.2.3 Personas

Over the last few years, personas have become a common feature of marketing and segmentation strategies, to the point that personas are often taken to represent a segmentation strategy. Segmentation refers to the range of techniques addressed in the previous section. Segmentation divides a market into segments (or clusters) that display similar behaviours.

Personas are an illustration of those segments. Personas are useful because they give a human representation of a segment and allow marketers to project themselves better into their consumers' minds. Therefore, personas are not a segmentation technique as such.

The Internet provides several templates that can be used to develop personas. For a persona to be useful, it is important to provide information on the persona itself (age range, sex, profession), the persona's leisure habits, holidays consumption habits and expectations, frustrations of daily life, etc. The persona has to be useful in giving an idea of who this segment is, how the segment behaves, its typical way of thinking, the segment lifestyle, etc. (see the example on Smaply in Section 6.6.2 thereafter).

6.3 Position the experience within some of the ten consumer trends

In Chapter 4, ten major current trends were reviewed, and we shall not detail them again in this section. As a reminder, they are represented in Figure 6.3. These trends bring another dimension to experience design by providing clues about the themes that can inspire the experience creation process. Integrating

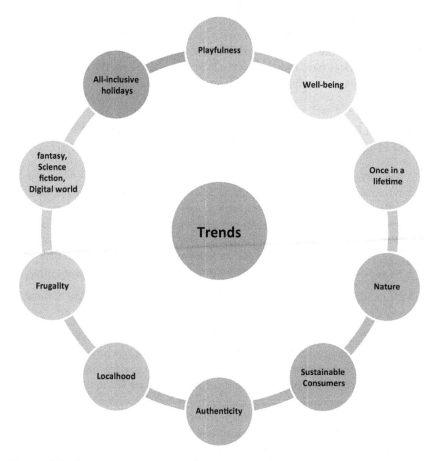

Figure 6.3 The ten consumer trends. Source: Author.

those trends into experience design helps give a sound basis to experiences by placing them in the context of what consumers expect nowadays. It might also bring another layer of creativity by engaging experience designers to contemplate other dimensions in their design. A destination might not have all the necessary components, in its resources and DNA, so the trend identification needs to integrate the resource capacities of the destination/enterprise. Finally, if a destination or company has a marketing strategy that has aimed to ascertain the positioning of its products and develop a branding strategy, the trends identified should be aligned to those strategic choices.

The objective in this experience design step is not necessarily to adapt the experience to each of the ten trends; a good experience is one that will resonate with one or two trends. For example, a tree house will combine a once-in-a-lifetime experience with a nature experience.

Trends should also be considered as adaptable themes depending on the experience context. For example, the trend for "all-inclusive holidays" might seem very remote for some destinations that aim to serve a more authentic product. However, the all-inclusive trend translates a deep need for a seamless holiday, one where services have been thought out in advance to ease the holiday process (see the following example of the delivery of food baskets).

EXAMPLE – CONTEXTUALIZING THE "ALL-INCLUSIVE" OFFER: DELIVERING LOCAL FOOD TO TOURISTS

A destination might want to promote local foods and develop an efficient system to deliver them directly to tourists. Tourists can book the delivery of a basket of local products every day or once a week. The basket might include local recipes that make the best use of the basket's products. This offer would suit tourists who have rented an appartement or villa and want to gain a sense of localhood. The basket contents and its delivery save tourists the effort of product sourcing, and the recipes guide them in the production of different meals.

A more "packaged" version of this approach could be the delivery of meals cooked by local chefs.

This experience might be contextualised even more by providing some information about the producers themselves (farmers, herb growers, chefs, etc.). This information would personalize the product, create more emotional connections with the producers and provide a deeper sense of connection with the destination. This offer would provide tourists with a sense of localhood (local products and local recipes) and of sustainability and well-being (organic ingredients, locally sourced), and it might bring an element of novelty and surprise (cooking new recipes, experiencing new dishes).

6.4 Integrate some of the six experience cues within the created experiences

The six experiential cues were addressed in Chapter 5 (see Figure 6.4).

When creating an experience, these six cues are useful but do not need to be all developed at once in the same experience. An experience that is impactful and touches consumers also has to be subtle. Often experiences will riff on one or two of those experiential cues, coupled with one or two of the trends (Figure 6.3). Examples of generating exercises were provided in Chapter 5 for each of the six components.

The experience can be developed via creative workshops that involve local tourism actors and stakeholders, greeters, local inhabitants, etc.

To lead efficient workshops, the groups need to have access to the range of resources available and the personas of the key clusters. It might be useful to

Figure 6.4 The experiential cues. Source: Author.

give to each group a specific cluster that they will concentrate upon. For example, the destination has identified that it wants to develop an experience on its natural resources for a specific persona. The range of resources previously identified are presented to the group, along with the persona, and the groups can then engage in an experience creative process.

6.5 Visualizing the experience

Once the experience creative process is engaged, the participants can also start visualizing the experience. This visualization process is useful to take a step back and be able to understand the extent to which the experience dynamics work, who the different stakeholders involved are, how the timing flows, etc.

The best approach to visualize an experience is to develop a story-board. The story-board divides the different steps of the experience, detailing what happens in every step, which actors are involved, the service components involved, etc. Polaroid cameras can be a useful tool to detail each step. Polaroids provide instant pictures that can be used to create the story-board and help participants to better visualize their experience.

Visualizing the experience is important, but it is equally important to analyse the repercussions of this creative process in terms of service delivery quality and the stakeholders involved.

6.6 The experience journey maps

One component of the experience design processes is to identify the journey map, and ideally one map will be produced for each consumer persona. The objective of these maps is to identify clearly the different steps that consumers undertake, the potential problems, the direction/information needs and ultimately the actors involved in each of the steps. Those various touchpoints allow experience designers to break down the experience into individual stages and identify problem areas and opportunities for innovation (Stickdorn and Schneider, 2011).

6.6.1 Identifying consumers' journeys: Observation

Stickdorn and Schneider (2011) advocate that "spending time within the service environment is often the only way to develop a truly holistic view of how the service is operating, as it provides an intimate understanding of the real-time interactions that take place between the various groups and touchpoints involved" (page 156).

If the experience is already in place, one approach to designing journey maps is to obtain feedback from consumers. Interviews are an option, but tourism experiences can include various encounters, and if consumers are interviewed afterwards, precious information about their journey will inevitably be lost. The best option is to follow consumers and take note of all their reactions as they evolve through the experience. This can be cumbersome for evaluators and intimidating for consumers. If tourism actors don't have the time or availability to undertake these consumer journeys, observation is another approach. It is not as rich as consumer journey feedback, but it can allow tourism actors to observe tourists while they are consuming an experience. Some information on observation was already provided in Chapter 2.

6.6.2 Collective shadowing

Another approach to customer journey creation is to engage various tourism actors to undertake the customer journey themselves. Experience collective shadowing involves taking two actors of different professions and engaging them in living an experience as tourists would do. For instance, they might undertake the booking of the experience themselves, find their own way through the experience, identify possible drawbacks as they undertake these tasks, etc. The objective is primarily for local tourism actors to gain a better understanding of the experience from the consumer viewpoint. This collective approach carries another interest, creating a better understanding of each actor's role in the experience process. It creates empathy between the different providers and allows them to understand how they interact with each other and the impacts that those interactions have on the final experience. Ultimately, this approach also helps to lower the barriers between different providers and helps to develop a seamless experience.

Another possibility is to involve staff in experiencing the product individually and commenting on all their actions. In this think-aloud protocol, a member of staff goes through all the steps of the experience, and another one observes them. The participant details aloud their perceptions, feelings, surprises, disappointments, etc. The observer takes notes and might even video the participant. An analysis of the experience process is then undertaken by both parties, aided by the notes, observations and video footage.

6.6.2.1 Mobile ethnography

Mobile ethnography is an approach that has emerged with the development of new technologies. Ethnography is a method that has been used for a long time to investigate peoples and cultures and is an extremely valuable but also a time-consuming approach. With the emergence of new technologies, the tourism industry quickly realized that mobile devices opened up new possibilities that were extremely valuable to accompanying and studying the experience as it unfolds: mobile devices have compasses, GPS, geolocalization services, cameras, recorders, video facilities, etc. Mobile devices can be used for various purposes and especially to provide information at the right moment: push mails, augmented reality to read a landscape, travel through time with archive videos, etc. Mobile ethnography also gives the opportunity to enter the intimacy of the tourist experience by collecting data about tourists' movements, views and major touchpoints (through pictures, recorded comments, videos, etc.) and recording their feelings and interpretations of lived experiences.

Digital devices now exist (see Chapter 2 – Section 2.3.7) that can allow experience designers to invite their consumers to record their feelings as they go across the different experience steps. Consumers can give indications about their feelings, the positive and negative experiences that occur at the most salient moments, explain why they expressed those feelings and take pictures or even videos. These live-action approaches are very rich (Hanington and Martin, 2019). Their main limitation is to ensure that consumers stay involved for the whole duration of the experience, and to this effect some bribes might be useful.

SMAPLY – THE EXTENDED JOURNEY MAPPING TOOL

Smaply is a new digital software, an online journey mapping tool that provides experience designers with a comprehensive tool. Smaply has several functions: it provides templates for creating personas, it creates customer journey maps and it also has the ability to design stakeholders' maps.

First and foremost, participating consumers contribute their information to construct their persona file (see Figure 6.5). The information collected might include travel preferences, service expectations, digital connection points, etc.

Image 1 – Participants' personas

Once participants are registered, they can enter information about their experience. The information uploads on a website, and the enterprise can access a profile page summarizing participants' information collected for each of those touchpoints. The system then provides a journey map that is extremely rich. An emotional curve allows the company to evaluate how consumers rate their emotions along their journey. For each touchpoint, consumers can also give a written description of their experience, upload videos and pictures than can help understand their perception of this touchpoint, etc.

Image 2 – Consumers' individual journey maps

The journey mapping tool identifies consumers' interactions with the service provider and the consumption universe. Through those various touchpoints, the consumer can indicate their feelings, points of satisfaction and dissatisfaction, etc.

When collating this information over the whole sample of consumers, companies can then identify the main contributors and the inhibitors to the experience by analyzing data per touchpoint (Figures 6.5, 6.6 and 6.7).

Source: https://www.smaply.com

Figure 6.5 Personas' profiles in Smaply. Source: https://www.smaply.com/

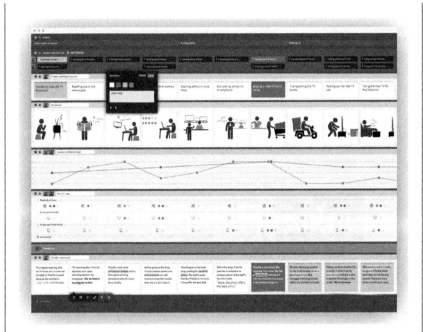

Figure 6.6 Journey maps in Smaply. Source: https://www.smaply.com/

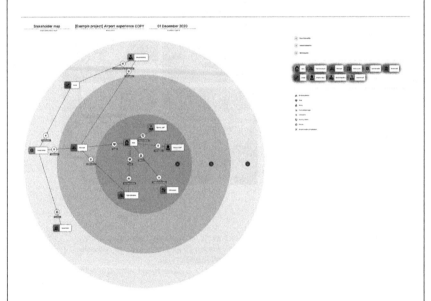

Figure 6.7 Stakeholders' maps in Smaply. Source: https://www.smaply.com/

6.6.3 The extended experience journey

Whilst it might be intuitive that the experience starts when consumers are at the destination, the experience encapsulates in fact a broader range of touch-points. The experience begins before the purchase, when consumers are seeking information, and it continues right up to after the consumption, once tourists have returned home. The various steps include:

- The experience before the consumption: research, plan, dream about the object of consumption, imagine the experience, etc.

- During the purchasing experience: choice, payment, packaging and meeting with staff.

- During consumption: sensations, satisfaction/dissatisfaction, flow in the experience, immersion in the world of consumption or irritation, etc.

- After consumption: memorability of the experience – even nostalgia, reactivated thanks to purchased souvenirs and photographs.

EXAMPLE – THE EXPERIENTIAL JOURNEY: AN EXAMPLE WITH GUIDED WILDLIFE TOURS

While all tourism experiences are different, there are some basic principles that can guide tourism actors in managing the customer experience. These basic principles are presented below, illustrated by an example on guided wildlife tours.

Before the purchase

Because tourism products are intangible and can only be truly perceived in situ, it is important to provide a range of insight/information upstream about the experience.

To this end, new technologies, and in particular websites and mobile applications, provide a wide range of tools to help the consumer access a more realistic view of the experience. These tools include videos, photos, real-time information (webcams, weather forecast, snow cover, etc.) and feedback from consumers who have already experienced the service (blogs, participatory sites, etc.). The tone and content of the texts provided on websites or in brochures will necessarily matter. It is already a question of surfing the register of emotions, referring to different senses, developing a story about the service/context and highlighting the key points that will fuel quality experiences for consumers. Preparing clients for the experience is essential. While it is crucial not to kill the surprise effect by giving too much information, the communication should tease, create interest and incite envy without revealing all the experience components. This communication can be compared to a trailer for a movie.

After the purchase and before the experience

If it is a subject/context with which consumers are not familiar, the pre-experience communication will aim to set the framework and provide reading keys which will subsequently improve the experience. In Chapter 2, Section 2.3.2 on nesting gives indications for the preparation for the experience.

For example, in Cairns (Australia), local tourism stakeholders have developed "Reef talks", two-hour information sessions that provide a better understanding of the coral reef ecosystem and the different species of fish, coral, algae and shells that can be observed there. This information session is an experience booster because it gives visitors on diving trips keys to understanding better what they will see during their dive. The knowledge provided will also give them a sense of satisfaction by allowing them to identify different elements encountered during their dive. They will thus approach their dive with the feeling of being able to make sense of what they will observe and come out of the experience with the feeling of having not only seen things but of having also learned things. At the end of the session, participants can buy plastic cards that list the main species encountered by category (shellfish, algae, fish, etc.) and that they can take with them on the boat (the cards are then kept as a souvenir of the experience). Other tourist attractions that run flora or fauna tours take advantage of the waiting time before the tour departs to show films that contextualize the tour.

During the experience

Numerous studies have identified that the professionalism and personality of the guide is essential to the success of an experience. The information provided by a guide during the experience will help to give meaning and understanding to the observed phenomena: explaining how a plant/animal endures an extreme climate, the strategies developed by fauna and flora to adapt to their environment, species' reproductive behaviour, their evolution, etc. When a consumer observes wildlife, (turtles in the Galapagos, sperm whales, orcas, etc.), this encounter can arouse very strong emotions. These emotions are aroused by the beauty of what is observed, its rarity, its wild dimension and its references to childhood wonder (fascination with certain animals such as whales). The function of the guide will also be to underline the rarity of the encounter and to highlight the beauty of the elements observed.

Other elements can help optimize the customer experience. Thus, knowledge about the environment of the experiment can be boosted in other ways during the experience. For example, experience providers can identify captive periods when consumers are available to absorb some more specific information (in a waiting room, on a bus or boat ride to the sighting location). In the first instance, it is important to situate the experience by contextualizing it. It might involve explaining the geological features of a destination which explains why some species have settled there or come to feed; migrating dynamics in wildlife; the evolution of a landscape, etc. Information needs to gradually immerse consumers into the experience context, from general to specific information. If possible, guides can also point out the best times to take pictures. For example, for the sighting of sperm whales (which remain mostly submerged), the guide can spot when a whale is about to dive and warn tourists, giving the best photo opportunity when its tail comes out of the water. Another key element is to involve participants in the experience by giving them the opportunity to help the guide spot wildlife (lend binoculars so that a participant can spot chamois or a golden eagle in the mountain, lend a hydrophone so that the participant can listen to and spot whales underwater, etc.). Surprise can also be orchestrated by a guide who will take clients to a site where encounters with a certain type of fauna are guaranteed but without warning them (placing a boat in a school of dolphins, surprising marmots in a valley, etc.). At this point, the guide can step back and let the participants appreciate the beauty of the animals.

After the experience

At the end of the experience, a major element for the guide is to summarize the experience: to clearly highlight all the elements that were seen during the experience, and to stress the rarity of the elements observed and the luck that the participants had to be able to witness these natural beauties.

The service provider can also continue the bond formed with participants by collecting their email addresses which will enable them to send them the newsletter, create a community on Facebook with regularly updated information, etc. This dynamic will not only encourage word of mouth and positive feedback on participatory sites, but also nourish the memorability of the experience.

The journey map allows experience designers to understand and analyse the different steps that consumers will go through. Another dimension to the experience is to understand the implications in terms of service provision in relation to the actors involved.

6.7 Identify actors' networks

Once the journey has been identified, the different touchpoints are then discussed with the tourism actors involved in the experience to identify, collectively, paths for improvement and increased fluidity. The outcome of this process is to identify a seamless experience flow; this fluidity will allow tourists to fully immerse themselves in the experience and not be distracted by functional details that could dampen their mood and enjoyment.

Following on from the example on Smaply in the previous section, this software also provides a tool to identify stakeholders. Stakeholder maps (Figure 6.7) allow experience designers to visualize the actors' ecosystems, i.e., all the tourism stakeholders who are involved in the experience provision.

6.7.1 The blueprint model

Some traditional methods such as blueprint models can also be used to visualize and understand the implications of the different journey touchpoints by analysing different experience dimensions. The blueprint model has been used for some time, its objective being to decouple the experience analysis by identifying, for each touchpoint, which functions within a destination or company are involved in the service delivery. The model usually deconstructs each step into physical facilities, customer actions, front-stage interactions, back-stage actions and support processes.

- **Physical facilities**: All the physical elements that are important to deliver the service. Physical elements refer to all those elements that are physically visible (employees' uniforms, shop setting, furniture, etc.). Because services are intangible, those elements are important as they give quality cues to consumers.

- **Customer actions**: Steps, choices, interactions and activities undertaken by consumers at each stage of their experience process (seeking information, purchasing, experiencing and post-experiencing).

- **Front-stage interactions**: Any activities, services or tasks undertaken by a frontline employee. The front-stage window of the blueprint looks at all the direct actions that will take place between the consumer and the frontline staff.

- **Back-stage interactions**: All the steps and actions that are directly invisible to the consumer but are directly connected to the experience. Those elements might pertain to process elements: the agent has been trained to master global distribution systems, communicates with other services, etc.

- **Support processes**: Steps and internal actions that are backstage and support the whole service process.

On top of those categories, it might be useful to time the experience, and identify the length that customers devote to each touchpoint and how those might be reduced. Touchpoints might even be cancelled by anticipating some of them through booking online before the experience. For example, a consumer might book a bike rental that will be delivered to the holiday accommodation, thereby saving time upon arrival.

The blueprint also needs to include the digital dimension that will allow an efficient delivery and connections between the different services and actors involved.

If the blueprint is a fairly classical approach, it is a useful one because it invites the actors involved in the experience to appreciate better how their collective and connected actions contribute to the experience flow. Beyond identifying the strengths and weaknesses of the experience provision, it also allows providers to identify paths for improvement.

The blueprint can be more complex for destinations because the range of stakeholders involved and their nature (public or private) creates other challenges. If the blueprint is important for a private business, it is even more important for destinations because the range of actors need to understand fully how they collectively contribute to the consumer experience.

6.8 Experience monitoring

Once the experience has been developed, it will need to be monitored on a fairly regular basis in order to evaluate its quality.

Service quality is a very large field, and the notion of quality has been defined and evaluated over the years through various techniques and models. We have seen in this book that what lies at the heart of experiences is of an emotional nature. Deep experiences also point to the role of personal growth and learning in this process. Nonetheless, experiences also rely on physical service provision. The fluidity of those services is an important dimension, as we have addressed in the previous section, as is their quality. Service providers need to design quality monitoring systems that will regularly provide them with an evaluation of their service delivery and identify potential pitfalls. Various tools and methods exist, and the field of service quality is very broad.

In its most basic but useful form, quality can be assessed with quality surveys. Those might be collected during the experience, but they are more commonly sent out to consumers 1–2 weeks after the experience. To identify which components should be integrated in those questionnaires, the SERVQUAL approach (Parasuraman, Zeithaml and Berry, 2002) is a traditional approach but a useful one to assess quality. Over the years, similar scales have been developed and adapted to specific contexts. Quality scales can be implemented to measure quality on a regular basis and thereby provide a quality barometer that allows providers to follow and rapidly identify quality pitfalls.

In a more prosaic approach, providers might also want to monitor consumers' comments on the Internet. Tripadvisor and Google Advice, among other sources of information, provide an interesting window into consumers' service evaluations.

The notion of quality, however, is broader than evaluating its components. It is not the object of this book to detail all its dimensions, but if providers want to investigate further the notion of quality, several elements need to be considered. Rather than measuring service quality, it might be interesting to integrate the notion of thresholds; a service provision might only impact visitors' evaluation if it is above or under a threshold. In this approach the work of Kano et al. (1984) is particularly interesting. Kano identified that service components respond to different evaluation processes and can be classified in three categories:

- **Basic attributes**, also called *dissatisfiers*, refer to service delivery components that consumers expect at a minimum. In the eyes of the consumer, a service needs, at a minimum, to provide those features. Any service delivery that does not perform on those attributes will be evaluated negatively. For example, the towels in a hotel bathroom or restroom facilities in a tourist site are service components that are expected and have to be present.

- **Satisfiers**: These are attributes that consumers do not necessarily expect. If the attributes are present in the service delivery, they create satisfaction; if they are absent, they do not create dissatisfaction. For example, a family with young children has booked an apartment in a seaside resort. The local tourist office might decide to develop some free entertainment, a street theatre event targeted at younger children. If this event does not happen, the family would most probably experience a satisfactory holiday, and this would not create dissatisfaction. If the event takes place, however, it will increase consumers' satisfaction.

- **Performance attributes**: The increase in consumer satisfaction is proportional to the service improvement. For example, a pool at a resort will be satisfactory, but it will bring more satisfaction if it is larger.

Kano's model is different from traditional quality scales and it offers a very interesting insight into consumers' evaluative processes. For a more detailed explanation of the model, please refer to https://www.mindtools.com/pages/article/newCT_97.htm.

6.9 The experiential marketing mix

Once the experience has been created and its various components and side aspects have been identified, the experience needs to be processed with marketing strategy in mind and cultivated in line with the four marketing principles.

Traditionally, and to keep it simple, the project needs to integrate the four Ps: product, place (distribution), price and promotion.

6.9.1 Product

The notion of product refers to either a physical product, a service or an experience. In the context of this book, we will limit our analysis to the experience. This dimension of the marketing mix has been addressed earlier in this chapter along with its design and monitoring.

6.9.2 Promotion

The promotion sphere is wider and larger that it has ever been. The objective of promotional strategies is to inform, persuade and/or remind target customers of the experience. Beyond providing information, promotional strategies need to persuade customers about the attractivity of the experience and its suitability for their holiday needs. Traditional communication strategies include promotional channels such as advertising, personal selling, public relations, etc. Its targets are the end consumers, tourists who are potential consumers or have already booked a holiday at the destination where the experience takes place. The channels used are equally wide: from TV to radio to leaflets in hotels, tourist information centres, etc. Nowadays, promotional tools have largely expanded with the advent of the Internet and all the possibilities that it offers: targeted advertising on Internet websites and podcasts, emails, blogs, notifications, destination and tourism actors' own websites, user-generated content websites, influencers, etc. Word of mouth is another promotional strategy weapon. This is the source that has the biggest impact upon decision making, so it should not be overlooked, especially when it resonates through the Internet.

Beyond the shape of the message and promotional support, the timing of the promotional campaign deserves some attention. One important criterion, for instance, is to identify when consumers start booking their holiday in order to time the promotion correctly.

Another useful component is to detect where consumers are most likely to come in contact with the promotional material. For example, international independent visitors are more likely to pick up leaflets in their accommodation (hotels, B&Bs, AirBnBs, etc.), on top of being bigger users of guide books. Local visitors might be an interesting target, but they rarely use information targeted to tourists. They might be more receptive to promotion circulated on local radio and newspapers, targeted magazines or signage.

Finally, familiarization trips are another interesting source. An individual divulging information will do it more positively and will elaborate more if she/he has experienced a service. Travel agents, tourist information staff, journalists, guide writers, hotels, restaurants and B&B owners are powerful information diffusers, advising their customers on key tourist experiences nearby or via their media. They need to be included in the promotional strategy and can be targeted off season to familiarization trips, when the experience premises have less tourists. Locally, tourist offices often organize networks events where tourism producers meet and present their offers to each other. This is an old and simple strategy, but one that still proves efficient to diffuse information among providers who will ultimately influence tourist demand.

6.9.3 Place

Place refers to the distribution dynamics of the experience(s) created. The distribution strategy needs to reflect an understanding of the networks that consumers traditionally use to become aware of a product and book it.

The experience designer might choose a direct sales approach or rely on intermediaries. For instance, the experience might be included in a package sold by a local travel agent, hotel, resort or tourist information centre. The experience might be sold directly through phone or via Internet bookings.

Asserting the distribution strategy requires an intimate knowledge of consumers, especially in regard to their booking procedures and their relative timing. It also needs to be tied in with the promotional components by investigating where consumers are more likely to seek information.

Considering that an increasing number of tourists no longer go to tourist offices' premises, some tourist offices and local experience providers have decided to embrace a mobile strategy whereby they install temporary information outlets while other destinations train local businesses (newsagents, etc.) as information providers. These approaches provide the ability to get much closer to visitors and engage in efficient selling outcomes.

6.9.4 Price

The pricing strategy includes various components, some of which have already been addressed in this section.

The price is always a thorny question: how much is an experience valued in the eyes of the consumers?

The price needs to reflect a good understanding of the experience cost structure. The starting point in pricing is to identify the fixed and variable costs associated with the production of the experience. But prices are also identified in relation to competitive experiences (direct and indirect competition).

The experience designer might also want to consider how to manage prices over different seasons. Revenue management is now a well-defined competence that masters the task of moderating prices according to consumer demand. In tourism, the notion of weather is another question that might be integrated into this reasoning. For instance, a tourism operator might decide to reduce its prices when the weather turns bad and the experience traditionally attracts fewer consumers. Prices are also set according to target customers; different targets will be responsive to different prices.

Options associated with a loyalty card or group prices might be another option in tourism experiences. Loyalty cards can be a good investment since they will lead to repeat visits, either in the same site or across a cluster of sites. They can be an attractive feature for a destination.

Willingness to pay is another element to consider. For example, in the Alps, summer consumers have a much lower willingness to pay than winter tourists. In winter, consumers will purchase ski-lift passes even though they can be quite expensive. In summer, they are more reluctant to pay for activities. When the price of experiences is included in a packaged offer or is free (the cost is "hidden" in the tourist tax), then participation in various tourist pursuits increases drastically. Considering that those activities can create a stronger attachment to the destination/brand, it is a strategy that is worth considering.

6.10 The experience identity matrix

With all the information collected through the steps we have addressed so far, the last step aims to summarize the most important strategic information into an experience identity card. This card brings together the key information that is necessary to identify the experience and its main components (Table 6.1).

In order to illustrate the experience creation process, an example is presented as the last feature of this book. This example takes the reader through the ten steps of the experience generating process.

6.11 Designing experiences in historic houses: An example of an experience generating process

To illustrate this chapter, an extended example will be developed to detail an experience generating process. We will use as a central example the context of historic houses in Great Britain. These houses have always been a key feature of British heritage and they have been portrayed in television series and films over the years. Whether in *Gosford Park* or *Downtown Abbey*, historic houses refer to a period in British history that has always attracted a lot of attention.

Table 6.1 The experience identity matrix

Experience identity card		
Resources used	**Activities used in the experience**	**Service assistance** Is the experience assisted by a human being (guide, etc.) or a digital device?
Key experiential cues (see Figure 6.4, page 165) • The five senses • Creating a surprise • Involving consumers • Creating souvenirs • Contextualising • Relatedness	**Consumer target profile(s)** Local/domestic/ international ? Which nationalities? Experiences sought? **Illustrate segments with personas** Mrs Amber Mr Wood Ms Watson	**Trends (see Figure 6.3, page 163)** • Playfulness • Well-being • Once-in-a-lifetime • Nature • Sustainable consumers • Authenticity • Localhood • Frugality • Fantasy • All-inclusive holidays
Competition Who are my direct competitors for this experience? (Identify other destinations/ enterprises providing an experience that might be perceived as similar)	**Co-construction** Which part of the service is the responsibility of the service provider and which part is controlled by consumers?	**Value proposition** A statement presenting the benefits of your experience and why they should purchase it
Nesting Do consumers need some form of "training" to access the experience?	**Sustainability issues** To what extent does the experience design include sustainability principles? To what extent does it use local and/or organic resources? How does the experience fit with the destination's economic and social profile?	**Governance** Who are the actors involved in the experience? Is it totally managed by private or public actors, or perhaps a mix of both? What are the responsibilities of each actor in the experience?
	MARKETING MIX	
PROMOTION	**PLACE**	**PRICE**

Source: Author

Those houses are either privately owned or under the management of heritage trusts. Beyond their heritage value, historic houses allow visitors to immerse themselves in the life of affluent families as they lived in the Georgian or Victorian era. The houses offer an immersion in various rooms, and visitors can project themselves in the lifestyle of that era, from the lavish dining rooms to the kitchens. The houses are usually set within a park which might have some free-roaming deer. They usually have a garden and some temporary exhibitions. The properties normally have a restaurant, often located in a heritage building or in the old stables. They also have shops that sell souvenirs connected to the property, as well as various other items (books, decorations, etc.). The properties might run some events, usually at weekends, either associated with the property or not (classic car shows, street theatre, art fairs, etc.).

Considering the financial pressures associated with the costs of running and restoring those sites, some properties have aimed to diverse their earnings. They might have chosen to open up to the wedding market and/or to the business market (adapting rooms for seminars and business events). They might also tie in with their local roots by opening a farm shop or garden centre.

Their consumer markets are varied, ranging from international to domestic tourists to local visitors. They usually have developed close links with local schools, which opens up an interesting off-season market and creates attachment with the adult visitors they will become.

In order to design experiences for those properties, each step developed in the experience generating process will be detailed thereafter. In order to constrain the reasoning to a delineated market, we shall focus only on the excursionist and tourism market. We shall not address the business market, which is an interesting one but responds to different dynamics.

6.11.1 Identifying resources

The houses' features have already been described earlier in this section. We shall summarize them as follows:

- **Natural resources**: A large park with some wild or tamed animals, and some monumental rare trees, some of which may have been brought back from the family's travels. The house might also have a walled garden, again with some rare plants and flowers. A pond might provide visitors with a restful view and water-based animals and birds.

- **Cultural resources**: Almost any feature in these houses provides a rich cultural base, from the buildings to the paintings and furnishings. The history of the family, the evolution of the house through the years and the culture associated with the era (dressing, cooking, travel souvenirs, etc.) offer a rich and diverse source of cultural assets.

- **Activities**: Historic houses have always devoted their efforts to providing a broad range of interpretation materials. The site will have some information panels, leaflets or guides that will provide an insight into the history of the property and some of its specific features.

    The house might have already developed alternative visits: discover the walled garden with the gardener, take behind-the-scenes tours of attics, cellars, etc. Other forms of creative activities might already be developed (embroidery workshops, etc.).

- **Service facilities**: The property can identify a range of services nearby that will assist its commercialization to different consumers. For example, the access option is interesting especially in relation to the types of consumer markets targeted: private car and public transport are essential components to assess. Beyond simple issues of access, properties will also need to estimate their catchment area, as we will address later on in the example. The properties also need to establish the range of local accommodation and catering facilities that will constitute a supplementary appeal to their visitors. They might also want to establish links with tour operators managing organized trips in their area (Figure 6.8).

Figure 6.8 A traditional British historic house. Source: Photo by Hulki Okan Tabak on Unsplash.

- **Collating consumer market intelligence**: As we discussed in Section 6.2, consumer intelligence can be sourced in various elements. The historic house might want to compile previous studies and surveys that have been collected on its consumers. It might also source more general reports conducted on heritage and historic house consumers. This assessment will be assisted by an analysis of spontaneous comments collected over UGC sites on the Internet, etc. These comments might concern the property itself, but it might also be interesting to assess how other similar properties are being assessed by their consumers. This information is extremely valuable; it will provide properties with an interesting insight into consumer evaluations and it might also give some indications of the potential segments of interest for the property. For instance, reports on other properties will have already produced some segmentation studies, and there will also be a rich range of academic papers investigating consumer markets.

- **Sourcing market intelligence**: In order to identify resources, some focus groups/interviews might be conducted with the staff at the property to collect their perceptions of current consumer sources of satisfaction and potential frustrations. They might also be a key resource to identify experiences that could be developed. Equally, local inhabitants and greeters might be another source of strategic information.

6.11.2 Identify target consumers

We have already addressed the notion of market intelligence. This information will be useful because it will offer some interesting pointers as to the range of consumers potentially attracted to historic houses. It might also give some key strategic insights into their segmentation.

Another approach is to conduct a segmentation strategy on consumers of historic properties. This is necessarily more costly and takes longer, involving skills in market analysis and segmentation, but it is a rich and valuable approach. The example thereafter gives an illustration of a segmentation on historic houses based on benefit segmentation. In order to help the reader understand this segmentation approach, they are encouraged to first analyse the data by themselves through different tasks, and then the results will be discussed.

The data provided in Table 6.2 are the results of a benefit segmentation analysis. The numbers should read as follows: The number 5 indicates that the visitor rated this benefit as very high and 1 that it was not important to this visitor. For example, Cluster 1 has a very small interest in plants and flowers (1.20) but a high demand for relaxation (4.10). The clusters read vertically; for each cluster it is easy to quickly understand the type of experience sought. To understand the dynamics of a cluster, analyse what are the most important motivations for that cluster. Human beings define themselves as much by what they want than by what they don't want. In order to profile a cluster, therefore, also investigate the motivations that received a low score. Once this work is done, name the cluster with a maximum of two words/adjectives. Then summarize the type of experience sought in three lines maximum.

- **Task 1: Describe and name each of the clusters (Table 6.2)**

- **Answers to Task 1:**

Cluster 1 is named the *Casual Historians*. This cluster groups those visitors interested in the historical side of the property but who also consider their visit as a casual outing; that is, learning is important, but the visit is also undertaken on a casual basis and spending time with one's family is equally important. There is the feeling that this cluster seeks a leisurely stroll through the property.

Table 6.2 Benefit clusters

Benefits sought	Cluster 1	Cluster 2	Cluster 3	Cluster 4
I have an interest in plants and flowers	1.20	3.0	1.09	2.05
I have an interest in gardens	1.84	3.80	1.35	2.30
To be outdoors, in nature	2.37	4.18	1.26	4.41
To enjoy a walk in the park	2.41	4.21	1.41	4.65
For relaxation	4.10	4.43	2.30	4.59
As part of a day out	4.53	4.42	1.72	4.20
For the atmosphere of the place	3.05	4.30	2.12	3.32
I have an interest in history	4.14	3.86	4.80	1.29
For the pleasure of viewing	3.60	3.90	3.42	2.74
To see how people lived in other times	4.27	3.95	4.34	1.37
To develop my knowledge	3.26	3.36	4.33	1.04
I have a particular interest in old items, paintings and furniture	3.66	3.65	4.51	1.06
To spend time with my family	3.42	3.76	1.83	3.76
To observe animals	1.29	3.22	1.05	3.31
To see something authentic and not commercialised	2.65	4.17	2.61	2.62
Proportion of each cluster in total sample	23.42%	17.42%	36.8%	22.36%

Source: Author

Cluster 3 might appear similar to Cluster 1 at first sight but it is in fact quite different. Cluster 3 is named *The Historians*. This cluster differentiates itself from the *Casual Historians*, grouping visitors who are mainly interested in history, old items, paintings and furniture and who are keen to improve their knowledge. The other features of the property seem to have little appeal to them.

Cluster 2 is named *The Browsers* because it groups those visitors who are motivated by a wide range of elements. Clusters such as this one are complex to analyse because they are not very explicit about the type of consumers they represent, but they need to be taken into consideration because in this case they represent 17% of the sample.

Cluster 4 is fairly easy to read, grouping visitors interested in spending a relaxing time with their family and enjoying the outdoors; they are called the *Family Trippers*.

It is interesting to note that each cluster is present in reasonable proportions in the properties investigated.

Once the clusters have been identified, the visitors' profiles will be detailed for each cluster. Profiling clusters consists of describing clusters with some outside information. For instance, Table 6.3 provides socio-economic information for each cluster. If the segmentation technique has been correctly developed, all the

Table 6.3 Visitors' socio-demographic profiles for each property

Socio-demographic characteristics	Casual Historians	Browsers	Historians	Family Trippers
Origins (percentage of each cluster)				
Domestic visitors	92.4	96	58.7	98.1
Overseas visitors	7.6	4.0	41.3	1.9
Purpose of visit				
Day trip from home	62.6	82.4	29.6	88.3
Visiting friends and relatives	6.9	1.6	2.7	4.9
On holiday in the area	29.9	16	67.7	6.8
Distance travelled				
Up to half an hour	23.2	25.4	11.9	50.6
Between half and one hour	32.5	44.3	32.6	31.7
One to two hours	12.5	11.4	10.0	6.3
More than two hours	31.8	18.9	52.3	11.4

Source: Author

information uncovered in the following step should align with the description of the benefits sought by each cluster.

- **Task 2: Profiling clusters**

In this second task, with Table 6.3 you will aim to describe the tourist profiles for each cluster. This table includes the types of tourists in each cluster, their origin and their commuting time to the property (for tourists, this time is calculated from their last place of accommodation).

- **Answers to Task 2:**

The *Casual Historians* are mostly domestic visitors and 2/3 are excursionists, 55% travel less than one hour to reach the historic house.

The *Historians* have a higher proportion of tourists (2/3), and 41% are international (in fact international visitors overall are concentrated in this segment only). They are willing to travel much longer distances to access to the property, which is in line with their tourist status.

The *Family Trippers* are very local excursionists, half of whom travel no more than 30 minutes. This small catchment area can be explained by the fact that this cluster seeks mostly an outdoor experience in a park. Beyond a 30-minute radius, they are likely to choose another park.

The *Browsers* are mostly domestic excursionists and 70% travel for a maximum of 1 hour to reach the site.

This step is already giving some strategic information about consumers. Table 6.4 provides even more information and provides a deeper understanding of each cluster.

- **Task 3: Keep on profiling clusters**

With the information given about consumers' group sizes, their information search and their behaviour at the properties, the profile of each cluster can be clarified even more. One word of caution, though; for the majority of the properties investigated, the gift shop was located at the end of the visit, and consumers had no other choice but to go through it after the house visit. This might explain the particularly high attendance at the souvenir shop.

As a supplementary task, consider which questions you would have liked to add to the survey in order to gain even more strategic information.

Table 6.4 Visitors' behavioural profiles for each property

Behavioural profiles	Casual Historians	Browsers	Historians	Family Trippers
Number of previous visits (including present visit)				
One	72.6	57.1	85.4	21
Two	9.7	7.1	8.0	21
Three	4.6	7.0	4.6	10.5
Four or more	13.1	28.7	1.9	47.5
Group size (average number of visitors constituting each group interviewed)	2.3	2.6	2.1	2.9
Group composition				
Single person	0	1.6	6.4	0
Family without children	57.5	51.2	57.9	38.4
Family with children	32.8	32.3	15.1	50.6
Group of friends	6.3	13.4	14.7	6.7
Organised group	3.4	1.6	6.2	4.3
Information about the property				
Loyalty card	13.8	31.7	5.4	15.9
Property leaflet	17.8	13.8	24.4	7.9
Been here before	6.3	13.8	5.4	17.1
Guide book	9.8	1.6	24.8	1.2
Signpost	4.0	4.9	5.0	4.9
Newspaper/magazine article	2.3	4.9	3.1	1.2
Personal recommendations	18.4	9.8	12.0	12.8
Tourist information centre	2.9	4.1	5.4	0
Always known about it	23.0	15.4	10.1	38.4
Organised tour	1.7	0	4.3	0
Parts of the property visited				
House	97.7	83.5	100	9.8
Gardens	40.0	63.8	24.1	38.0
Exhibition	14.9	22.0	10.3	8.6
Park	50.3	67.7	23.0	90.2
Restaurant	65.7	83.5	53.6	58.9
Shop	89.1	90.6	93.9	68.1
Time spent at the property	**2.36**	**2.53**	**2.20**	**2.15**

Source: Author

- **Answers to Task 3:**

Table 6.3 provides some very interesting information that can be read as follows:

The *Casual Historians* are on their first visit in 2/3 of cases, and 60% form groups without children (1/3 are visiting with children). They know about the property through personal recommendations or having already heard about it; leaflets are another information source, and 13% have a loyalty card. They visit a wide range of the sites on the property, including the gardens and park, and 90% visit the restaurant.

The *Historians* are in their majority on their first visit. They compose smaller groups (an average group size of 2.1 people), and 57% are in a family group without children. They mostly source their information through guide books and leaflets, which aligns with the high proportion of international or domestic tourists in this cluster. Their interest seems to lie mostly in the visit to the house, and the other parts of the property carry less interest for them (they are even the smallest proportion of restaurant consumers), and their average length of stay is the shortest of all the clusters (2h 20 min).

The *Family Trippers* are a very different cluster, as we have addressed already. They are the visitors who stay for the least amount of time at the property (2h 15 min on average) and mostly visit the outdoors (the park). Half of this cluster includes families with children with an average group size of 2.9 individuals. Half of them have visited the site more than four times, and their knowledge about the property is mostly acquired through word of mouth. This group does not usually pay an entry price (access to the grounds is free or, at the most, a small parking fee is charged). However, they attend the shop (68%) and the restaurant (58%), which constitutes another source of earning for the properties. This cluster also visits different parts of the site than the *Historians*, so if a property aims to attract both those clusters, it will not put the whole property under visitor pressure.

The *Browsers* have so far been difficult to understand; they don't have a profile and behaviour that allows their specificities to be identified. Browsers are consumers who stay the longest at the property, visit all the sites and are big consumers of the shop and restaurant. They are the second-highest repeat visitors. More than 30% of them have a loyalty card, but further investigation would be needed to investigate to which extent the card leads these consumers to behave differently. They visit the site frequently since 30% of them have visited the property more than four times. If the loyalty card plays an important role in their behaviour, it means that the ticket price that they did not pay to access the property is not totally lost since they are heavy consumers of the restaurant and shops – an interesting point to consider.

Which other questions could be added to the survey? It would be pertinent to know how much consumers have spent on site. The season in which they made their visit would be another interesting piece of information. Knowing the age of the children would also be of interest in order to target better services. Information searched for on the Internet would need to be further analysed (which websites were visited, etc.).

Which strategic knowledge is gained from the segmentation? This analysis carries a lot of learning for the properties surveyed. Most commonly, heritage sites often consider that their main consumer segment is composed of *Historians*. The results of this study show that in fact four different clusters exist and each of them carry their own specificities. The four clusters can be targeted by the properties but will require different strategies.

For example, the *Family Trippers* represent a very local market who will source information in their vicinity (radio, signposts, parents' magazines, school trips, etc.). They might require more products and services targeted to the needs of their children. They might also be easier to attract off-season.

The *Historians* are the usual consumer one would expect at a heritage site; they mostly have a tourist status and their sources of information mean that they can be reached through specific tourist channels (distributed leaflets in local hotels and accommodation, develop relationships with guide books especially in line with the nationalities concerned, develop links with tour operators, etc.). Organizing visits off-season with local accommodation providers and tourist information centres' front-line staff might also help in diffusing this information. Further information provided in the survey necessarily showed these tourists' keen interest in history and thirst for information.

The *Casual Historians* are another market to consider; they represent 23% of the sample, are fairly local, visit several parts of the property and might be another interesting market to target. Their thirst for historical knowledge is less pronounced than for the *Historians*, and they might be more receptive to alternative forms of experiences.

Lastly the *Browsers* are an interesting market; they are repeat visitors, they are big consumers of the property's sites and the loyalty card appears to impact their behaviour.

- Task 4: Design personas for each cluster

You will find on the Internet various websites that provide interesting templates for designing personas. Now that you have understood each cluster in detail, you can design a persona illustrating the typical consumer representing each cluster.

To finish this exercise, we shall summarize the following steps of the experience creation process with two experiences. Each of those experiences is presented via the experience matrix that summarises its main components.

Example 1: Land art

This first experience relies on the creation of works of art in the shape of land art. Land art aims to develop art from raw material sourced in nature. The participants in the workshop (maximum 20 people) will attend for half a day. This experience will be run by a guide from the historic house and an artist specializing in land art. After an introduction to this specific type of art, participants will be encouraged to source natural components in the park. A place dedicated to their creation will have been identified. Once they have finished, the guide will take pictures to share on social networks about their creative process. The works of art created will then be on show outside, and other tourists will be able to walk among them and appreciate the creativity of each production. Each piece of art will be identified; the name of the creator and a few words explaining the idea behind the piece will be indicated. This workshop can be conducted with a wide range of ages and can be conducted across the four seasons with different materials (the works can even be ephemeral if creating with snow or ice) (Table 6.5).

Example 2: Victorian gastronomic experience

This experience is focussed on eating habits and practices in the Victorian era. It is mostly targeted at the *Casual Historians* segment although it could be appealing to the *Historians*. Around the gastronomy theme, various experiences can be created. The objective in this experience is to use all the elements, within the property, that can be associated with gastronomy: sourcing products, preserving, cooking, recipes, the roles of the kitchen staff, service protocols, etc. In the second step, the participants take part to a workshop where they will learn some basic cooking skills, allowing them to learn how to cook and preserve food in the most natural way. They will also have a nice souvenir to take home, and the skills that they have learned can be reused in their daily lives and passed on to their friends and children (Table 6.6).

Table 6.5 Land art experience

Land art		
Resources used	**Activities used in the experience**	**Service assistance**
All the natural resources present on the grounds in the park and garden.	Creative skills to make a work of art from the pieces collected.	A guide will explain the principles of land art and will show some examples.
Key experiential cues (see Figure 6.4, page 165)	**Consumer target profile(s)**	**Trends (see Figure 6.3, page 163)**
• The five senses • Involving consumers • Creating souvenirs • Contextualising	Local/domestic/schools Land art creative workshop can be run in each of the four seasons with different materials.	• Playfulness • Nature • Sustainable consumers • Simplicity
	Illustrate segments with personas 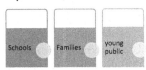	
Competition	**Co-construction**	**Value proposition**
Identify if other parks, historic sites local rangers are running similar activities in the area.	Fairly high: this is an interactive experience where the consumer is the main creator of the work of art.	Creating beauty with what nature offers.
Nesting	**Sustainability issues**	**Governance**
Not as such, although a few basic principles of land art might be welcome at the start of the experience.	This experience is totally sustainable: it sources local materials. Ultimately all materials will return to nature unchanged.	Mostly the guides from the property. If a local ranger or artists have expertise in land art, they might be leading the experience.
	MARKETING MIX	
PROMOTION	**PLACE**	**PRICE**
Contact schools directly, parents' magazines, gardening/outdoors magazines, art magazines, local radio and media, social networks, etc.	Mostly through the property's website.	Usual workshop price for a 2h 30 min activity. Special group price for schools. Could be commercialised as a team-building exercise.

Source: Author

Table 6.6 Victorian gastronomy experience

Period eating		
Resources used All elements associated to cooking: the cuisine itself, old cooking tools, table settings, etc.	**Activities used in the experience** Run a visit based on Victorian cooking culture and practices. The visit will be followed by a preserve workshop: making elderflower champagne in spring, sweet and sour courgette pickles in summer, spiced blackberry jam in autumn and Christmas cake in winter.	**Service assistance** A guide will accompany the tourists step by step through the visit and then the workshop.
Key experiential cues (see Figure 6.4, page 165) • The five senses • Involving consumers • Creating souvenirs • Contextualising • Relatedness	**Consumer target profile(s)** Local/domestic/schools Groups of friends, same-sex groups, etc. Workshops can be run in each of the four seasons with different ingredients. **Illustrate segments with personas** 	**Trends (see Figure 6.3, page 163)** • Well-being • Nature • Sustainable consumers • Authenticity • Simplicity
Competition Identify if other historic sites are running similar activities in the area.	**Co-construction** Fairly high: this is an interactive experience where the consumer is co-creating their food items, helped by the guide.	**Value proposition** Sourcing and preserving natural food through the ages.

Table 6.6 (Continued)

Nesting	Sustainability issues	Governance
An introductory visit focusses specifically on the gastronomic elements within the house. This workshop does not require special skills, although a few basic principles of the recipes need to be presented/reminded.	This experience is sustainable; it sources local foods and aims to preserve them in their simplest and most natural forms.	Mostly the guides from the property.

	MARKETING MIX	
PROMOTION	**PLACE**	**PRICE**
Contact schools directly, parents' magazines, cooking magazines, art magazines, local radio and media, social networks, etc.	Mostly through the property's website.	Usual workshop price for a 2h 30 min activity.

Source: Author

Example 3

We shall not develop Example 3 but rather set it as a challenge. This third experience proposition is targeted at a complex market for historic houses, that of teenagers Can you think of an experience that could cover one or several afternoons, and would be particularly attractive to teenagers? You could design an escape game, but this is not what I had in mind. I am thinking of an experience that is very creative and uses some of the characteristics of the historic house. It is also an experience that needs to be attractive to teenagers. I already have an idea, but I would like to hear your suggestions. If you have come up with a creative idea, and I am sure you have, contact me on Linkedin; I am keen to hear your project and I will share with you what I had in mind.

Conclusion

This conclusive chapter has combined together some of the key information addressed in the book. It has aimed to provide experience designers with ten steps and one identity matrix that will assist them and guide them through their creative process.

Generating experiences is a very creative and exciting process and the previous chapter has presented many possibilities for engaging in this process. Experiences are also a service that is marketed to a target audience, involves various providers and relies on traditional marketing tools to guarantee its success. The matrix provided towards the end of the chapter provides a useful summary of the major components addressed in this book. It allows designers to reposition their experiences within a more strategic approach that will truly assist them in developing a successful experience from creation to marketing.

Conclusion

Experiences carry strong emotional luggage and can be very impactful on consumers. They feed consumers' cherished memories and fuel word-of mouth and place attachment. Experiences are more than just products and services; they are the soul of the holidays, the core moments that will elicit strong emotions and that will bring more value to the whole holiday than any other encounters. This book has aimed to provide a broad understanding of what experiences consist of and how they can be designed. In order to efficiently design tourism experiences, tourism providers need to master a broader understanding of what experiential marketing involves and the subtleties of consumer behaviour. Years of academic knowledge also provide a solid base for understanding what are the most important dynamics within the experience and how they impact consumers.

This book has aimed to demonstrate the depth and value of experiential marketing, especially for the marketing of tourism products. Experiential marketing is a powerful technique that provides a pertinent structure and knowledge basis to create, build and develop tourism experiences. Over the years, experiential marketing has also developed a range of tools that can be particularly useful for the creation of experiences.

The last two chapters of the book aim to provide a framework and tools that experience designers can integrate into their creative process. These will be developed into a business game, *The Experience Generator*, in 2022.

Experiential marketing resonates with consumers, resonates with emotions, resonates with the surrounding world. Experiential marketing nests within the realm of passion and creativity. It is also a marketing act that is deeply rooted in connections with human beings. For these various reasons, experiential marketing is an extremely rich, genuine and creative field, and designing experiences is extremely fulfilling.

Knowledge on experiences will keep on evolving and it will remain a rich field of information. Currently, academia is increasingly developing research testing methods (electrodermal measures, for example) and more connections are also being established with neuroscientists. These connections allow researchers to gain a more intimate understanding of experiences. Various forms of experimentation are also being conducted which will bring a more acute knowledge of experiences. Experiential marketing is here to stay, because it brings an understanding of the elements that truly impact consumers and because it brings some magic to the consumption universe. The pandemic that paralyzed the world in 2020 has led consumers to question their lifestyles, and they have increasingly turned to life experiences that are more meaningful and where they feel more connected to others. This evolution will lead to an even bigger demand for experiences. Tourism consumption stopped on an international scale during the pandemic, but it did not disappear, and domestic tourism remained a strong component of national tourism economies. In this context, experiences were in demand more than ever. Experiential marketing offers opportunities for consumers increasingly eager to temporarily leave stressful and unfulfilling lives. It is also a way to reenchant the world, society and the lives of individuals. The months and years to come will witness a sustained interest in tourism experiences that we can all learn from; keep your eyes open!

References

Ackerman, D. (2011) *Deep Play*. Vintage.

Arnould, E. J., & Price, L. L. (1993) River magic: Extraordinary experience and the extended service encounter. *Journal of Consumer Research*, 20(1): 24–45.

Belk, R. W. (1988) Possessions and the extended self. *Journal of Consumer Research*, 15(2): 139–168.

Bargeman, B., & van der Poel, H. (2006) The role of routines in the vacation decision-making process of Dutch vacationers. *Tourism Management*, 27: 707–720.

Bitner, M. J. (1992) Servicescapes: The impact of physical surroundings on customers and employees. *Journal of Marketing*, 56(2): 57–71.

Boorstin, D. (1964) *The Image: A Guide to Pseudo-Events in America*. New York: Harper.

Borrie, W. T., & Roggenbuck, J. W. (2001) The dynamic, emergent, and multi-phasic nature of on-site wilderness experiences. *Journal of Leisure Research*, 33(2): 202–228.

Bourdieu, P. (2018) *Distinction: A Social Critique of the Judgement of Taste*. Routledge.

Cai, W., McKenna, B., & Waizenegger, L. (2020) Turning it off: Emotions in digital-free travel. *Journal of Travel Research*, 59(5): 909–927.

Campbell, C. (1987) *The Romantic Ethic and the Spirit of Modern Consumerism*. Oxford: Basil Blackwell.

Carù, A., & Cova, B. (2006) How to facilitate immersion in a consumption experience: Appropriation operations and service elements. *Journal of Consumer Behaviour*, 5: 4–14.

Cave, J., & Jolliffe, L. (2012) Visitor interpretation, key concepts in tourism, in Robinsin, P. (Ed.), *Key Concepts in Tourism*. London: Routledge: 273–275.

Celsi, R. L., Rose, R. L., & Leigh, T. W. (1993) An exploration of high-risk leisure consumption through skydiving. *Journal of Consumer Research*, 20(1): 1–23.

Cheng, T. M., &; Wu, H. C. (2015) How do environmental knowledge, environmental sensitivity, and place attachment affect environmentally responsible behaviour? An integrated approach for sustainable island tourism. *Journal of Sustainable Tourism*, 23(4): 557–576.

Cohen, E. (1972) Toward a sociology of international tourism. *Social Research*, 164–182.

Cova, B., Carù, A., & Cayla, J. (2018) Re-conceptualizing escape in consumer research. *Qualitative Market Research: An International Journal*, 21(4): 1–20.

Cova, B., & Dalli, D. (2009) Working consumers: The next step in marketing theory. *Marketing Theory*, 9(3): 315–339.

Crompton, J. L. (1979) Motivations for pleasure vacation. *Annals of Tourism Research*, 6(4): 408–424.

CSA/Télérama (2003) Les vacances des Français, Sondage du 30/07/03, Paris: CSA.

Csikszentmihalyi, M. (1991) *Flow: The Psychology of Optimal Experience*. New York: Harper & Row.

Dann, G. M. (1977) Anomie, ego-enhancement and tourism. *Annals of Tourism Research*, 4(4): 184–194.

Direction du Tourisme (2002) *Voyageurs et non-partants en 2002*. Ministère délégué au Tourisme, Juin.

Dixon, R. (2018) Open and shut case: Why the package holidays are back. *The Guardian*, Tuesday 14th August.

Duerden, M. D., & Witt, P. A. (2010) The impact of direct and indirect experiences on the development of environmental knowledge, attitudes, and behaviour. *Journal of Environmental Psychology*, 30(4): 379–392.

Frochot, I., Elliot, S., & Kreziak, D. (2017) Digging deep into the experience – flow and immersion patterns in a mountain holiday. *International Journal of Culture, Tourism and Hospitality Research*, 11(1): 81–91.

Frochot, I., Kreziak, D., & Elliott, S. (2018) Home away from home: A longitudinal study of the holiday appropriation process. *Tourism Management*, 71: 327–336.

Frochot, I., & Morrison, A. M. (2000) Benefit segmentation: A review of its applications to travel and tourism research. *Journal of Travel & Tourism Marketing*, 9(4): 21–45.

Gilbert, D., & Abdullah, J. (2004) Holidaytaking and the sense of well-being. *Annals of Tourism Research*, 31(1): 103–121.

Gordon, B. (1986) The souvenir: Messenger of the extraordinary. *Journal of Popular Culture*, 20(3): 135–151.

Goulding, C. (2001) Romancing the past: Heritage visiting and the nostalgic consumer. *Psychology & Marketing*, 18(6): 565–592.

Guivarc'h, J. M. (2002) Havas voyages, pionnier du marketing olfactif. *Espaces Tourisme et Loisirs*, 193(May): 38–39.

Haley, R. I. (1968) Benefit segmentation: A decision-oriented research tool. *Journal of Marketing*, 32(3): 30–35.

Hallé, M. C. (2012) Le pouvoir du storytelling dans une approche marketing. Globeveilleur- Tourism Intelligence Network. https://veilletourisme.ca/2012/02/24/le-pouvoir-du-storytelling-dans-une-approche-marketing/.

Ham, S. (1992) *Environmental Interpretation – A Practical Guide for People with Big Ideas and Small Budgets*. Golden: North American Press.

Hanington, B., & Martin, B. (2019) *Universal Methods of Design Expanded and Revised: 125 Ways to Research Complex Problems, Develop Innovative Ideas, and Design Effective Solutions*. Beverly: Rockport Publishers.

Hetzel, P. (1992) *Planète Conso – Marketing expériential et nouveaux univers de consommation.* Paris: Editions d'Organisation.

Holbrook, M. B., & Hirschman, E. C. (1982) The experiential aspects of consumption: Consumer fantasies, feelings, and fun. *Journal of Consumer Research,* 9(2): 132–140.

Hosany, S., & Witham, M. (2010) Dimensions of cruisers' experiences, satisfaction, and intention to recommend. *Journal of Travel Research,* 49(3): 351–364.

Huang, S., & Choi, H. S. C. (2019) Developing and validating a multidimensional tourist engagement scale (TES). *The Service Industries Journal,* 39(7–8): 469–497.

Husemann, K. C., & Eckhardt, G. M. (2019) Consumer deceleration. *Journal of Consumer Research,* 45(6): 1142–1163.

Jafari, J. (1987) Tourism models: The sociocultural aspects. *Tourism Management,* 8(2): 151–159.

Jansson, A. (2007) A sense of tourism: New media and the dialectic of encapsulation/decapsulation. *Tourist Studies,* 7(1): 5–24.

Jauréguiberry, F., & Lachance, J. (2011) *Le voyageur hypermoderne.* Toulouse: Erès.

Juvan, E., & Dolnicar, S. (2014) The attitude–behaviour gap in sustainable tourism. *Annals of Tourism Research,* 48: 76–95.

Kahneman, D., Fredrickson, B. L., Schreiber, C. A., & Redelmeier, D. A. (1993) When more pain is preferred to less: Adding a better end. *Psychological Science,* 4(6), 401–405.

Kano, N., Seraku, N., Takahashi, F., & Tsuji, S. (1984) Attractive quality and must-be quality, *Hinshitsu. The Journal of the Japanese Society for Quality Control,* 14: 39–48.

Keinan, A., & Kivetz, R. (2011) Productivity orientation and the consumption of collectable experiences. *Journal of Consumer Research,* 37(6): 935–950.

Kellert, S. R., & Wilson, E. O. (1995) *The Biophilia Hypothesis.* Washington: Island Press.

Keltner, D., & Haidt, J. (2003) Approaching awe, a moral, spiritual, and aesthetic emotion. *Cognition and Emotion,* 17(2): 297–314.

Kemp, S., Burt, C. D., & Furneaux, L. (2008) A test of the peak-end rule with extended autobiographical events. *Memory & Cognition,* 36(1): 132–138.

Kim, J., & Fesenmaier, D. R. (2017) Sharing tourism experiences: The posttrip experience. *Journal of Travel Research,* 56(1): 28–40.

Kim, J.-H., Ritchie, J., & McCormick, B. (2012) Development of a scale to measure memorable tourism experiences. *Journal of Travel Research,* 3(2): 123–126.

Kirillova, K., Lehto, X. Y., & Cai, L. (2017) Existential authenticity and anxiety as outcomes: The tourist in the experience economy. *International Journal of Tourism Research,* 19(1): 13–26.

Kozinets, R. (2009) *Netnography: Doing Ethnographic Research Online.* SAGE Publications Ltd.

Kozinets, R. (2012) Rituals without Dogma: A burning man videography. https://www.youtube.com/watch?v=ZA6LEsJXYzg (21/05/2021).

Kozinets, R. V. (2002) Can consumers escape the market? Emancipatory illuminations from burning man. *Journal of Consumer Research,* 29(1): 20–38.

Kreziak, D., & Frochot, I. (2011) Co-construction de l'expérience touristique: les stratégies des touristes en stations de sport d'hiver. *Décisions Marketing*, 64: 23–33.

Krippendorf, J. (1987) *The Holidaymakers: Understanding the Impact of Leisure and Travel*. London: Heinemann.

Laing, J. H., & Frost, W. (2017) Journeys of well-being: Women's travel narratives of transformation and self-discovery in Italy. *Tourism Management*, 62: 110–119.

Larsen, J. (2008) De-exoticizing tourist travel: Everyday life and sociality on the move. *Leisure Studies*, 27(1): 21–34.

Lenglet, F., & Frochot, I. (2021) Expériences touristiques immersives: le rôle clé de l'état de déconnection sur la memorisation et le bien-être perçu. 19–21 May, *Congrès International de l'AFM*, Angers, Online.

Lumsdon, L. (1997) *Tourism Marketing*. Boston: International Thomson Business Press.

MacCannell, D. (2013) *The Tourist: A New Theory of the Leisure Class*. Oakland: University of California Press.

Markwell, K. W. (1997) Dimensions of photography in a nature-based tour. *Annals of tourism Research*, 24(1): 131–155.

Maslow, A. H. (1964) *Religions, Values, and Peak Experiences*. London: Penguin Books Limited.

Masset, J., & Decrop, A. (2017) Tomorrowland festival: A heteropia of deviation. *Vimeo*. https://vimeo.com/222471926.

Masset, J., & Decrop, A. (2020) Meanings of tourist souvenirs: From the holiday experience to everyday life. *Journal of Travel Research*, 60: 718–734.

Mayo, E., & Jarvis, L. (1981) *The Psychology of Leisure Travel*. Boston: CBI Publishing.

McKercher, B., & Lui, S. L. (2014) Becoming a tourist. *International Journal of Tourism Research*, 16(4): 399–406.

Mergoupis, T., & Steuer, M. (2003) Holiday taking and income. *Applied Economics*, 35(3): 269–284.

Ministry of Agriculture (2015) *Forestry Standards Manual, Forest Service*. Dublin: Department of Agriculture, Food & the Marine.

Mitchell, T. R., Thompson, L., Peterson, E., & Cronk, R. (1997) Temporal adjustments in the evaluation of events: The "rosy view". *Journal of Experimental Social Psychology*, 33(4): 421–448.

Moutinho, L. (1987) Consumer behaviour in tourism. *European Journal of Marketing*, 21(10): 3–44.

Nawijn, J., Marchand, M. A., Veenhoven, R., & Vingerhoets, A. J. (2010) Vacationers happier, but most not happier after a holiday. *Applied Research in Quality of Life*, 5(1): 35–47.

Newman, D. B., Tay, L., & Diener, E. (2014) Leisure and subjective well-being: A model of psychological mechanisms as mediating factors. *Journal of Happiness Studies*, 15(3): 555–578.

Oberg, K. (1960) Cultural shock: Adjustment to new cultural environments. *Practical Anthropology*, 4: 177–182.

OECD (2018) Megatrends shaping the future of tourism, in *OECD Tourism Trends and Policies*. Paris: OECD Publishing: 1–380.

Oh, H., Fiore, A. M., & Jeoung, M. (2007) Measuring experience economy concepts: Tourism applications. *Journal of Travel Research*, 46(2): 119–132.

Oliver, R. L. (1980) A cognitive model of the antecedents and consequence of satisfaction decisions. *Journal of Marketing Research*, 17(4): 460–469.

Orsoni, T. (2007) Cap vers l'incomparable! La nouvelle stratégie du Club Med. *Cahiers Espaces – Revue Espaces Tourisme et Loisirs*, 94(August): 16–20.

Parasuraman, A., Berry, L., & Zeithaml, V. (2002) Refinement and reassessment of the SERVQUAL scale. *Journal of Retailing*, 67(4), 114–139.

Pearce, P. L. (1981) Environment chock: A study of tourists' reactions to two tropical islands. *Journal of Applied Social Psychology*, 11(3): 268–280.

Pearce, P. L. (1982) Tourists and their hosts: Some social and psychological effects of inter-cultural contact, in Bochner, S. (Ed.), *Cultures in Contact. Studies in Cross-Cultural Interactions*, Vol 1. Oxford: Pergamon Press: 199–221.

Peter, J. P., & Olson, J. C. (1987) *Consumer Behaviour*. Homewood: Irwin.

Pine, B. J., Pine, J., & Gilmore, J. H. (1999) *The Experience Economy: Work Is Theatre & Every Business a Stage*. Boston: Harvard Business Press.

Plog, S. (2001) Why destination areas rise and fall in popularity: An update of a Cornell quarterly classic. *Cornell Hotel and Restaurant Administration Quarterly*, 42(3): 13–24.

Plog, S. C. (1974) Why destination arise and fall in popularity. *The Cornell Hotel and Restaurant Administration Quarterly*, 14(4): 55–58.

Prahalad, C. K., & Ramaswamy, V. (2004) Co-creation experiences: The next practice in value creation. *Journal of Interactive Marketing*, 18(3): 5–14.

Richards, G. (1999) Vacations and the quality of life: Patterns and structures. *Journal of Business Research*, 44(3): 189–198.

Rokeach, M. (1973) *The Nature of Human Values*. New York: Free Press.

Rosa, H. (2013) *Social Acceleration*. New York: Columbia University Press.

Schmitt, B. (2000) *Experiential Marketing: To Get Consumers to Relate to Your Brand*. New York: The Free Press.

Seligman, M. (2018) PERMA and the building blocks of well-being. *The Journal of Positive Psychology*, 13(4): 333–335.

Sherry, J., Kozinets, R., & Borghini, S. (2007) Agents in paradise: Experiential cocreation through emplacement, ritualization and community, in A. Carù & B. Cova (Eds.), *Consuming Experience*. Oxon: Routledge: 17–33.

Shiota, M. N., Keltner, D., & Mossman, A. (2007) The nature of awe: Elicitors, appraisals, and effects on self-concept. *Cognition and Emotion*, 21(5): 944–963.

Stickdorn, M., Schneider, J., Andrews, K., & Lawrence, A. (2011) *This Is Service Design Thinking: Basics, Tools, Cases*. Hoboken: Wiley.

Strauss-Blasche, G., Ekmekcioglu, C., & Marktl, W. (2000) Does vacation enable recuperation? Changes in well-being associated with time away from work. *Occupational Medicine*, 50(3): 167–172.

Taheri, B., Hosany, S., & Altinay, L. (2019) Consumer engagement in the tourism industry: New trends and implications for research. *The Service Industries Journal*, 39: 7–8, 463–468.

Thellier, I. (2012) Esprit de Picardie. Le storytelling au service d'une marque expérientielle et relationnelle, *Espaces Tourisme et Loisirs*.

Turner, V. (1969) *The Rituals Process. Structure and Anti-Structure*. Chicago: Aldine.

Turner, V., & Turner, E. (1978) *Image and Pilgrimage in Christian Culture*. Oxford: Basil.

Uriely, N. (2005) The tourist experience: Conceptual developments. *Annals of Tourism Research*, 32(1): 199–216.

Urry, J. (1990) The "consumption" of tourism. *Sociology*, 24(1): 23–35.

Usborne, S. (2017) Just do it: The experience economy and how we turned our backs on "stuff". *The Guardian*, 13th May.

Van Gennep, A. (1960) *The Rites of Passage*. Chicago: University of Chicago Press.

Vargo, S., & Lusch, R. (2004) Evolving to a new dominant logic for marketing. *Journal of Marketing*, 68: 1–17.

Wang, L., Zhang, G., Shi, P., Lu, X., & Song, F. (2019) Influence of awe on green consumption: The mediating effect of psychological ownership. *Frontiers in Psychology*, 10: 2484.

Wang, N. (1999) Rethinking authenticity in tourism experience. *Annals of Tourism Research*, 26(2): 349–370.

Wermes, R. (2007) La formule Club Med – Le succès d'un concept qui a su évoluer. *Cahiers Espaces- Revue Espaces Tourisme et Loisirs*, 94(August): 10–15.

Westman, M., & Eden, D. (1997) Effects of a respite from work on burnout: Vacation relief and fade-out. *Journal of Applied Psychology*, 82(4): 516.

Williams, F. (2017) *The Nature Fix: Why Nature Makes Us Happier, Healthier and More Creative*. New York: W.W. Norton & Company.

Wong, J., Wai, I., & Tao, Z. (2019) Sharing memorable tourism experiences on mobile media and how it influences further travel decision. *Current Issues in Tourism*, 23(14): 1–15.

Woodside, A. G., & King, R. I. (2001) An updated model of travel and tourism purchase–consumption systems. *Journal of Travel & Tourism Marketing*, 10(1): 3–27.

Index

Printed in the United States
by Baker & Taylor Publisher Services